Frontiers of Artificial Intelligence, Ethics and Multidisciplinary Applications

Artificial Intelligence is now present in numerous spheres of our everyday lives. It is poised to lead new and efficient business models for effective and user-centric services in the private and public sectors. Advances in AI in deep learning, (deep) reinforcement learning, and neuroevolutionary techniques can pave the way forward for artificial general intelligence (AGI). However, the development and use of AI also present challenges. Inherent biases prevalent within data corpora used to train AI and machine learning systems attribute to most of these challenges. In addition, multiple instances have highlighted the need for privacy, fairness, and transparency in AI-powered decision-making. This book series will provide an avenue for researchers, leaders, decision-makers, and policymakers to share research and insights on the forefronts of AI, including its use in an Ethical, Explainable, Privacy-Preserving, Trustworthy, and Sustainable manner.

The series has relevance across disciplines and be multi-disciplinary. Advances in AI, explainability AI, privacy-preserving AI, and ethical AI explored in this book series are unexplored areas for research and competence building. Such developments can reduce hesitancy for AI integration in many domains. The book series thus fits in well as an essential and growing need among those who work on artificial intelligence in academia, business and industry, and the public sector to exploit the opportunities in the constantly evolving field of AI.

The series publishes research monographs, authored works by practitioners and case studies to highlight innovative and best practices, and edited volumes putting together varied perspectives.

Sadaf Fahim

Ethico-Legal Aspect of AI-driven Driverless Cars

Comparing Autonomous Vehicle Regulations in Germany, California, and India

Springer

Sadaf Fahim
Faculty of Law
Chanakya National Law University
Patna, Bihar, India

ISSN 2731-8125 ISSN 2731-8133 (electronic)
Frontiers of Artificial Intelligence, Ethics and Multidisciplinary Applications
ISBN 978-981-97-6882-0 ISBN 978-981-97-6883-7 (eBook)
https://doi.org/10.1007/978-981-97-6883-7

This Springer imprint is published by the registered company Springer Nature Singapore Pte Ltd.
The registered company address is: 152 Beach Road, #21-01/04 Gateway East, Singapore 189721, Singapore

This Book

Is Dedicated To The

Memories Of My Father

Late Md. Fahim Ahmad

Preface and Acknowledgements

No research work is possible without cooperation and collaboration. The book could not have been completed without the great support that I have received from so many persons. I would like to offer my most heartfelt thanks to the following persons. I would like to thank my mentors **Dr. Aparajita Bhatt**, Assistant Professor of Law, and Co-supervisor **Prof. (Dr.) G. S. Bajpai**, Vice-Chancellor of Rajiv Gandhi National University of Law, Punjab, and Ex-Registrar of National Law University, Delhi, for allowing me to find my way through this exercise and for giving valuable input from time to time. I am highly indebted to them for providing me with constant support and supervision despite their busy schedule. Their support and swift responses have been a great source of inspiration in the completion of the research work.

I would further like to acknowledge the help and assistance extended by the Library staff of the National Law University, Delhi, in aiding me in my research work.

Finally, I must express my very profound gratitude to my parents, Late **Md. Fahim Ahmad** and **Bilquis Fahim**, who have been a great source of strength all through this work, my siblings, *Shahla Fahim, Kausar Fahim, Nausheen Fahim, Arshi Fahim,* and *Nazish Fahim*, and my friends, *Akhter Hemayoun* and *Karan Chaudhary*, for providing me with unfailing support and continuous encouragement throughout the process of completing this book. Without them, this achievement would not have been feasible. Their devotion and encouragement throughout my long workdays and evenings were invaluable to me.

Patna, India Dr. Sadaf Fahim

About This Book

This book examines the ethical and legal implications of artificial intelligence in general, focusing on the realities of the context in which it was extensively discussed—autonomous automobiles. This book's chapters each present a true story. The development of AI and the problems it has caused for society and industry as a whole are the subject of the narrative.

Data protection, privacy, security, and social concerns all become very important issues that need to be handled thanks to the policies on AI. The book is divided up into six chapters that each cover a different area of law, ethics, and policy issues to artificial intelligence.

Chapter 1 of the book titled: "Artificial Intelligence—An Overview of the Legal Status" discusses the legal concerns of artificial intelligence regulation. To convey opinions on artificial intelligence's legal personality and standing before the law, the author has cited a number of jurists. This chapter seeks to provide the argument that artificial intelligence should not be accorded personhood due to the moral and ethical issues that surround it, as well as the fact that it lacks human intelligence, emotions, and values and may contain both intentional and unintentional prejudice.

Chapter 2 of the book titled: "Introduction and Evolution of Self-driving Cars" This chapter discusses the issues and problems that arise from AI technology. As the scope of AI is vast and applicable in diverse sectors; hence, for the purpose of determining tortious and criminal liability, the scope of this chapter is limited to study only the regulation of Autonomous Vehicles.

Chapter 3 of the book titled: "Determining Tortious Liability of Artificial Intelligence Technology—A Study of India, California, and Germany" This chapter extends to the legal and regulatory framework of Germany, California, and India. The chapter has tried to make a comparative study of the legal and regulatory provisions in determining the tortious liability of AI within three jurisdictions—Germany, California, and India. Germany has a developed market for AI and is also a leading manufacturer of AI-enabled systems including AVs. It is one of the leading automotive industries considering the new developments in autonomous driving vehicles and other areas.

Chapter 4 of the book titled: "Determining Criminal Liability of Artificial Intelligence Technology—A Study of India, California, and Germany" The chapter discusses how artificial intelligence (AI) machines are subject to criminal law. The chapter focuses on whether the machines can conduct crimes and whether they can be held accountable. The chapter also addresses the question of who is responsible for an AI-related crime—the makers or users, or both.

Chapter 5 of the book titled: "Ethical Issues Related to Artificial Intelligence in Autonomous Cars" This chapter discusses the ethical issues that arise from AI technology. It highlights the idea that bias refers to any predisposition or prejudice, whether for or against one person or a group, particularly when done in a way that is deemed unfair. Data that has been tampered with or is biased may be racial, gendered, or ideological in nature. The chapter discusses the problem of prejudice in artificial intelligence and provides a case study of the discriminatory AI employed by businesses like Tesla, BMW, Google Cars, and many more like Facebook, Apple, Amazon, and Google.

Chapter 6 also offered insightful suggestions and recommendations for laws that would better utilise artificial intelligence in Indian governance.

Academics, legal professionals at the advanced, undergraduate, and graduate levels, as well as individuals looking to deepen their grasp of legal and policy challenges in artificial intelligence will find this book to be relevant across the common law globe. The jurisprudence and policy of AI can be better understood by reading this book, which will be of great interest to law students and authors in both fields. Policymakers, economists, lawyers, and technocrats can all benefit from this book.

Highlights of the Book

This book deals with how India follows the Common Law like US, England, and Canada, unlike Germany, which follows the Civil Law. The objective behind studying and researching into Indian jurisdiction is to identify the risks and challenges in the deployment of AI systems, identify the loopholes in the law, and learn from the best practises adopted by advanced countries like Germany and California. Thus, the limitations of this research study are limited to discussing and determining the liability of self-driving vehicles or autonomous vehicles in particular.

This book provides, clearly and concisely, the general philosophical principle on which problems relating to artificial intelligence may be handled are presented in this book in a straightforward and lucid manner because of the fact that the State of California is well-known for its technological and new innovative digital inventions since Facebook, Apple, Amazon, and Google is headquartered in California as these are not only the biggest and thriving rather than the most valuable high-tech IT companies. California gives its industry a very flexible, active, and cutting-edge legislative framework, which comes into play with the help of active collaboration with the economy and the legislators.

This book discusses how companies like Google, Amazon, Facebook, and Microsoft invested extensively in artificial intelligence because they think it will shape the future. Hence, Artificial Intelligence has been exponentially expanding as a subject of study and as an important component of global economies.

Contents

About the Author

Sadaf Fahim is a faculty of Law, at Chanakya National Law University, Patna. In 2014, she graduated with a B.A., LL.B. (Hons.) from Aligarh Muslim University in Aligarh. She holds a master's degree in Law with specialisation in cyber law and cyber security from National Law University, Jodhpur and has a doctoral degree in Artificial Intelligence and Law from National Law University (NLU), Delhi. She has been teaching subjects such as cyber law and cyber security, artificial intelligence and law, telecommunications, press and media law, and international humanitarian law and refugee, and IPR law. She was involved in curriculum development and academic administration in her institution and is also enrolled with the Advocates' Association, High Court in Patna, and has full-time litigation experience. Dr. Fahim has published articles in reputable journals and also has other publications to her credit such as book chapters, magazine articles, and blogs. She has been presenting her AI and Law policy, crafted during her Ph.D. studies, to policymakers.

Acronyms and Abbreviations

&	And
ADAS	Advanced Driver Assistance System
ADF	Automated Driving Function
AGI	Artificial General Intelligence
AI	Artificial Intelligence
and others i.e.	that is
ANI	Artificial Narrow Intelligence
ANN	Artificial Neural Networks
Anr.	Another
Ar.	Article
ASI	Artificial Super Intelligence
AV	Automated Vehicle
AVT	Automated Vehicle Technology
CDEP	Committee on Digital Economy Policy
DL	Deep Learning
DMV	Department of Motor Vehicles
E.U	European Union
EC	European Community
ed(s)	Editor(s)
et. al.	Edition
ML	Machine Learning
NHTSA.	National Highway Traffic Safety Administration
NLP	Natural Language Processing
OECD	Organisation for Economic Cooperation and Development
U.K	United Kingdom
U.S	United States of America
UN	United Nations
UNICRI	United Nations Interregional Crime and Justice Research Institute
v.	Verses
Vol.	Volume

Chapter 1
Artificial Intelligence—An Overview of the Legal Status

Abstract This chapter talks about how Artificial Intelligence primarily deals with three strategies. They are Symbolic AI, Data Driven, and Future turn of events. It has been given many rules, and it will carefully follow the best in a compelled climate. In fluffy rationale, it is a generally evident or bogus technique and applied in charge frameworks. In Data-driven AI, Neural organisations and profound learning algorithms are applied to cycle the pool of information-by-information mining and enormous information and are applied in Natural Language Processing. It is critical to recognise various techniques and apply the correct one to their degree of development. In this subject, the author will find out about How Artificial Intelligence Systems (AVs) Work. This chapter provides an overview of the legal situation of artificial intelligence (AI), which is a system that can sense its surroundings and take measures to increase its chances of success. AI can be divided into two kinds, Weak or Strong, depending on how it is used and for what purpose. The personhood claim made by AI systems is discussed in this chapter. This claim can be investigated by examining the definitions offered by various legal scholars and theories of intelligence.

1.1 Introduction

1.1.1 Background

The history of artificial intelligence can be traced back to the classical era of Greek mythology when the idea of machines and mechanical men was well developed.

John McCarthy first used the term ‘artificial intelligence’ in 1956 at the Dartmouth Conference. The first AI laboratory was built in 1959, three years after it was founded. The era of AI research began during this time. The MIT lab, which is currently open for business, served as the first AI research centre. The first robot was added to the ‘GM assembly line in 1960’.

In 1961, the first chatbot was developed. Alexa and Siri are now commonplace. Eliza, a chatbot, was first created in 1961. The renowned IBM Deep Blue came next.

S. Fahim, *Ethico-Legal Aspect of AI-driven Driverless Cars*, Frontiers of Artificial Intelligence, Ethics and Multidisciplinary Applications,
https://doi.org/10.1007/978-981-97-6883-7_1

In 1997, word spread that 'IBM's Deep Blue' had defeated chess world champion 'Garry Kasparov'. This was regarded as an early success for artificial intelligence.

The Stanford racing team's robotic car Stanley, which was constructed for the DARPA Grand Challenge in 2005, took first place. That was yet another significant achievement for Artificial Intelligence. Brad Rutter and Ken Jennings, the two greatest Jeopardy winners, were vanquished by IBM's question-answering machine, Watson, in 2011. Thus, the idea of Artificial Intelligence was first introduced in an imaginary setting. One of the most relevant technologies in use today is artificial intelligence. Many things surrounding today are powered by AI deep learning or machine learning, if one looks around. Since artificial intelligence (AI) first appeared in the 1950s, it has grown exponentially and has enormous potential. In addition to other closely related topics, AI encompasses disciplines including "*machine learning, deep learning, neural networks, natural language processing, knowledge-based systems, and expert systems.*" AI is being used in image processing and computer vision. Now, if artificial intelligence has been around for more than 50 years, why has it now grown to be so significant and well-liked?

The first reason is because individuals now have access to massive computational and data storage power, allowing them to harness AI's capabilities. Processing power requirements for artificial intelligence are high. Artificial Intelligence is now commercially viable for solving problems that affect a wide range of daily activities thanks to numerous recent advances in exponentially increasing 'computational and data storage capabilities' while exponentially reducing the costs associated with those 'computational and data storage capabilities'.

The second most significant factor is that as the world has grown more and more digitalised, people now have access to a vast amount of data that has been produced through time. It has been churning out data at an unfathomable rate. It collects data through social media, Internet of Things (IoT) devices, and any other ways available. So, it needed to come up with a way or a solution to help analyse this massive amount of data to enable individuals to extract relevant insights and expand their businesses based on those insights. For instance, to develop a useful AI agent that is capable of intelligent choices like anticipating what products to recommend next when shopping online or figuring out how to recognise an object from a picture. All these things are conceivable when artificial intelligence is taught on large data sets, and big data makes this even easier.

The third reason is that it now has more powerful algorithms for extracting information from massive data sets. These powerful algorithms are based on neural network concepts. This is the central principle of deep learning. The need for AI has increased as a result of better algorithms that can perform better and faster computations with greater precision, resulting in more and better commercial opportunities and enhanced profitability.

In this chapter, the author study's scope is confined to Germany, California, and India where the author has highlighted when Artificial Intelligence deserves legal personhood and when they are required to be granted legal standing. Secondly, in this chapter, the author has highlighted the civil and criminal legal liabilities arising when the AV is involved in an accident. Lastly, the author has highlighted the ethical issues of AI.

Moreover, the author will discuss further whether there are challenges and problems arising from AI technology that can be addressed within existing civil and criminal laws—procedural and substantive law—or whether ***a sui generis law*** on AI technology is required. It is a juxtaposition study of the laws involving the legal and ethical issues related to AI for self-driving cars in Germany, California, and India, determining the legal liabilities of the designer, developer/programmer, manufacturer, producer, users, or AI in the case of autonomous vehicles (AVs).

The author chose this topic because AV technology seeks to revolutionise the mobility ecosystem by reducing accident rates and by offering additional advantages, such as *the potential to reduce traffic, increase safety and mobility, lower energy usage, and generate free time*. The nature of the study for the chapters is doctrinal and qualitative.

Now, why discussing Germany in particular? Because Germany is legally set or prepared to remain in the market as one of the top automotive industries considering the new developments in autonomous driving systems and other areas.

Furthermore, discussing California next, the State of California is a city that is well-known for its technological and innovative digital inventions since Facebook, Apple, Amazon, and Google are headquartered in California. Considering that these aren't just the most valued high-tech IT companies, but also the largest and booming ones. California provides a particularly adaptable, dynamic, and cutting-edge legal framework for its industry, which is put into action with the aid of active collaboration between the economy and the legislators.

Lastly, why India? So the reason is that our country follows the Common Law like the U.S., England, and Canada, unlike Germany, which follows the Civil Law. Although there is no specific legislation on Artificial Intelligence technology/systems to date, there will be a legislative framework covering all the legal liability issues.

Thus the scope of this book is limited to the discussion and determination of liabilities of autonomous vehicles specifically and not all kinds of AI in general.

1.1.2 What is Artificial Intelligence?

'John McCarthy' first used the term "*artificial intelligence in 1956 at the Dartmouth Conference.*" It was the year that artificial intelligence was born.

John McCarthy explains AI in the following words: "***AI as the science and engineering of making intelligent machines.***" In other terms, the key to creating computer frameworks that can perform tasks that ordinarily require human knowledge, such as discourse acknowledgement, visual discernment, navigation, and language interpretation, is sentient thinking.

Thus, Artificial Intelligence (AI) is a family of technology for trains machines to think and act similarly to people. Artificial intelligence has recently made this possible by producing tools and automated systems that are utilised in many different industries, including healthcare, drones, agriculture, and so forth. The Google predictive search engine is one of the most well-known examples of artificial intelligence in work. When users begin typing a search query, Google suggests options for them to choose from. Therefore, predictive searches are based on information that Google has gathered about users, including browsing history, location, age, and other private data. Google uses artificial intelligence to try to deduce what it is looking for.

1.1.2.1 Application of Artificial Intelligence in Diverse Fields

Moving on, the Contract Intelligence Platform from JPMorgan Chase analyses legal documents using "ML, AI, and Image Recognition Software." For instance, it took over 36,000 h to hand examine about 12,000 agreements, which is a long time for work that could have been done more quickly for a better company. However, once an AI system took over this task, it was finished in only a few seconds. So that's how AI differs from natural intelligence; despite the fact that AI cannot think or reason as people do, it has much greater computational capability than humans do due to the sheer processing power of computers needed to run machine learning algorithms and robust learning. The most complex of complex issues may now be calculated by AI in only a few seconds.

'IBM' is one of the industry leaders who created AI software exclusively for the medical field. IBM Artificial Intelligence Product, which is essentially 'IBM Watson', is utilised by over 230 healthcare facilities. In 2016, 'IBM Watson' was able to quickly compare 20 million oncology records and properly identify a patient's uncommon leukaemia disease. In essence, 20 million records were processed in a matter of seconds to minutes. This demonstrates how significant Artificial Intelligence has become because it has begun to affect every aspect of people's lives. Another project involves Google collaborating with an Indian network of eye care facilities to create an 'artificial intelligence system' that will analyse 'retinal images' and be able to diagnose conditions.

Another example is the use of artificial intelligence in face recognition on social media sites like Facebook, where it uses the "principles of machine learning and deep learning" to identify both can-tag friends and include face features. People rarely realise how frequently artificial intelligence (AI) is used in their daily lives, yet the auto-tagging tool that they use in Facebook is actually powered by "machine learning, deep learning, and neural networks." In fact, artificial intelligence plays a significant role in the daily operations of all social media platforms, including Instagram, Facebook, Twitter, and others. Another illustration of this is the AI employed by Twitter to identify any 'terrorism-related and hate content'. Recently, Twitter found nearly 300,000 accounts connected to terrorism, and 95 per cent of those accounts were actually made by non-humans, implying that these accounts were made by artificially intelligent machines.[1]

---

[1] *See* <https://www.cbinsights.com/research/autonomous-driverless-vehicles-corporations-list/>, accessed on October 21, 2023.

Another well-known application of AI is the virtual agents Siri and Alexa. The recently released Google Duplex virtual assistanthas astounded millions of people worldwide. It can not only answer calls and make appointments for specific people. But it may also sound incredibly lifelike by applying human filters to add a human touch to its operation. As a result, it can be difficult to tell it apart from humans when speaking on the phone.[2]

Autonomous Vehicles are another well-known application of artificial intelligence. These fully automated self-driving cars use "computer vision, image detection and processing, and deep learning in conjunction with artificial intelligence to automatically detect any objects or obstacles and navigate around them." Many Big Tech firms, including Google, Apple, Microsoft, Tesla, Facebook, and others, are essentially data-driven businesses that heavily rely on AI technology.[3]

Artificial intelligence is evolving into a more human-like communication tool by responding contextually and mimicking human speech patterns. AI is evolving into a very human-like being, expressing itself through artistic creations and the swiftly developed solutions it comes up with. The degree to which AI mimics human behaviour and can fool us with persuasive content despite our knowledge that it is delusional is proof that it is evolving into a human. Will we be able to accept that AI is evolving into a human? Or will our demise result from humanising AI? The catalyst for humanity's cataclysmic demise. However, we will undoubtedly need to shape, navigate, assess, mitigate, integrate, validate, and, most crucially, govern if AI is to become human.

1.1.2.2 Definitions of Artificial Intelligence

John McCarthy, the discipline's founder, stated the concept in 1955 as "***that of making a machine behave in ways that would be called intelligent if a human were so behaving***."[4]

---

[2] *Ibid.*

[3] *See* <https://www.cbinsights.com/research/autonomous-driverless-vehicles-corporations-list/>, accessed on October 21, 2023.

[4] Kaplan, J. (2016). *Artificial Intelligence* (2016 ed.). 198 Madison Avenue, New York, NY 10,016, United States of America: Oxford University Press 2016.

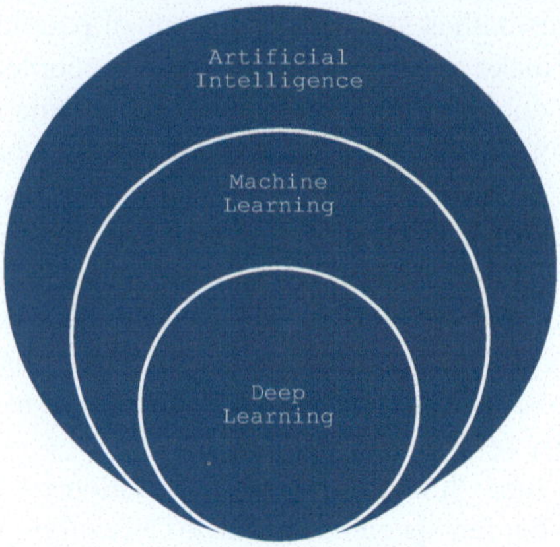

Artificial Intelligence

AI is a technology which is designed to mimic how a human brain thinks.

Machine Learning

ML is a "subset of AI", where the machine learns from a set of data and predicts decisions.

Deep Learning

It is a "subset of ML", that seeks to artificially imitate human cognitive abilities.

What is 'Artificial' aND 'Intelligence'?

Artificial Intelligence is a study of how to make a system, which can think, behave, and act exactly or better than what a human being can act or react.

Black's Law Dictionary

'Black's Law Dictionary's' explanation of artificial intelligence is ***"software used to make computers and robots work better than humans. The systems are rule based or neutral networks. It is used to help make new products, robotics, human language understanding, and computer vision*."**

Bellman *explained it as "the automation of activities that we associate with human thinking, activities such as decision-making, problem-solving, and learning*."

Kurzweil *explained it as "the art of creating machines that perform functions that require intelligence when performed by people*."

Author's Understanding of AI

AI is basically a man-made system, processed and created in such a fashion that made things autonomous in nature, either partial or full automation, in conformity with the ethical rules and deep neural network norms.

According to the author's view, AI is an intelligent technology. However, that intelligence is artificial, which is being processed by humans through the help of algorithms (which is step-by-step) mathematical calculations, i.e., algorithms. The nature of computer programs is such that they flow data. It makes patterns out of similar data, which is very much known as machine learning, learning through the help of big data making similar patterns out of massive data, which eventually make sense out of it at the end and helping machines to adapt, act, and behave in the same way, whenever the situation demands, or act in the same way whenever the similar situation comes in.

Algorithms → Machine Learning which includes (Deep learning + Neural networks + Speech recognition + voice recognition + virtual agents = Artificial Intelligence).

Now, the question is who is programming the algorithms?

It is a human being who is putting all efforts to make the machine learn! Learn from its experiences. Ultimately, humans are mastering the machine to make it intelligent so that it functions on its own with time. However, making a machine intelligent and independent would paralyse the human soon, losing its control and giving all reliance on the machine for their respective work, so how much reliance should individuals have on AI algorithms? Suppose the system is working ideally 99 times. On the 100th attempt if it crashes or fails in the system, then can it be said that it can completely rely and depend on AI? The failure of the 100th attempt made people realise that the reliance on AI algorithms system needs a careful check and accuracy in the system with no glitch of whatsoever nature.

The majority of AI authors concur that the approach taken is just as crucial as if the problem is solved. So, another mark of intelligence is how it fails gracefully. Understanding and respecting human limits and making plausible errors are hallmarks of expertise.

Types of Artificial Intelligence: Living in the Age of Artificial Narrow Intelligence

Artificial intelligence is classified into three distinct evolutionary stages, or one could say that AI is in three stages. It naturally has narrow artificial intelligence followed by artificial general intelligence, followed by artificial super-intelligence.

Types of AI:

Artificial Narrow Intelligence

Focuses on one area and a single problem—*Machine Learning*

Example: Siri, Alexa, Cortana, and AVs.

Artificial General Intelligence

Refers to a computer that is completely equal in intelligence to a person—*Machine Intelligence.*

Artificial Super Intelligence

An intellect that, in almost every discipline, is significantly smarter than the best human minds. —*Machine Consciousness.*

1.1.2.3 Needs Revisiting—Personhood[5]

Artificial Intelligence is the central factor for the disruptive shift of the 4.0 industrial revolution. Similarly, Artificial Intelligence frameworks are still at an exceptionally beginning stage. The attribution of any rights, duties, or obligations to AI frameworks is a troubling position that the Indian legal system seems unaware of. The legitimate status of an individual or substance is straightforwardly connected to its autonomy. This status is not simply conceded to people yet collaboration, companies just as associations or organisations.

However, with regards to artificial intelligence, then, at that point, it is anything but perceived at this point by any general set of laws as a lawful substance aside from "Saudi Arabia wherein a robot called Sophia," which the state has interpreted as a falsely intelligent humanoid with rights and obligations that are the same as those of humans and as a respectable person residing within the state. Artificially intelligent robots or programs may be given legal status depending on whether it is possible to grant them specific rights and obligations that a living person is typically reliant upon.

In the House of Lords,[6] the UK constituted the AI Committee. Concerning AI's legal definition and legal status as a person, the US government does not struggle to consider these issues.

"Section 3 of the European Bill, 2017" on AI gives the general definitions of AI as follows[7]:

- "Artificial systems capable of performing tasks without human presence (autonomous systems)."
- "Systems that think as by analogy with the human brain and are able to pass the Turing test[8] or another comparable test by processing natural language, representing knowledge, automated reasoning, and learning."
- "Systems that act rationally achieve goals through perception, planning, reasoning, learning, communication, decision-making, and action."[9]

As per European Union countries, they pay very particular attention to making legal regulations for self-driving cars. The German Traffic Act[10] puts the responsibility on the *owner* to manage and work on an automated or semi-automated car as it contemplates only a partial involvement of the 'Federal Ministry of Transport and the Digital Infrastructure'. As presented in the EU resolution on robotics ('European

[5] In the UK, the term 'legal personality' is more common, whereas in the US 'personhood' seems to be preferred. In the book, the terms 'personality' and 'personhood' are used interchangeably.

[6] Shead (2017).

[7] Ibid. at 6.

[8] "The Turing test, also known as the imitation game and first used by Alan Turing in 1950, measures a machine's ability to exhibit intelligent behaviour that is comparable to it or indistinguishable from that of a human. If the tester is unable to consistently discriminate between the machine and the person, the machine is said to have passed the test".

[9] Cantwell (2017).

[10] Czarnecki (2017).

Parliament Resolution, 2017 on Civil'), it talked about the most current, comprehensive, and conducive approach to the definition of present and potential legislation in *robotics*. It explains the types of AI use and ethics, covering all the liability issues, and for operators, developers, and manufacturers in robotics, it provides basic rules of conduct. These norms are based on three 'laws of robot technology'.[11]

Is it possible to give AI Legal Personality?

A collection of obligations and rights—Legal personality is a fiction created by individuals through the legal system or general laws. In this way, it has the freedom to decide what it should apply and what its composition should be. A key US decision from the eighteenth century focused on corporations' and companies' unique legal personalities, '*Trustees of Dartmouth College v. Woodward*,[12] Chief Justice Marshall' communicated the idea as follows:

A corporation is an 'artificial personality' that only exists in the eyes of the law and is intangible and elusive. Being a straightforward creature of law, it has only the characteristics that the approval of its formation bestows onto it, whether intentionally or accidentally. The rights and obligations of the latter are consequently functionally tied to those of the former. Persons in charge of or acting on behalf of the organisation are held accountable for both the physical and mental components of any wrongdoings. In this context, it's important to recognise that the legal personhood of corporations is not without limitations because the corporate curtain can be lifted to ignore it. A corporation may be penalised in order to punish those who oversee, manage, or possess it. Corporations and people that conceal themselves behind incorporation are subject to administrative, civil, and even criminal responsibility regimes. In the modern environment, where evolution is occurring at a faster rate than ever before, it is simple to see how constrained systems using artificial intelligence are made to do specific tasks in a timely manner.

A live person is independent or autonomous and has the capacity to make their own decisions. But an AI framework is established by persons and fills in according to the bearings of the projects that have been added to its framework to execute target jobs in a specific way. Companies and corporations are nonetheless accountable to their partners for any risk that may later develop as a result. Even if companies portray the situation as a different legal entity, they are nonetheless accountable to their partners for any risk that may later develop as a result of the trades that these businesses or organisations/corporations have made.

Challenges to AI as a Separate Entity—Not Equal to Human Being

Treating AI as a brand-new legal field that requires its own set of legal standards is a difficulty. The EU resolution does not nudge into this issue which is very much possible in the robotic application.[13]

---

[11] Azimov (1942.

[12] 17 U.S. (4 Wheat.) 518 (1819).

[13] *Id.* at 7–8.

The question of granting legal status is seen chiefly as theoretical. Legal persons, according to Joanna Bryson,[14] Mihalis Diamantis, and Thomas Grant, are "fictive, divisible, and not necessarily accountable." They claim that "legal personality is an artifice," and that "[l]egal people need not possess all the same rights and obligations, even within the same system."[15]

A legal person serves as a tool to help natural persons more effectively pursue their objectives. What objective—and whose objective—would be served if AIs were given legal status or specific rights? No matter how 'aware' or 'intelligent' the AI is, it will never be able to acquire legal status. Intentionality, free will, and consciousness are only a few examples of human characteristics that are thought to be necessary for moral and legal responsibility but are not present in any machine. Of course, it is feasible to question this approach's metaphysical underpinnings.

Although intentionality and free will are typically the foundations of legal accountability, 'guilty mind' and 'autonomy' frequently, they get treated as if they are real physical entities. Purely human traits, such as intention and free will, are only 'things' that people assign to one another in order to preserve order in their social relationships. It is a conceptual construct, not a thing that is 'actual', and its presence may be verified and quantified. Therefore, it cannot be a prerequisite for legal (or moral) culpability. Specific human characteristics, like consciousness and self-awareness, have been deemed unimportant from a legal standpoint, which immediately discards the limiting approach. Some people have traditionally been denied legal standing, whereas states or corporations that do not possess any human traits have been given such persons.

Therefore, it is not required to determine what computers must be able to do (in regards to imitating human characteristics or abilities) or what attributes they must possess in order to be recognised as individuals, writers, or innovators. Anyone may be given rights by the law. In the past, some legal systems have refused to acknowledge some individuals as legal persons or denied them a fundamental right, while acknowledging other entities as persons or granting them rights—even when the latter did not possess any human qualities. The legal system does not recognise something as a legal person based only on its inherent qualities since legal personhood is a fiction. Because of this, any item, including algorithms and computer systems, could be given legal personality, regardless of its level of creativity, intelligence, or consciousness. Reiterating that this grant is not based on any inherent qualities of the algorithm or machine, the legislature is entitled to introduce any legal interpretations that they deem necessary to achieve their goals. Despite the foregoing, anything other than a human cannot be given legal personality without specific arguments or 'good reasons'. The following inquiries come up: What would be the point of giving an algorithm individual identity? What would the advantages and hazards be? It would be necessary to choose the criteria for differentiating between algorithms that require personhood and those that do not since there are neither natural nor legal requirements for personhood.

[14] Bryson et al., "Of, for, and by the People".

[15] Ibid.

Another quality would have to be chosen because the vague notion of autonomy is inappropriate—if only because it is gradable and necessitates choosing the degree of autonomy that validates personhood. Would it have to do with how an artificial intelligence (AI) work is judged in terms of its creativity, originality, or emotional resonance? Which component of the system would be viewed as a human from a technical standpoint? Remember that an AI never exists in a vacuum and that its interests are just one component of a much larger system. How much, if any, liability would the algorithm's designer still bear for the algorithm's performance?

Furthermore, it is necessary to consider that algorithms do not generate themselves and that autonomous systems are not the result of the technological equivalent of a technically perfect idea.

In conclusion, giving AIs legal personhood raises a plethora of practical and technical issues. Last but not least, it's imperative to keep in mind that the law must be logically consistent.

1.1.3 The Legitimate Status of AI: Concluding Remarks

So, according to the study, Artificial Intelligence cannot be awarded legal personhood until and unless it becomes highly and fully autonomous in nature, in terms of autonomous vehicles, and in general, when it reaches the "level of Artificial General Intelligence and Artificial Super Intelligence, where Artificial Intelligence can make decisions on its own independently."

Otherwise, even for granting the status of electronic personality, or legal personality, it must meet the criteria of being independent in its own actions and decisions, being able to sue and be sued, and "*Artificial Intelligence is still at the stage of Artificial Narrow Intelligence*," where it is not even capable of perceiving and making decisions without human intervention.

Bibliography

Abbott R (2018) The reasonable computer: disrupting the paradigm of tort liability, 86 Geo. Wash. L. Rev. 1

A J Kurki V (2017) Legal Personhood: animals. Artifi Intell Unborn (2017 Ed.). (T. Pietrzykowsk, Ed.) Cambridge, Uk: Springe

Artificial Intelligence, The Law Dictionary (N.D.) https://Thelawdictionary.Org/ArtificialIntellAgence/[Https://Perma.Cc/5bpn-Ybte

David R (2016) Lawrence; Cesar Palacios-Gonzalez; John Harris, Artificial Intelligence The Shylock Syndrome, 25 Cambridge Q. Healthcare Ethics 250:261

Dremliuga R, Pavelkuznetcov, Mamychev A (2019) Criteria for recognition of AI as a legal person, 12 J. Pol. & L. 105

Dremliuga R, Pavelkuznetcov, Mamychev A (2019) Criteria For Recognition Of Ai as a legal person, 12 J. Pol L 105

European parliament, European civil law rules in robotics, (Dec. 8, 2019, 11:30 Pm) Regulation (Eu) 2016/679 Of The European Parliament And Of The Council Of Apr. 27, 2016

Goksu BB, Oze U (2020) Responsibility for damages caused by artificial intelligence. 23 Gsi Articleletter 64

Halkimoral R (2019) Responsibility of robots and hybrid agents the monist 102(2):259–275

Iriagiuffrida FL, Vermeys N (2018) A legal perspective on the trials and tribulations of AI: how artificial intelligence, the internet of things, smart contracts, and other technologies will affect the law, 68 Case W. Res L Rev 747

Ilková V, Ilka A (2017) Legal aspects of autonomous vehicles—an overview. Conference: 21st International Conference On Process Control (Pc)At: Štrbské Pleso, Slovakiahttps://doi.org/10.1109/Pc.2017.7976252

Iriagiuffrida FL, Vermeys N (2018) A legal perspective on the trials and tribulations of ai: how artificial intelligence, the internet of things, smart contracts, and other technologies will affect the law, 68 Case W. Res. L. Rev. 747

Kaplan J (2016) Artificial intelligence (2016 Ed.). 198 Madison Avenue, New York, Ny 10016, United States Of America: Oxford University Press

Keller P (2018) Autonomous vehicles, artificial intelligence, and the law. J Robot Artif Intell Law 1:101–109

Kuner C, Cateexpanding *FH (2018) The artificial intelligence-data protection debate international data privacy law 8(4)

Karen Yeungfive Fears about mass predictive personalization in an age of surveillance capitalism international data privacy law 8(3) (2018)

Khoury AH (2017) Intellectual property rights for Hubots: on the legal implications of human-like robots as innovators and creators, 35 Cardozo Arts &Ent. Lj 635

Marchant G, Bazzi R (2020) Autonomous vehicles and liability: what will juries do? Boston Univ J Sci Technol Law 26(1):67

Metz R, And the award for most nauseating self-driving car goes to … I Rode In A Bunch Of Autonomous Cars, So You Don't Have To"

Nick Bostrom Eliezer Yudkowsky The Ethics Of Artificial Intelligence Cambridge Handbook Of Artificial Intelligence, Eds. William Ramsey, And Keith Frankish Cambridge University Press (2011)

Nunez C (2017) Artificial intelligence and legal ethics: whether Ai lawyers can make ethical decisions, 20 Tul. J. Tech Intell Prop 189:204

On the protection of natural persons about the processing of personal data and the free movement of such data, and repealing directive 95/46/Ec (General Data Protection Regulation) (Dec. 9, 2019, Karen Yeungfive Fears About Mass Predictive Personalization In An Age Of Surveillance Capitalism International Data Privacy Law 8(3) (2018)

Pagallo U (2013) The laws of robots (2013 Ed.). Torino, Italy: Springer Dordrecht Heidelberg New York London, ISBN: 978-94-007-6563-4, Pg

Populism FLA (2018) Artificial Intelligence, jobs, and politics in the nearterm oxford review of. Economic Policy 34(3):393–417

Ryan Calo, Robots as legal metaphors, 30 Harv. J. L. & Tech. 209 (2016)

R. George Wright, The constitutional rights of advanced robots (And Of Human Beings), 71 Ark. L. Rev. 613 (2019)

Richter K (2019) Product liability, legal transplants, and artificial intelligence, 2019 harmonious: J Legal Soc Stud Se Eur 292

Rzeczycka H, Kovac M, Autonomous self-driving vehicles—the advent of a new legal era? King's Student Law Rev 10(I)

Santa Clara Law Review, Volume 33; Ronald B. Desilets, Jr., Note, Software Vendors' Exposure To Products Liability For Computer Viruses, 9 Computer/L.J.509,524 (1989)

Sartor G (1998) Judicial applications of artificial intelligence (Reprinted From Artificial Intelligence And Law 6(2–4)1998 Ed.). (K. Branting, Ed.) Aa Dordrecht, The Netherlands: 1998 Kluwer Academic Publishers

Scherer MU (2016) Regulating artificial intelligence systems: risks, challenges, competencies, and strategies. Harv J Law Technol 29(2). Spring

Turner J (2019) *Robot Rules*-regulating artificial intelligence, London,-Uk: Palgrave Macmillan, ISBN: 978-3-319-96234-4, Pg

The Future Computed: Artificial Intelligence And Its Role In Society, Microsoft (2018)

Us Defence Science Board, "*Summer Study On Autonomy*," (Us Department Of Defence, 2016. Executive Office Of The President (2016) *Artificial Intelligence, Automation And The Economy*," Washington, Dc, Usa

Vladeck DC (2014) Machines without principals: liability rules and artificial intelligence, 89 Wash L Rev 117

Walton D (2013) Argumentation methods for artificial intelligence in law (2013 Ed.). Winnipeg, Manitoba R3b 2e9, Canada: Springer Berlin Heidelberg New York

Walpert JD (2017) Carpooling liability: applying tort law principles to the joint emergence of self-driving automobiles and transportation network companies, 85 Fordham L Rev 1863

Wither R, The Eu Is trying to decide whether to grant robots personhood. European commission high-level expert group on artificial intelligence, policy, and investment recommendation on trustworthy Ai

Statutes And International Agreements

UN Convention on Road Traffic, 1948

Vienna Convention on Road Traffic, 1968

German Road Traffic (Amendment) Act, 2017

German Civil Code,1900

German Product Liability Law, 1989

California Civil Code,1872

California Vehicle Code,1993

California Code Of Civil Procedure,1872

Consumer Protection Act, 2019

Motor Vehicle Act, 1988

Motor Vehicle (Amendment) Act, 2019

Consumer Protection Act 1986

Law Of Tort

Bharatiya Nyaya Sanhita, 2023

Constitution Of India

Reports

National Strategy for Artificial Intelligence #AIFORALL—Discussion Paper (NITI Aayog, June 2018)

2016–2019 Progress Report: Advancing Artificial Intelligence by Artificial Intelligence Research & Development Interagency Working Group, November 2019

Working Document: Enforcement Mechanisms for Responsible #AIforAll 2020: Towards Responsible AI for All (Part 1)

Mckinsey Global Institute—Notes From The AI Frontier Modeling The Impact Of AI on The World Economy, September 2018.

Corporate Partnership Board Report: Governing Transport in the Algorithmic Age by International Transport Forum, December 2018 at the OECD in France.

Recommendation Report of the Council on Artificial Intelligence—OECD Legal Instruments 2020.
NTDPC, India Transport Report: Moving India to 2032.
Future of Jobs in India: A 2022 Perspective, 2017.

Websites

http://legalinstruments.oecd.org
https://www.nitrd.gov/pubs/National-AI-RD-Strategy-2019.pdf
https://www.whitehouse.gov/ai/ai-american-innovation/, https://www.nitrd.gov/about/.
www.mckinsey.com/mgi.
www.medium.com
www.CSRankings.org
https://heinonline.org/HOL/License
www.harvardbusinessreviewpress.com
www.nytimes.com/section/technology
https://www.bloomberg.com/technology
https://www.sae.org/standard

Chapter 2
Scope of Artificial Intelligence

Abstract In this chapter, the author has analysed the potential of constituent technologies involved in AI and how it helps make AI valuable and successful. This chapter has explained why the peculiarities of artificial intelligence, potential ethical and legal conundrums, and solutions to these problems are discussed. This raises three major concerns: responsibility, or who is responsible if AI causes harm; rights, or the debatable moral and practical justifications for bestowing legal identity upon AI; and the ethics surrounding AI decision-making. AI is the technology used to make machines work like real human beings. The potentials of AI are many—like, it reduces errors and increases the chances of achieving accuracy, due diligence, and prediction technology. So, in the coming ten years, technologies in narrow fields such as speech recognition will continue to improve and reach the human level. In 10 years, AI will be able to communicate better with a human in unstructured English using text or voice, navigate(not perfect) in an unprepared environment, and have some rudimentary common-sense—and domain-specific intelligence. However, the field of artificial consciousness remains in its infancy, so the early years of the twenty-first century should see dramatic strides forward in this area, however. In October 2017, Saudi Arabia conceded 'citizenship' to a humanoid robot named Sophia. Only days after the Saudi declaration, Tokyo's Shibuya locale reports that an AI framework had been allowed 'residency'.

S. Fahim, *Ethico-Legal Aspect of AI-driven Driverless Cars*, Frontiers of Artificial Intelligence, Ethics and Multidisciplinary Applications,
https://doi.org/10.1007/978-981-97-6883-7_2

2.1 Introduction and Evolution of Self-driving Cars

Initially,[1] the desire to develop self-driving cars[2] stemmed from concerns about national security.[3] The purpose was to develop unmanned military vehicles.[4] In 2004,[5] the 'Defence Advanced Research Projects Agency (DARPA)' of the Pentagon issued a challenge to innovators to develop self-driving vehicles capable of traversing the Mojave Desert.[6]

The 142-mile course was not completed by any of the competitors; the top-scoring car travelled fewer than 8 miles.[7] DARPA held a competition incorporating traffic signals and barriers in a simulated city just three years later, and six out of eleven teams passed the test.[8]

Self-driving vehicles[9] are based on cutting-edge technology, but in their most basic form, they use comprehensive maps and sensor data[10] to understand their location and how to respond.[11] Sensors detect objects around the car,[12] and software classifies them based on their movement patterns, sizes, and forms.[13] The advanced Program uses predictive technologies to forecast how things in the immediate vicinity of the

---

[1] Walpert, J. D. (2016). Carpooling liability: applying tort law principles to the joint emergence of self-driving automobiles and transportation network companies. *Fordham L. Rev.*, *85*, 1863. See also <https://ir.lawnet.fordham.edu/flr/vol85/iss4/12/, accessed on October 21, 2023.

[2] *Supra* note 1; See also <https://ir.lawnet.fordham.edu/flr/vol85/iss4/12/, accessed on October 21, 2023.

[3] *Supra* note 1; Press Release, U.S. Dep't of Def., The DARPA Grand Challenge: Ten Years Later (Mar. 13, 2014), http://www.dod.mil/pubs/foi/Reading_Room/DARPA/15-F-0059 _ DOC_22_NEWS_GC_10_YRS_LATER.pdf [https://perma.cc/4BCD-P5A7]. This initial motivation mirrors the original impetus for the Internet. See Barry M. Leiner et al., Brief History of the Internet, INTERNET SOC'Y 2 (Oct. 15, 2012), http://www.internetsociety.org/ sites/default/files/ Brief_History_of_the_Internet.pdf [https://perma.cc/M58L-2B8Y].

[4] *Supra* note 1; See Press Release, U.S. Dep't of Def., supra note 1. ("The longer-term aim was to accelerate development of [autonomous vehicles] that could ultimately substitute for men and women in hazardous military operations, such as supply convoys.").

[5] Ibid.

[6] Ibid.

[7] DARPA held another competition the next year, where five vehicles out of 195 teams completed the course.

[8] *Supra* note 1.

[9] Ibid.

[10] Ibid.

[11] Technology, WAYMO, https://waymo.com/tech/ (last visited Feb. 16, 2020) [https://perma.cc/ P326-3XXD].

[12] *Supra* note 1.

[13] Ibid.

car would behave or move.[14] Finally, the software in the car decides what to do based on its surroundings[15] and pertinent situations.

A Stanford University[16] team led by Sebastian Thrun,[17] a Google developer and co-inventor of the company's 'Street View' mapping tool,[18] won the second DARPA competition using an early version of this technology.

Thrun and his technical team, together with Google co-founder Larry Page, were early proponents of self-driving vehicles'[19] promise to reduce energy costs and make roadways safer.[20]

As a result, the technology industry has become a crucial player in the development of self-driving vehicles.[21]

2.1.1 Technologies that Make Self-Driving Cars a Reality[22]

While autonomous vehicles (AVs) will combine a wide range of technological advancements, this chapter will focus on the technologies that enable automated driving. AVs must first sense the environment in which they work, then understand it, and adjust their movement accordingly. It goes into the technology underlying each of these tasks briefly, because an AV's potential liability is frequently determined by the capability of these systems.[23]

a. **Sensors**: The three primary kinds of sensors used by Autonomous Vehicles to sense their surroundings are radar, lidar, and cameras. Additionally, Global positioning system information and thorough environment maps are used to enhance sensor data in order to acquire a more complete picture of the surroundings. Other

---

[14] Ibid. *See* also, for example, the software might predict that a pedestrian standing at a crosswalk is waiting to cross the street.

[15] Ibid. *See* also Circumstances include, for example, road work, closed lanes, railroad-crossing indicators, and cyclists' hand signals.

[16] *Supra* note 1.

[17] Ibid.

[18] John Markoff, Google Cars Drive Themselves, in Traffic, N.Y. TIMES (Oct. 9, 2010), http://www.nytimes.com/2010/10/10/science/10google.html [https://perma.cc/RT8E- 9SXV].

[19] *Supra* note 1.

[20] *See id.* (noting "Dr. Thrun sounds like an evangelist when he speaks of robot cars" and the technology's potential to "reduce fuel consumption" and "reduce[] [the] possibility of accidents").

[21] *See* Ujjayini Bose, Note, The Black Box Solution to Autonomous Liability, 92 WASH. U. L. REV. 1325, 1328 (2015) (describing how Google's participation in the DARPA challenges spurred its desire to develop self-driving vehicles for the public).

[22] MARCHANT, G., & BAZZI, R. AUTONOMOUS VEHICLES AND LIABILITY: WHAT WILL JURIES DO?.

[23] *Supra* note 22.

environmental sounds and emergency alarms are also picked up by AVs using audio sensors.[24]

i. **Radar**: Radar creates a picture of the surroundings by producing *'radio waves'* and receiving the *'reflected waves'*.[25] It can also be used to determine the speed of moving objects in the environment.[26] Radar works effectively in bad weather and at night and can detect objects at a distance, although it provides images with low quality.[27]
ii. **Lidar**: Lidar uses a *'pulsed laser light'* source and sensors to detect the *"reflected light and create a three-dimensional picture of objects"* in the surroundings.[28] In general, Lidar can give maximum-resolution pictures than radar.[29]It also has the benefit of being able to operate at night because it is not reliant on external light.[30] In addition, Lidar systems offer a larger field of view than radar systems.[31] Lidar, on the other hand, does not perform well in inclement weather and is prone to hacking.[32] With the exception of Tesla, most self-driving car manufacturers use Lidar.[33]
iii. **2D Cameras**: Two-dimensional cameras catch visible light to create a 2D image of the environment, which is then translated by algorithmic approaches to generate a 3D image of the scene's image. Cameras have the benefit of being inexpensive sensors, but they struggle in dim light.[34] Recent efforts have started to investigate the possibility of supplementing

[24] WAYMO, WAYMO SAFETY REPORT: ON THE ROAD TO FULLY SELF-DRIVING 14 (2018), https://storage.googleapis.com/sdc-prod/v1/safety-report/Safety%20Report%202018.pdf [https://perma.cc/77KA-QJFY]; see, e.g., NURO, DELIVERING SAFETY: NURO'S APPROACH 12 (2018), https://static1.squarespace.com/static/57bcb0e02994ca36c2ee746c/t/5b9a00848a922d8eaecf65a2/1536819358607/delivering_safety_nuros_approach.pdf.

[25] WAYMO, *supra* note 24, at 14. See generally Guilio Reina, David Johnson & James Underwood, Radar Sensing for Intelligent Vehicles in Urban Environments, 15 SENSORS 14,661 (2015).

[26] NURO, *supra* note 24, at 19.

[27] Jelena Kocić, Nenad Jovičić & Vujo Drndarević, Sensors and Sensor Fusion in Autonomous Vehicles 1, 2 (26th Telecomms. Forum TELFOR 2018), https://ieeexplore.ieee.org/stamp/stamp.jsp?tp=&arnumber=8612054.

[28] Jeff Hecht, Lidar for Self-Driving Cars, 29 OPTICS & PHOTONICS NEWS 26, 41 (2018).

[29] *Id.*

[30] Phillip Lindner & Gerd Wanielik, 3D LIDAR Processing For Vehicle Safety and Environment Recognition, 2019 IEEE WORKSHOP ON COMPUTATIONAL INTELLIGENCE IN VEHICLES AND VEHICULAR SYSTEMS 66, 66 (2019), https://ieeexplore.ieee.org/stamp/stamp.jsp?tp=&arnumber=4938725.

[31] Hecht, *supra* note 28, at 33.

[32] Mark Harris, Researcher Hacks Self-driving Car Sensors, IEEE SPECTRUM (Sept. 4, 2015), https://spectrum.ieee.org/cars-that-think/transportation/self-driving/researcher-hacks-selfdriving-car-sensor [https://perma.cc/KG2G-EPS8].

[33] Hecht, *supra* note 28, at 29.

[34] *Id.*

existing cameras with *'infrared thermal imaging spectrum'* for increased safety.[35]

b. **Recognising and interpreting the surroundings**: To get a complete picture of their surroundings, data from all of an AV's sensor inputs are combined.[36] To create a model of objects and their motions in the environment, radar velocity data is combined with lidar imagery.[37] To precisely establish the position of the vehicle and other objects in the environment, this information is combined with the camera, Global positioning, and the database of saved maps. Using computer vision[38] and machine learning approaches,[39] interpreting the environment entails recognising things in the environment. Machine learning is defined[40] as "a set of methods that can automatically find patterns in data and then utilise the uncovered patterns to forecast future data or perform various types of decision-making under uncertainty"[41] at a high level.[42] The training data is the data that is used in learning (or training set).[43] Scene understanding and forecasting the behaviour of other vehicles are both done using machine learning techniques. While AVs have come a long way in terms of comprehending their surroundings, extreme weather conditions like sandstorms, heavy rain, fog, or snow still present challenges.[44]

Companies developing self-driving cars use cryptic algorithms. The effectiveness of machine learning systems is influenced by the quality of the training data, which must be representative of the various situations in which the system will be used. Additionally, machine learning systems are vulnerable to adversarial attacks. A method of modifying an input to a machine learning system that is undetectable to humans but leads the system to understand or anticipate the input wrongly is known

---

35 *Id.*

36 *Supra* note 22.

37 Ibid.

38 Sayanan Sivaraman & Mohan Manubhai Trivedi, Looking at Vehicles on the Road: A Survey of Vision-based Vehicle Detection, Tracking, and Behavior Analysis, 14 IEEE TRANS. INTELLIGENT TRANSP. SYST. 1773, 1775 (2013).

39 Andreas Geiger, Philip Lenz & Raquel Urtasun, Are We Ready for Autonomous Driving? The KITTI Vision Benchmark Suite, IEEE CONF. ON COMPUTER VISION AND PATTERN RECOGNITION (2012), https://ieeexplore.ieee.org/abstract/document/6248074 [https://perma.cc/S4XL-66E7].

40 Markus Kuderer, Shilpa Gulati & Wolfram Burgard, Learning Driving Styles For Autonomous Vehicles From Demonstration, IEEE INT'L CONF. ON ROBOTICS AND AUTOMATION 2641, 2641–22 (2015); Moritz Menze & Andreas Geiger, Object Scene Flow for Autonomous Vehicles, IEEE CONF. ON COMPUTER VISION AND PATTERN RECOGNITION (2015), available at http://cvlibs.net/publications/Menze2015CVPR.pdf [https://perma.cc/V8N5-8FHG].

41 Kevin P. Murphy, MACHINE LEARNING: A PROBABILISTIC PERSPECTIVE 1 (2012).

42 Liangzhi Li, Kaoru Ota & Mianxiong Dong, Humanlike Driving: Empirical Decision- Making System for Autonomous Vehicles, 67 IEEE TRANS. VEHICULAR TECH. 6814, 6815–16 (2018).

43 *Id.*

44 Tom Krisher, *5 Reasons Why Autonomous Cars Aren't Coming Anytime Soon*, ASSOC. PRESS (Feb. 4, 2019), https://www.apnews.com/b67a0d6b6413406fb4121553cdf0b95a [https://perma.cc/E8TC-RJB2].

as an adversarial attack.[45] Adversarial attacks are a sign that current machine learning systems are not sufficiently secure, which makes evaluating machine learning-based systems challenging.[46]

The automation levels were made and divided into six levels in 2016 by the Society of Automotive Engineers (SAE International) by the US Department of Transportation, the general public of car manufacturers, which has since become the business standard when alluding to independent vehicles. Likewise, it has been observed that these levels have portrayed other mechanical frameworks when examining levels of self-sufficiency.

Level 0 requires complete control from the driver *(no driver automation)* as the vehicle has no emotionally supportive networks.[47]

Level 1 includes essential help highlights or features in case of driver assistance. Level 1 vehicles are regularly outfitted with an electronically monitored slowing mechanism/automated base system (ABS) and journey control. The driver is still in full control of the vehicle yet gets a few types of help.[48]

Level 2 relates to semi-self-autonomous driving, i.e., *partial driving automation.* This means advanced driver assistance systems (ADAS). At this level, the vehicle can drive straight, remain in its path, and control the good ways from vehicles in front entirely all alone. For instance, in abrupt gridlocks out and about, the vehicle can assume responsibility for guiding and slowing down.[49]

Level 3 characterises the second level when the installed frameworks can assume control over every driving capacity in specific circumstances. So, the jump from Level 2 to Level 3 from a technological perspective is very substantial but very subtle if it is not negligible from a human perspective. So, in any case, the driver must stay at the station constantly and be prepared to dominate, i.e., manual intervention.[50]

Level 4 is an entirely autonomous experience (high driving automation), with somebody in the driver's seat.[51]

Level 5 vehicles are fully self-driving vehicles *(full driving automation).* They work autonomously in all conditions. There is no requirement for individuals in the vehicle to make any move, but have to keep their hand on steering while driving as instructed by Tesla and other companies. It is accepted that such vehicles will not be furnished with components, for example, a directing wheel.[52]

---

[45] Alexy Kurakin, Ian Goodfellow & Samy Bengio, *Adversarial Examples in the Physical World* (Feb. 11, 2017), https://arxiv.org/pdf/1607.02533.pdf [https://perma.cc/XN85- BDAX]; Christian Szegedy et al., Intriguing Properties of Neural Networks (Feb. 14, 2014), https://arxiv.org/abs/1312.6199 [https://perma.cc/N7Y9-XKAM].

[46] Cumhur Erkan Tuncali et al., Simulation-based Adversarial Test Generation for Autonomous Vehicles with Machine Learning Components (Jan. 7, 2018), https://arxiv.org/pdf/1804.06760.pdf [https://perma.cc/Y3ZA-Y46F].

[47] *Supra* note 22.

[48] Ibid.

[49] *Supra* note 22.

[50] Ibid.

[51] Ibid.

[52] Ibid.

Should a driverless vehicle glitch and cause a mishap, who will be blamed: The individual involving the driverless vehicle/ owner of the vehicle or the vehicle manufacturer? The innovation for driverless vehicles exists, and the idea will soon become a reality for most drivers, vehicle manufacturers, and collision protection companies around the globe.[53] They concocted a type of guidelines and protection terms and conditions that best suits vehicles that drive themselves. Notwithstanding, it is just a short time before we discover, and up to that point, everything else is just a conjecture.[54]

2.1.2 *Artificial Intelligence and Its Types*

Artificial Intelligence's primary purpose is to help machines become more human-like. As a result, the basic technique for depicting AI is based on how well it can reproduce human-like actions. There are two categories of artificial intelligence, both of which rely on simulating the workings of the human brain. One type of request that the 'Based on Functionality' AI group receives is on the basis of their similarity to the human mind and its capacity for thought and emotion independently. The next representation technique, 'Based on Capabilities' of AI opposite Human Intelligence, is dynamically indisputable in the tech industry.[55]

1. **Receptive Machine**

They are the most important and well-known type of artificial intelligence. They simulate how a person would react to certain stimulation. Because this type of AI lacks memory capacity, they have recently had trouble using the data they have collected to produce improved results. These AI types cannot therefore prepare themselves like the others can. The perfect example of these machines is IBM's Deep Blue, a supercomputer that can play chess. It is praised for defeating international chess champion Garry Kasparov in the latter half of the 1990s. Dark Blue has the ability to identify different chess pieces and their movements. It is able to discriminate between all possible legal actions for both itself and its opponents. It decides on the best course of action in light of the alternative. In any case, as these technologies lack internal memories, they are unable to learn from their prior actions.[56]

2. **Limited Theory**

Along with the capability of Reactive Machines, this type of AI has memory capabilities, allowing it to draw on historical information to make wiser decisions in the future. This category includes the vast majority of everyday applications that are

---

[53] *Supra* note 22.

[54] *See* <https://www.cbinsights.com/research/autonomous-driverless-vehicles-corporations-list/>, accessed on October 26, 2023.

[55] *See Supra* note 55, accessed on October 17, 2023.

[56] Ibid.

present around us. A substantial amount of preparatory data that is saved in these AI programs' memory can be used as the source of the viewpoint model. Example: There are several applications for limited memory technology in self-driving cars. They keep track of a hundred various types of information to enable them to drive as naturally as a human does, including GPS location, nearby vehicle speeds, and the nature of obstructions.[57]

3. **Theory of Mind**

These kinds of AI are typically maintained in research labs and are in the 'Work in Progress' stage. Once developed, these sorts of AI will significantly minimise human characteristics such as needs, preferences, sentiments, viewpoints, and so on. The AI will have the opportunity to alter its response once Human personalities and their inclinations are taken into account. Example: In his research, author Winston showed a model of a robot that can go through a small hallway with other robots coming from the opposite direction. The AI can foresee various robot developments and can take a different route or veer right or left to avoid a potential collision with the advancing robots. Wilson claims that this robot chooses its action based on the 'presence of mind' of how different robots will move.

4. **Autonomous AI**

The final type of AI is this. As of right now, it only exists in theory and is only found in science fiction movies. These AI can evoke human emotions and understand them, in addition to having their own sensations. AI sceptics like Elon Musk are cautious about this type of AI. The reason for this is that once an AI enters self-preservation mode, it may begin to perceive humanity as a potential threat and, implicitly or explicitly, may want to eradicate humanity.[58]

Classification of AI

1. **Artificial Narrow Intelligence (ANI)**

This category encompasses all current AI applications that humans encounter in their daily lives. Artificial Intelligence is far from human abilities and has expertise only in some areas. It does not have thinking and perception abilities. *'Artificial Narrow Intelligence'* incorporates an AI framework that can perform barely characterised explicit assignments simply like people. These machines cannot perform assignments for which it was not modified beforehand, so they fizzle at playing out the phenomenal task. In light of this framework is the mix of all responsive and restricted memory artificial intelligence. ANI computations, which a person uses in this day and age for completing the most complex predictions, fall under this classification.[59]

---

[57] *See Supra* note 55, accessed on September 17, 2023.

[58] *See* id.

[59] Ibid.

2. **Artificial General Intelligence (AGI)**

AGI can prepare, learn, comprehend, and perform works simply like a normal individual would. These frameworks will have multi-practical abilities cutting across various areas. When confronted with extraordinary conditions, these frameworks will be more nimble and respond and improvise like people. There is no concrete example of this kind of AI. Yet, in this field, substantial advancements have been made.[60]

3. **Artificial Super Intelligence (ASI)**

The most important objective of AI development will be to develop counterfeit Super Intelligence. The most important sort of knowledge in the world will be ASI. Due to its outrageously unequalled information preparation, memory, and dynamic capability, better than humans, it will be able to complete every duty. Many experts worry that the introduction of ASI will bring about the 'Technological Singularity'. It is a speculative scenario where creativity will reach a saturation point and cause an unfathomable transformation in Human Civilisation. The future's shape is now difficult to anticipate once a more potent sort of AI materialises.[61]

However, since humans are just in the early stages of improving cutting-edge AI, it is certain that it will take a while to reach that stage. For proponents of artificial intelligence, it might be said that people are only now beginning to unearth what lies beneath to reveal AI's true potential. For AI sceptics, the Technological Singularity is still a long way off. It may be viewed as a threat to humanity in the future.[62]

2.2 Artificial Intelligence and Its Constituent Technologies/Potentials Involved

Artificial intelligence (AI) is a combination of science and computing that enables any machine—framework, software, or otherwise—to perform intelligent and innovative functions. Devices using artificial intelligence and deep understanding provide an investigative report that helps to improve the clarity of planning, thinking, critical thinking, and learning.[63]

---

[60] *See Supra* note 55, accessed on September 17, 2023.

[61] Ibid.

[62] *Id.*

[63] *Supra* note 22.

2.2.1 Frontiers of AI—Constituent Technologies Involved

Advancements utilised in artificial intelligence—constituent advancements associated with artificial intelligence are as per the following:

1. **Natural Language Processing**

Natural Language Processing (NLP) is a technique for teaching machines or assisting them in understanding the standard language in which humans communicate. A primary distinguishing factor between humans and other animals is our ability to use language. It uses words to communicate and help us think, remember, assign things to categories, and label individuals. Language serves not only to describe but also to educate, create, imagine, indicate intentions, make commitments, and identify people of similar heritage, among many other things. Wherein Natural Language Processing (NLP) is used to understand given data's meaning (semantics). For example, someone found a wallet near the bank. The task of NLP is to understand in the end that 'bank' refers to a financial institute or 'riverbank'. Text analytics or text mining is a process of extracting hidden information inside text data through pattern recognition and is used to understand the structure of given text data (syntax).[64]

The self-driving car NLP must interpret what the human has said and then inform the human of any concerns. The self-driving car should repeat what was said and then express any concerns, such as whether the request is impossible, dangerous, or illegal, or whatever other issues may exist. NLP applications for personal applications (e.g., Alexa, Cortana, Google Assistant, and Siri) and home assistant/entertainment applications have recently evolved in user devices (e.g., Amazon Echo, Apple Home Pod, and Google Assistant).[65]

To focus on the automated driving experience, the autonomous vehicle industry is leveraging AI and very advanced computing capabilities with network and cloud connectivity. With *Level 5 of the International Society of Automotive Engineers by the US Department of Transportation* full autonomous 'no driver' vehicles, there is an opportunity to improve the interactive experience for passengers who will be the only occupants. Focusing on streaming HD video content and bringing VR to the car can also improve the passenger experience. NLP has enormous potential in these and many other areas. To make this happen, the ecosystem needs NLP actors to boldly join the AV actors and extend their platform APIs, bringing NLP to every car. Natural Language Processing (NLP) applications enable not only a richer passenger experience, but also a trust relationship between the passenger and the autonomous vehicle.[66]

---

[64] Odukha, O. (2018). 'How Machine Learning Algorithms Make Self-Driving Cars a Reality', Intellias Blog Post, updated on May 13, 2024, accessible at https://intellias.com/how-machine-learning-algorithms-make-self-driving-cars-a-reality/, accessed on September 21, 2023.

[65] *Supra* note 65.

[66] *Supra* note 65.

2. **Machine Learning**

Machine learning is a powerful technology when used in a self-driving car. The future of transportation will be defined by self-driving cars that use machine learning. And it's no secret that they're a match made in heaven.[67] In autonomous vehicles, machine learning algorithms are most commonly used for perception and decision-making. However, there are many more algorithms and possibilities for self-driving cars that can be discovered using machine learning. For example, machine learning can be used for autonomous navigation and recognising a driver's state. Self-driving cars are made possible by machine learning algorithms. They enable a car to collect data from cameras and other sensors about its surroundings, interpret it, and decide what actions to take. Machine learning even enables automobiles to learn how to perform these tasks as well as (or better than) humans. In self-driving cars, machine learning algorithms are used. The feature transform is scale-invariant.[68]

(SIFT)

Think of a vehicle that is concealed behind a tree. Could an automated vehicle notice it? If SIFT was employed, yes. The scale-invariant feature transform allows for image matching and object recognition for objects that are only partially visible. Using an image database, the program extracts the important features (or salient points) of an object. These are features of the thing that remain the same regardless of how it is rotated, cluttered, or noisy. Self-driving car machine learning algorithms compare each new image to the SIFT features that were derived from the database. It finds a correlation between items to identify them. An autonomous vehicle uses the three corners of a triangle road sign as feature points. A self-driving car employing SIFT would recognise a triangular road sign regardless of damage or bend back because of the sign's fundamental properties.[69]

AdaBoost[70]

A decision matrix algorithm called AdaBoost makes sure that learning is boosted adaptively. In essence, it assesses how well the results of other regression and classification algorithms match up with accurate predictions. Multiple algorithms' performance is combined and enhanced using AdaBoost so that they cooperate and enhance one another. Although individual algorithms are probably not very good, their combined performance can help learning. AdaBoost helps self-driving cars make decisions and recognise objects more precisely. It is particularly helpful for identifying faces, people on foot, and moving automobiles.

---

[67] Ibid.

[68] Ibid.

[69] *Supra* note 65.

[70] *Supra* note 65.

TextonBoost[71]

Similar to AdaBoost, TextonBoost enhances picture recognition using texton labelling. Textons are collections of visual data that share similar traits and react similarly to filters. In a machine learning-based self-driving automobile project, the TextonBoost algorithm combines data from appearance, shape, and context. Simply put, it's not always possible to accurately label an object based solely on its look. Actually, TextonBoost improves object recognition for self-driving automobiles. The object detection and object recognition abilities of autonomous cars are enhanced by the machine learning method.[72]

Histogram Oriented Gradient (HOG)[73]

Histogram of directed gradients is one of the most fundamental machine learning methods for computer vision and autonomous driving (HOG). HOG connects the computed gradients in each cell and counts the occurrences of each direction. The Support Vector Machine (SVM) is then given these features in order to classify data.

Images are essentially characterised by HOG as distributions of picture intensity. In addition to being more than just a collection of pixels, it creates a coded and compressed version of an image that has a useful image gradient. HOG can also assist autonomous vehicles because it is a potent first step in the image identification process. It's intriguing that HOG is so good at spotting people. Without the use of machine learning in autonomous vehicles, this sector is hard because of the range of appearances humans have and stances they can adopt. Surprisingly, this issue is resolved for driverless automobiles with the HOG algorithm.[74]

YOLO[75]

A machine learning method called YOLO (You Only Look Once) is used to categorise items including vehicles, people, and trees. In actuality, it uses an algorithm other than HOG. Segmenting the full image after analysis, YOLO assigns labels to each kind of object in accordance with its distinct set of attributes. The algorithm produces bounding boxes and predictions for each image segment. It just does one network evaluation and takes into account each prediction in light of the complete image. On the other hand, alternative detection techniques use detectors and classifiers to numerous locations and sections of a picture. Consequently, YOLO is quicker and more accurate than HOG. The YOLO method is a great tool for autonomous vehicles' object detection. It guarantees fast processing and vehicle response to real-world scenarios.[76]

---

[71] Ibid.

[72] *Supra* note 65.

[73] *Supra* note 65.

[74] Ibid.

[75] *Supra* note 65.

[76] Ibid.

3. **Artificial Neural Networks**[77]

Artificial Neural Network (ANN) utilises the preparation of the cerebrum as a premise to create calculations that can be utilised to display complex examples and forecast issues. How about if it starts by first agreement, on how the cerebrum measures data: In our cerebrum/brain, there are billions of cells called neurons, which measure data as electric signs. Outside data/boosts are gotten by the neuron's dendrites, handled in the neuron cell body, changed to yield, and went through the Axon to the next neuron. The next neuron can decide to either acknowledge it or reject it relying upon the sign's strength.[78]

4. **Robotic Process Automation**

It makes use of content to simulate the human cycle and enlists the help of a robot to complete it properly. So, what does Robotics entail? Robotics should be self-explanatory; it entails creating machines that are capable of carrying out real-world tasks. Making a single device capable of handling a wide range of shapes, loads, and delicacy, on the other hand, remains a challenge at the cutting edge of AI. The main problem here is responding to constantly changing or confusing conditions. The autonomous vehicle, which explores roads and manages places in collaboration with human-controlled automobiles, bikes, and other vehicles, is the apex of advanced mechanical research in this regard.[79]

5. **Facial Recognition**

It helps in the perception of the human face via development. In order to find a match using biometric features, human faces are built from video or photos and integrated with the database. The security issue is a huge test when it comes to implementing this advancement. The process of sensing and recognising an object or feature in a digitised image or video is known as image acknowledgement. Artificial Intelligence is being placed on top of this innovation on a regular basis, with remarkable results. The human credits and genuine highlights of a body's shape and structure are distinguished and broken down by this innovation.[80]

6. **Speech Recognition**

SIRI is the best case of speech recognition which comprehends and connects with the voice reaction of human language by portable applications. When artificial intelligence (AI) was developed, it contacted practically all features of life and environmental factors. Speech recognition is one such innovation that AI enables to add comfort to its clients. This innovation can change over voice messages to messages.

[77] Ibid.

[78] Ibid.

[79] Kaplan, J. (2016). *Artificial Intelligence* (2016 ed.). 198 Madison Avenue, New York, NY 10,016, United Sttes of America: Oxford University Press 2016, pg. 62–64.

[80] Ibid.

Furthermore, it likewise can perceive an individual dependent on their voice order. Consequently, this AI-powered innovation speech recognition picked up mammoth significance among tech goliaths, for example, Apple, Microsoft, Amazon, Google, Facebook, and so forth. Amazon Echo, Siri, and Google Home are some applications and gadgets that overwhelmed the market with speech recognition highlights. For instance, Microsoft Windows added the voice included in its update empowering clients to direct messages at the speed of typical human discourse. Subsequently, optional exploration affirmed that before 2020, most web crawlers would utilise voice innovation to oblige the pursuit of necessity. Likewise, it has been anticipated that the quantity of voice-actuated brilliant speaker proprietors will increase in the years to come. Effectively 2,600 voice applications exist for shoppers to download and utilise. In 2009, a gathering of analysts at the University of Toronto teamed up with IBM Research to apply AI strategies to the issue, decreasing blunder rates by an astounding 30%.[81]

7. **Virtual Agents**

Presently, the voice recognition abilities are planning gatherings, overseeing messages, setting up contact with the retailers, overseeing playlists, requesting food, and working web crawlers on the web. Such offices are effectively accessible on every single individual gadget. Apple's Siri—Home Pod, Amazon's Alexa—Echo, Microsoft's Cortana—Invoke, Google Assistant—Google Home, and Facebook—Oculus computer-generated reality headset.[82]

The Chatbot is an appropriate model that is modified to communicate with a human. Applications for voice recognition are widely used in public spaces. Many platforms for digital assistants connect with users and deliver information content tailored to their demands on all aspects of the planet. The most widely used digital assistant software programs include Siri (Apple), Alexa (Amazon), Google Now, Cortana (Microsoft), Facebook Messenger, Blackberry Assistant, Teneo, Speaktoit Assistant, Hound, and Braina. This software is either integrated into consumer electronics like smartphones and tablets or sold separately as devices like the Amazon Echo, Google Home, and so on.[83]

Decision Management

Smart machines intend to outline new principles and rationale to Artificial Intelligence frameworks for setting up delayed upkeep and ideal tuning and make us run a productive association. The two different ways of finding clients' reactions to things are as follows:

1. Content-based proposals comprehend clients' advantage dependent on the input accommodated a couple of things and recommend comparative things to them.
2. Collaborative sifting centres on recognising comparative clients and suggesting things favoured by different comparative clients.

---

[81] *Supra* note 80.

[82] Ibid.

[83] Ibid.

8. **Deep Learning Platform**

Deep learning is a subtype of AI that entails computations that allow a product to self-train to do tasks like image and speech recognition by exposing multi-layered neural structures to large amounts of data. It has the potential to have a significant impact on a variety of industries, including money, automobiles, aircraft, media transmission, data innovation, oil and gas, modern, protection, media and promotion, clinical, and others.

Deep Learning in Self-Driving Automobiles Neural Nctworks was used in the first self-driving car to detect lane lines, segment the ground, and drive. It was created in 1989 and was known as ALVINN. Deep Learning has dominated the major autonomous driving subfields.

It's even crazier in 2021. Deep Learning has dominated the major autonomous driving subfields. All four pillars of autonomous driving, as well as how Deep Learning is used in each.

In a Nutshell:

- In *Perception*, find the environment and obstacles around individuals.
- In *Localisation*, individuals define their position in the world at 1–3 cm accuracy.
- In *Planning*, individuals define a trajectory from A to B, using perception and localisation.

Deep Learning is used in all four modules.

9. **Emotion Recognition**

By utilising sophisticated image preparation or sound handling, the technology enables the product to 'verify' the angles on a human face. It can now take in 'miniature articulations', which are intricate nonverbal communication concepts, as well as vocal emphasis that expresses a person's feelings.[84]

10. **Marketing Automation**

Exposing marketing automation gives businesses the ability to increase commitment and enhance execution. It uses programming to automate customer division, information coordination, and mission management for executives, as well as smooth out repetitive tasks, allowing key personalities to focus on what they do best.[85]

---

[84] *Supra* note 80.

[85] Ibid.

2.2.2 *Potentials of Artificial Intelligence in the Context of Autonomous Vehicles*

Potentials or Advantages of Artificial Intelligence:

AI is now capable enough to make differences in it, in terms of making their own 'independent developments', meaning thereby systems which possess at least one of the qualities that are as follows:

i. The ability/capability to learn from its own data sets and make patterns out of those given data which the AI system's designers do not plan; and
ii. The capability/ability of AI systems to improvise themselves and help in making a new AI system in a better version of itself should not look like the replication of the original 'seed' program.[86]

Potential of AI in the Indian scenario:

All industries, including "*e-commerce, biotechnology, disease diagnosis, the military, mathematics and logistics, heavy industry, finance, transportation, telecommunication, aviation, digital marketing, telephone customer service, agriculture, and gaming,*" have successfully embraced AI.

1. **Smart Transportation and Mobility**

In today's India, roads are the most common means of transportation. They transport about 85% of passenger traffic and more than 60% of freight in the country. In the financial year 2019, road freight transit accounted for over 64% of total freight transportation in India. Rail's role in freight transportation in India has been declining since 1951, according to the report. It was only 18 per cent in 2020, compared to 71 per cent for roads.[87] If there aren't considerable changes in the policy initiatives in this area, it's anticipated that this reliance on these means of transportation will persist as the economy expands. The necessity to employ intelligent methods in their AI implementation is further increased by the fact that these modes of transportation produce significantly more pollution than air and maritime transportation combined. Apart from the present problems, the Indian transportation sector faces various difficulties.[88]

---

[86] TURNER, J. (2019). *ROBOT RULES-Regulating Artificial Intelligence*, London-UK: Palgrave Macmillan, ISBN-978-3-319-96,234-4, Pp. 82–102.

"Legal personality is a technical label for a bundle of rights and responsibilities instead of being a single notion", Joanna Bryson, Mihalis Diamantis, and Thomas Grant write that *"legal persons are fictive, divisible, and not necessarily accountable."* They observe "legal personality is an artifice," with the effect that "legal people need not possess all the same rights and obligations, even within the same system".

Legal protections for humans have changed over time and continue to shift.

[87] *See* <https://pib.gov.in/indexd.aspx>, accessed on July 20, 2023.

[88] Ibid.

(a) *High number of traffic deaths:* According to a '*PIB (Press Information Bureau)*'[89] release by the '*Ministry of Road Transport and Highways (MORTH)*' as of March 2017, there have been 501,423 traffic accidents nationwide in 2015, leaving 146,133 people dead. '*The National Highways (NHS)*' were responsible for 35.0% of all fatalities and 29.1% of all traffic fatalities. Although the current NHS only makes up about 1.9 per cent of the entire road network, they nonetheless handle about 40 per cent of all traffic. According to '*MORTH statistics*', there has been a steady increase in on-road accidents over the years.[90]

(b) *Assisted vehicle technologies:* The cost of a driver per kilometre is currently too cheap in India for autonomy to be economically sustainable. However, India has a large economic opportunity to capitalise on by investing in the range of autonomous car technology and exporting such vehicles. It would be wise for Indian manufacturers to invest in research and development of the wider range of technologies that are necessary for assistive AI as the same technologies may play a significant role in lowering fatalities and alleviating congestion. By making driving decisions that it has a high degree of confidence in and informing the driver if it has a low degree of confidence in any decision, these technologies can help the driver. The sophisticated cruise control found in modern Tesla vehicles is a prime example of such commercially viable assistive AI. This may start and stop in response to traffic, follow highway traffic, and follow curves in the road. The driver, however, takes control of the system the moment they make any input. This hybrid method is far safer than unaided human driving and avoids any potential risks associated with having a fully autonomous system. Another reason why India shouldn't completely disregard research into assistive vehicle technology has to do with the creation of new public infrastructure. It has the advantage of hindsight because a significant portion of the overall demand for greenfield infrastructure has just recently started to be built.[91]

(c) *Need for sustainable transportation:* The current problems with urban mobility, such as traffic congestion, effective traffic flow, and the movement of products, can in fact be resolved utilising AI technology, even though such initiatives may take some time to have a discernible influence. By scheduling public transportation systems, enhancing access to public transportation infrastructure based on users' decision behaviours, and offering real-time travel mode advice based on anticipated traffic scenarios, AI can power multimodal integration. Mobility solutions with AI capabilities can help the Indian automotive and transportation industries overcome a number of difficulties.[92]

(d) *Autonomous trucking:* Trucking could change significantly as a result of the use of autonomous technologies. Through intelligent platooning, in which trucks form a platoon and drivers are free to rest while the platoon is still driving, AI can help improve safety and hauling efficiency. Additionally, by ensuring

---

[89] Ibid.

[90] *See* <https://morth.nic.in/>, accessed on July 20, 2023.

[91] Ibid.

[92] Ibid.

optimal road space utilisation, such a system increases the capacity of the road infrastructure.[93]

(e) *Intelligent Transportation Systems:* 'Real-time dynamic decisions on traffic flow', such as 'lane monitoring, access to exits', 'toll pricing', 'allocating right of way to public transportation vehicles', and enforcing 'traffic regulations' through 'smart ticketing', can be made through the use of an 'intelligent traffic management system' that uses 'sensors, CCTV cameras, automatic number plate recognition cameras, speed detection cameras, signalised pedestrian crossings, stop line violation detection systems, and the use of AI'. 'Using accident data' and 'driving behaviour' at specific areas on the road network connected to 'topology, geometric road design, speed limit', etc., accident heat maps might be created, and necessary actions could be performed beforehand to prevent potential accidents. Additionally, AI might be used to develop complex urban traffic control systems that can enhance junction, zonal, and network-level signal timings as well as provide services like autonomous vehicle detection for red/green phase extension or intermittent priority.[94]

(f) *Travel route/flow optimisation:* By minimising the whole route time, which includes access time, waiting time, and travel time, AI can assist in making accurate forecasts for trips taken on public transportation with access to traffic data at the network level. AI can transform first-last-mile travel, which could alter how it views public transportation journeys today. AI can consider elements like accessibility to the closest mode of transportation and the most convenient access path depending on local conditions and preferences. A variety of traffic data sets and preferences could be used by AI to simulate human decision-making when choosing a route for personal transportation. The dependence on overhead Variable Messaging Systems (VMS) could be minimised with knowledge of changing tolls and traffic patterns on lines, lowering significant infrastructure costs. On a systemic level, AI can assist with network-level traffic flow prediction and offer alternate flow methods to reduce congestion, relieving cities of this serious problem.[95]

(g) *AI for Railways:* According to official figures, more than "500 train accidents occurred between 2012–2017, 53% of them due to derailment." Train operators can obtain situational intelligence through real-time operational data and analyse them in three different dimensions: *"spatial, temporal, and nodal. Fleet management and asset maintenance, including that of rolling stock, are pertinent AI use cases."* Recently, the 'Ministry of Railways', 'Govt. of India' has decided to use AI to undertake remote condition monitoring using 'non-intrusive sensors for monitoring signals, track circuits, axle counters, and their sub-systems of interlocking, power supply systems including the voltage and current levels, relays, and timers'.

[93] Ibid.

[94] Ibid.

[95] Ibid.

(h) *Community-Based Parking:* The availability of parking is a significant issue for Indian cities. AI can help optimise parking, likely by minimising vehicle downtime and maximising driving time. With the advent of electric vehicles, AI will be needed to mediate the 'complex vehicle grid interactions (VGI)' and for charging optimisation. Parking guidance systems help drivers find vacant parking spaces while using the road network and approaching close to their destination. 'Community-based parking using AI' helps cars in 'traffic collect data' on vacant parking spaces and allocates cars to spaces such that the demand is always met. Globally, research on "autonomous cars has sparked advancements, particularly in the robotics and computer vision disciplines of artificial intelligence." The majority of significant investments in AI over the past two years have been made in the field of autonomous vehicles due to the exceptionally high market potential. Autonomous vehicles are widely expected to be the first extensively used commercial application of AI.[96]

Moreover, AI algorithms developed using driving data from India have the potential to be incredibly reliable due to the congested and unpredictable conditions of Indian traffic.

According to the Stanford AI index,[97] since 2010, product categorisation error rates have decreased from 28.5 per cent to 2.5 per cent. As a result, existing methods are developed sufficiently to be applied in Indian circumstances. Additionally, the key technologies utilised in AI have a great potential for transfer. It is possible to spot malignant cells in a pathological image using the same template that is used to detect items on the road.[98]

Artificial Intelligence's Potential in the Face of a COVID-19 Pandemic

Artificial Intelligence—Need of an Hour in the Era of COVID-19 Pandemic.

Artificial Intelligence (AI) is changing each part of our lives. It impacts how it works and plays. It vows to help unravel worldwide difficulties like environmental change and admittance to quality clinical consideration. However, AI additionally brings genuine difficulties for governments and residents. As it pervades economies and social orders, what kind of strategy and institutional systems should manage AI plan and use, and how might it guarantee that it benefits society in general?

The OECD upholds governments by estimating and breaking down the monetary and social effects of AI advances and applications and drawing in with all partners to distinguish excellent practises for public arrangement.

[96] Ibid.

[97] Zhang, D., Mishra, S., Brynjolfsson, E., Etchemendy, J., Ganguli, D., Grosz, B., … & Perrault, R. (2021). The AI index 2021 annual report. *arXiv preprint arXiv:2103.06312. See* <https://aiindex.stanford.edu/wp-content/uploads/2021/03/2021-AI-Index-Report_Master.pdf, >accessed on July 29, 2023.

[98] Ibid.

In order to battle COVID-19, policymakers should guarantee that AI frameworks are reliable and lined up with the OECD AI Principles: they should regard common freedoms and protection; be straightforward, logical, vigorous, secure, and safe.[99]

2.2.3 *Limitations of Artificial Intelligence in Automobile Sector*

- In the case of a self-driving vehicle, the driver will be considerable, travel times will decrease altogether, and the option to face the traffic will be all the more effective, so living in suburbia will bode well. The idea is to have the option to sit in the vehicle's protection-having breakfast and get a head start to work while the vehicle does the self-driving. It is this thought alone that has made the car owners overjoyous about the driverless vehicles. Google, Mercedes-Benz, GM, and other companies are sinking a great many dollars in innovative work and the testing of these vehicles.
- In the recent past, India has had its own set of reservations about self-driving cars. The battle for self-driving cars is long, with numerous stakeholders in the mix. The government is concerned about job losses. Companies are concerned about high R&D costs and market viability. Consumers, on the other hand, are simply uninterested. Experimenting does not appear to be a viable option in one of the world's largest automobile markets. The government has made it clear in the past that anything that could jeopardise jobs will not be promoted. So, where do individuals stand on self-driving cars? Is India going to adopt the technology while the rest of the world waits for it to be commercialised? Or will we have to wait another decade or two?
- As of now, India appears to be hesitant to adopt self-driving vehicle technology. More than a crore of people's jobs may be jeopardised as a result of self-driving cars.
- Any decision that has an impact on employment[100] in such a large country could have serious consequences. According to a recent report by HR solutions[101] business PeopleStrong, India may lose a quarter of its workforce to automation by 2020. According to the company's research, India will account for about 23% of worldwide employment losses due to automation by 2021.[102]

---

[99] *See* OECD (2020), "Using artificial intelligence to help combat COVID-19", *OECD Policy Responses to Coronavirus (COVID-19)*, OECD Publishing, Paris, https://doi.org/10.1787/ae4c5c21-en; accessed on August 29, 2023.

[100] *Martand Mishra, Self-Driving Cars in India, All is Not Lost with Autonomous Cars, MAY 7, 2020. See* also <https://gomechanics.in/blog/self-driving-cars-in-india/>, accessed on August 29, 2023.

[101] Ibid.

[102] Ibid.

- According to the 2018 World Road Statistics Report,[103] India ranks first in the world in terms of the number of road accident-related deaths. In 2018, more than 1.5 lakh people[104] died as a result of road accidents in the country. Can autonomous cars ensure safety in a country where traffic signs are merely a shiny blue or green board? The entire technology behind self-driving cars is based on AI detecting its surroundings in order to function.[105] It isn't capable of predicting a reckless driver changing lanes while blasting loud music. However, this cannot be used as an excuse to not plan for the future. While things may appear to be bleak, there is a glimmer of hope. Although India may not see self-driving cars, self-driving tractors are undoubtedly on the way.[106]
- Escorts, a tractor manufacturer, is working on developing a Level 2 autonomous tractor.[107] The tractor will be able to auto-steer and use geofencing via GPS.[108] In September 2019, the tractor's prototype was unveiled. Mahindra & Mahindra[109] is also working on something similar. The world's largest tractor manufacturer is enthusiastic about taking farm automation to the next level.[110]
- India is ranked 24th out of 25 countries in KPMG's 2019 Autonomous Vehicle Readiness Index.[111] The list stated the countries' readiness to adopt autonomous vehicle practises. The Netherlands topped the list. Countries such as Germany, the United States, the United Kingdom, Japan, and China[112] are currently testing the vehicles.[113] China is on track to commercialise self-driving cars by 2025.[114] According to a recent survey conducted by the Beijing Innovation Centre for Mobility Intelligence, 77 autonomous vehicles (AVs)[115] have been tested for more than one million kilometres in the country. The Netherlands has been adamant about pushing technology forward. It intends to deploy a platoon of over 100 driverless trucks on specific roads.[116] Norway legalised autonomous car testing on public roads in January 2018, while Sweden is working on electric-charging roads, public transportation, and other projects. Meanwhile, Singapore has established a Centre of Excellence for Autonomous Vehicle Testing and Research.[117] The

103 Ibid.

104 Ibid.

105 Ibid.

106 Ibid.

107 Ibid.

108 Ibid.

109 Ibid.

110 Ibid.

111 Ibid.

112 Ibid.

113 *Id.*

114 Ibid.

115 Ibid.

116 *Id.*

117 Ibid.

Centre's goal is to expand research on AVs. According to a report by the marketing firm ABI, 8 million self-driving cars will be on US roads by 2025.[118]

- Technology, as it has seen in the past, does not wait for anyone. Individuals must adapt no matter how strict the restrictions are and what the situation is. People used to be extremely sceptical of electric vehicles, but now people embrace them.[119]

2.3 Recent Developments and Implications of Artificial Intelligence

- *The most relevant policy developments and implications that are in progress in Artificial Intelligence areas:*

Recommendation of the Council on Artificial Intelligence

22/05/2019—*the OECD's work on Artificial Intelligence and reasoning for building up the OECD Recommendation on Artificial Intelligence.*

The OECD Principles on Artificial Intelligence support AI that upholds democratic principles, human rights, and innovation. The OECD Council Recommendation on Artificial Intelligence was endorsed by OECD member countries in ***May 2019***, marking their adoption.

The OECD will host a debate on Artificial Intelligence, Data, and Competition in ***June 2024.*** The purpose of the discussion is to go over recent advancements in AI, investigate potential worries about future competition, and decide what steps authorities can do.[120]

Artificial Intelligence, the definition from the OECD Principles: AI system: ***"An AI system is a machine-based system that can, for a given set of human-defined objectives, make predictions, recommendations, or decisions influencing real or virtual environments. AI systems are designed to operate with varying levels of autonomy."***

Artificial Intelligence (AI) is a universally helpful innovation that can improve individuals' government assistance and prosperity, add to positive manageable worldwide monetary action, expand development and efficiency, and help react to fundamental worldwide difficulties. It is conveyed in numerous areas, from creation, account, and transport to medical care and security. Close-by benefits and AI likewise raise difficulties for our social orders and economies, remarkably concerning financial movements and imbalances, rivalry, changes in the work market, and suggestions for majority rule government and common liberties.

---

[118] Ibid.

[119] *Id.*

[120] *See* <https://www.oecd.org/daf/competition/artificial-intelligence-data-and-competition.htm#:~:text=In%20June%202024%2C%20the%20OECD,available%20for%20authorities%20to%20take>, accessed on June 11, 2024.

The Organisation for Economic Cooperation and Development (OECD) has attempted exact and strategy exercises on AI on the side of the approach banter in recent years, beginning with a Technology Foresight Forum on AI in 2016 and a worldwide gathering on AI: Intelligent Machines, Smart Policies in 2017. The organisation also led insightful and estimation work that gives a diagram of the AI specialised scene maps and economic and social effects of AI advances. Their applications distinguish significant strategy contemplations and depict AI activities from governments and partners at public and worldwide levels. This work has exhibited the need to shape a steady strategy climate worldwide to cultivate trust in and appropriation of AI in the public arena. Against this foundation, the OECD Committee on Digital Economy Policy (CDEP) consented to build up a draft Council Recommendation to advance a human-driven way to deal with reliable AI that encourages research, jelly monetary motivations to develop, and applies to all partners.

OECD Principles on Artificial Intelligence[121]–May 2019[122]

The OECD will have the new Global Partnership on AI (GPAI), an alliance that targets guaranteeing that Artificial Intelligence is utilised capably, regarding fundamental liberties and vote-based qualities. The GPAI will unite specialists from industry, government, common society, and the scholarly world to lead AI examinations and pilot ventures. Its goal, as set out by countries like Australia, Canada, the European Union, France, Germany, India, Italy, Japan, Korea, Mexico, New Zealand, Singapore, Slovenia, the United Kingdom, and the United States is to overcome any barrier among hypothesis and practise on AI strategy. The GPAI Secretariat would likewise liaise with Centres of Expertise in Montréal and Paris.[123]

India has joined the Global Partnership on Artificial Intelligence or GPAI as a founding member in June 2020. This multi-stakeholder international partnership will promote responsible and human-centric development and the use of AI.[124]

Functions and Implications of the Global Partnership on Artificial Intelligence

The G7's notion was conceived under the Canadian and French presidencies, and GPAI represents the realisation of that idea. It went live in June of 2020.

- Bridge the gap between theory and practise on AI by supporting cutting-edge research and applied activities on AI-related priorities.
- An example is how AI could help societies respond to and recover from the COVID-19 crisis.
- Bring together leading experts from industry, civil society, governments, and academia to conduct research and pilot projects on AI.

---

[121] *See* https://legalinstruments.oecd.org/en/instruments/oecd-legal-0449#:~:text=The%20Recommendation%20on%20Artificial%20Intelligence,Digital%20Economy%20Policy%2C%20CDEP), accessed on September 21, 2023.

[122] "Section 2.1: **Principles for responsible stewardship of trustworthy AI"**
"Section 2.2: **National policies and international cooperation for trustworthy AI"**
VIII. "The Committee on Digital Economy Policy".

[123] OECD to have Secretariat of new Global Partnership on Artificial Intelligence dated 15/06/2020.

[124] Law Minister Ravi Shankar Prasad tweeted on 18/06/2020.

- It will initially comprise four working groups focused on responsible AI, data governance, the future of work, and innovation and commercialisation.

GPAI will be able to take advantage of the OECD's expertise on AI policy and its leadership in setting out the first international standard for trustworthy AI—the OECD Principles on Artificial Intelligence.[125]

2.3.1 Recent Policy Initiative and Development in India—In the Field of AI

- India unveiled its National AI Strategy and National AI Portal in June 2018 and has also started leveraging AI across various sectors such as education, agriculture, healthcare, e-commerce, finance, and telecommunications, so forth. The National AI Portal has been developed jointly by the National e-Governance Division of the Ministry of Electronics and Information Technology (MeitY) and the National Association of Software and Service Companies (NASSCOM). The portal is meant to work as a 'one-stop digital platform' for all AI-related developments in India.[126]
- The National AI strategy was released in 2018 by NITI Aayog.[127] It is termed 'AIFORALL' as it is focused on leveraging AI for inclusive growth in line with the Government policy of Sabka Saath Sabka Vikas.[128]
- Kerala police inducted a robot for police work. Robot-themed restaurant in Chennai.
- Telerobotic coronary intervention in Ahmadabad; cardiologist performed the first-in-human telerobotic coronary intervention on a patient who is 30 km away.

On December 28, 2020, country's first-ever fully automated driverless train on the Magenta Line of the Delhi Metro was flagged off. The Delhi metro is now connected through the National Common Mobility Card (NCMC). NCMC, dubbed as 'One Nation One Card', is an inter-operable transport card that will allow the holders to also pay for their bus travel, toll taxes, parking charges, retail shopping, and even withdraw money.

---

[125] OECD to have Secretariat of new Global Partnership on Artificial Intelligence dated 15/06/2020.

[126] *See* <https://www.niti.gov.in/sites/default/files/2019-01/NationalStrategy-for-AI-Discussion-Paper.pdf>, accessed on July 30, 2023.

[127] Ibid.

[128] *See* id.

2.4 Conclusion

AI's relevance in society is inevitable. It is designed to help societal transformation on par with the industrial, digital, and information revolutions. Artificial Intelligence allows farmers, doctors, and rescue workers to impact society with the help of this technology positively. Artificial Intelligence remains the top driver of economic, geopolitical, and technological risks. The big tech giants like *'Google, Microsoft, and Facebook'* are hungrier for data in the case of 'Deep Learning'. Microsoft and Google are working on privacy issues by providing ways to use and train the ANN used in deep learning without needing to gobble up everything. They hope to introduce smarter software and convince the sensitive data guardian to use such systems. Artificial Intelligence based on security systems increasingly makes decisions for human individuals or assists them. This development is particularly worrisome, as currently, these systems do not have a moral code. Living in an age of rapid technological advances where artificial Intelligence (AI) is a reality, not a science fiction fantasy. In *"Data-driven AI, neural networks and deep learning algorithm"* are applied to cycle the pool of information-by-information mining and are applied in NLP. It is critical to recognise various strategies and apply the correct one to their degree of development.

The exhibition of AI-empowered applications radically decreases the opportunity for human mistakes to sneak in. These AI variants are quicker at computationally costly undertakings, particularly in logical exploration and tedious assignments. A large portion of the everyday practise, unimportant and redundant assignments can be mechanised with appropriate AI technology to improve operational efficiencies. It spares the work cost, decreases the possibility of blunder, and gives a most extreme yield in the least time. A machine may complete the same task in a few minutes which takes the man hours to complete by hand. The machines are modified to do a dull errand which expands profitability, and it is effectively utilised. Bomb defusing, space exploration, and customised management all tasks that are risky to be completed by people are the significant highlights of machines. The serious exploration of the machine is to actualise them with impact sensors, cameras, and ultrasound sensors to make them see, hear, and touch. The device is used in space exploration and is adaptable to the environment and mental conditions. Other than enthusiastic dealing, a machine is additionally modified to think intelligently and make successful choices. Artificial intelligence is used in science to configure tests, train the assets, decipher the information, and reduce complexity. In daily life, artificial intelligence is implemented and effectively developing around individuals in parts of correspondence, time the executives, instruction, perception, well-being, security measure, traffic signal, buying,promoting, and organising.

The future of AI in the domains of finance, healthcare, education, and military applications, where it might affect both the ways, either positively or negatively, is something that is both a blessing and a curse for society, as described earlier.

However, the author chose this topic because it can be seen how AV technology aims to revolutionise the mobility ecosystem by *"reducing the number of accidents and providing other benefits, such as the ability to reduce traffic, increase safety and mobility, reduce energy consumption, and generate free time.*" As a result, it's imperative to talk about the civil, criminal, and ethical responsibility issues that have evolved because of the usage of AI in AVs.

Chapter 3
Tortious Liability of Artificial Intelligence

If we wait for the moment when everything, absolutely everything, is ready, we shall never begin.
Ivan Turgenev, Father, and Sons
TORTS—'Mitigating product liability for artificial intelligence'

Abstract In this chapter, the author tries to investigate the tortuous liability issues from the perspective of looking into the claim of unliquidated damages under the purview of 'Negligence, Strict, and Product Liability and Vicarious Liability'. So, this chapter talks about the liability issues that may arise under three scenarios: first, when the sale of a product connects small parties like a manufacturer and a consumer, and second, when two parties are in a direct contractual relationship. The third case is when the user relies on information supplied by the computer system. However, the first scenario considered here is negligence and strict liability under the law of torts. In contrast, the second and third scenarios fell under both—express and implied, covering breach of warranties. Lastly, the third scenario again deals with negligence.

3.1 Introduction

Tort Law in India is a new development in common law—supplemented by its codifications of statutes, including statutes governing compensations. India mostly follows the United Kingdom's Common Law approach. The chapter discusses the issues and problems that arise from AI technology that can be addressed under the existing laws—procedural and substantive law. The chapter also looks into whether there is a need for a sui generis legislation on AI technology?

To construe and understand the tortious liability of AI, the scope of this chapter is limited only to make a comparative study of the tortious liability of autonomous vehicles in Germany, California, and India.

Germany has one of the leading automotive industry sectors considering the new developments in autonomous driving vehicles and other areas. Germany is to adopt fast—the new types of car technology in the United Nations treaty, since March

S. Fahim, *Ethico-Legal Aspect of AI-driven Driverless Cars*, Frontiers of Artificial Intelligence, Ethics and Multidisciplinary Applications,
https://doi.org/10.1007/978-981-97-6883-7_3

23, 2016, there have been many discussions over defining Article 8 of the Vienna Convention of 1968,[1] which deals with the necessity and capabilities of a driver. The convention is amended by a new subtitle, number 5b. So, Germany has adopted this very new provision and included it into the basic law (Constitution) of Germany under Article 59(2) Grudgesetz(GG).[2]

California gives its industry a very flexible, active, and cutting-edge legislative framework, which comes into play with the help of active collaboration with the economy and the legislators.

Lastly, India follows the Common Law like the U.S., England, and Canada, unlike Germany, which follows the Civil Law. Although in India there is no specific legislation on Artificial Intelligence technology/systems to date, it is expected that soon there will be a legislative framework to cover the legal liability issues of AI.

It is debatable whether AI is liable for the violations of the law. This question arose even 30 years ago in the case of ***the United States v. Athlone Industries.*** The court held that "robots cannot be sued" and discussed the manufacturer's liability in case of any machine defect.[3]

The determination of the tort liability can be understood in the context of the Levels of automation. Automation has been divided into six levels (L 0–5) by the Society of Automotive Engineers (SAE) J3016. Society of Automotive Engineers (SAE) is a global association committed to being the ultimate knowledge source for the engineering profession.[4]

The following are the levels of driving automation:

Level 0–2: where the car is fully under the control of the operator.[5]

Levels 3 and 4: where an operator controls the car manually only when an autonomous mode requests to do so.[6]

Level 5: where the vehicle/car turned into a driverless car and required no human intervention, that is, it turns into a fully automated car.[7]

---

[1] *"Article 8 No. 5 Vienna Convention of 1968"*.

[2] *"Grundgesetz/ Basic Law, (Bundesrepublik Deutschland / Federal State of Germany, 1949)"*.

[3] **US Court of Appeals for the Third Circuit—746 F.2d 977 (3d Cir. 1984).**

[4] *See* <https://timesofindia.indiatimes.com/auto/cars/adas-level-0-to-level-5-autonomous-cars-self-driving-level-2-kia-ev6-features-explained/articleshow/91762964.cms> , accessed on September 25, 2023.

[5] Ibid.

[6] Ibid.

[7] Ibid.

3.2 Position in Germany—Law of Negligence, Strict, and Product and Vicarious Liability

3.2.1 Law of Negligence in Germany

German Tort Law seems to be similar to the English concept of a duty of care.[8] And so is the expressive of judicial policy too.[9] Being a civil law framework, the law of torts has in principle been incorporated into the German Civil Code *(BGB).*[10] It comprises of 30 successive articles, called paragraphs, found in the second book of the Code as a component of the law of obligations.

In this chapter, the author is particularly concerned with the question of who will be held liable, particularly when an automobile runs on the road that has been programmed to operate by software. However, in such circumstances, there is a higher likelihood of negligence than of product failure by an AV. The responsibility to perform a legal duty is most commonly derived from the *Verkehrssicherungspflichten,* which means legal duties to maintain safety to protect the innocent.[11]

German law defines negligence, as described.

In, § 823 BGB (Bürgerliches Gesetzbuch) of the German Civil Code, 1900[12]:

The first and the most relevant of these tort provisions is *§ 823 BGB,*[13] which lays down the following two general rules:

(1) "*A person who, intentionally or negligently, unlawfully inquires the life, body, health, freedom, property, or another right of another person is liable to make compensation to the other party for the damage arising from this.*"[14]

(2) *"The same duty attaches to a person who infringes a statutory provision that is intended for the protection of others. According to the statute's purview, infringement is possible without fault, and the duty to make compensation arises only if some fault can be imputed to the wrongdoer."*[15]

---

[8] C v Bar, 'Limitation and Mitigation in German Tort Law' in J Spier (ed), *The Limits of Liability—Keeping the Floodgates Shut* (1996) 17, 22.

[9] B Markesinis, *The German Law of Obligations—Volume II the Law of Torts: A Comparative Introduction* (3rd edn, 1997) 75.

[10] *See* <https://www.gesetze-im-internet.de/englisch_bgb/englisch_bgb.pdf>, accessed on September 25, 2023.

[11] Cf Palandt-H Thomas, *BGB* (58th edn, 1999) § 823 Rn 35.

[12] *See Supra* note 10.

[13] Ibid.

[14] *See* <https://www.gesetz-im-internet.de/bgb/_823.html>, accessed September 25, 2023.

[15] Translation of § 823 taken from B Markesinis, *The German Law of Obligations—Volume II The Law of Torts: a Comparative Introduction* (3rd edn, 1997) 12.

'The German Civil Code, § 823 I BGB',[16] defines negligence as a type of fault. When '§ 823 I BGB' defines that careless conduct might render someone liable in Tort, it implies both acts and omissions.[17]

'§ 823 II BGB'[18] provides for the liability for the breach of a protective enactment or statute. The statute is for giving protection to others. It is not limited to protecting others but also protecting an individual's interest. German law does not require a legislative intent in protecting statute to create a civil remedy.[19]

Although '§ 823 I and II BGB'[20] are the most important provisions under the 'German Tort Law', even their wordings do not include any limitations attached to them, but their application or implementation differs from a private person to public authorities, and so their employees performing public functions.[21]

The second sentence of '§ 276 I BGB'[22] states about not exercising the reasonable care required in usual circumstances. However, omissions lead to liability where there is a legal duty to act but somehow fails to perform it. Though negligence is defined under '§ 276 I 2 BGB',[23] in contrast to English Law, subdivided into light, ordinary, and gross negligence. Though as is required under English law, the required standard of care is objective.[24]

It can be seen that the position of public authorities is different from that of private persons and so private legal entities who generally act for their benefits. This is one of the reasons they are made liable for the damage they have caused. Public authorities, in contrast to private persons, exercise statutory power and duties for the welfare of the people in society, having discretion as to how to carry out their duties and take a decision which may lead to open judicial review and can be questioned based on the principles and rules of public law. An extraordinary claim for a breach of official duty against public liability is given under '§ 839 BGB',[25] read with *"Article 34 of the German Constitution (GG). This conforms to Article 19 IV 1 GG–Grundgesetz (Constitution),"* which provides for the rights of an individual to have recourse to law where any public authority violates the rights of an individual.

'§ 839 I 1 BGB' states about the liability of an official who has wilfully or negligently breached the official duty. In case of negligence conduct,[26] '§ 839 I 2 BGB' will apply, which leads to the exclusion of the liability of the official or public

[16] *See* <https://www.gesetze-im-internet.de/englisch_bgb/>, accessed on June 15, 2023.

[17] *See Supra* note 10.

[18] Ibid.

[19] Ibid.

[20] Ibid.

[21] One exception in BGH NJW 1996, 3208, 3209.

[22] *See Supra* note 10.

[23] Ibid.

[24] MünchKomm-H Papier, *BGB* (3rd edn, 1997) §839 Rn 279, 284; B Bender, *Staatshaftungsrecht* (3rd edn, 1981) Rn 333, 334.

[25] *See Supra* note 10.

[26] Ibid.

body if the injured party has already obtained compensation otherwise.[27] '§ 839 III BGB' provides for the liability of public officials as the last resort to be able to avert the damage.[28] Understanding it in an easier example, like the police who will be exonerated for his negligent driving while pursuing a criminal rather than a fun-rider because the police action saves the greater interest than the latter.[29]

3.2.1.1 Liability of AI Under the Law of Negligence in Germany

The present research has tried to analyse whether these provisions under German law are adequate to determine the tortious liability in the case of Autonomous vehicles? The applicability of these provisions to AVs.

A comprehensive analysis of these provisions reveals that existing provisions such as *"§§ 823 BGB, 823 BGB I, 823 BGB II, 823 BGB III, 276 I BGB, 276 I 2 BGB, 839 BGB, 839 I 1 BGB, and 839 I 2 BGB"*[30] only apply to human drivers or car owners who are held liable for negligence and subject to punitive damages under tort law. Whoever causes a person's death by negligence faces a penalty of up to five years in prison or a fine. *Whoever* is considered as a natural and legal person in this context, which stands true to 'SAE Level 0–3' but not to a highly and fully autonomous system, because here autonomous system is independent in its actions and reasoning but in 'SAE Level 0–3', it is humans who is controlling and monitoring on its own, human intervention is present to control the AI agent/tool/machine.

As a result, the author observed that there is a gap in the legislation that does not specifically cover the highly and fully autonomous system. The author proposed that a proper law be put in place to address the current issue, namely 'SAE Levels 4 and 5'.

Now, because it must be viewed from the perspective of 'SAE Level 0–2', where the car is perfectly under the control of the human driver, the human driver monitors the driving environment in these scenarios. Now author will look at whether the same law applies in cases of negligence ranging from 'SAE Level 0 to 5'. According to the author, it will be used on a frequent basis whenever the situation necessitates it because it is entirely in the hands of the human driver/owner/user of a car, who can monitor the driving environment. When compared to existing provisions in the law of negligence, such as *"§§ 823 BGB, 823 BGB I, 823 BGB II, 276 I BGB, 276 I 2 BGB, 839 BGB, 839 I 1 BGB, and 839 I 2 BGB,"*[31] with 'SAE Level 0 to 5', the outcome is even.

---

27 Ibid.

28 *See* https://ouclf.law.ox.ac.uk/a-comparative-study-of-the-english-and-german-judicial-approach-to-the-liability-of-public-bodies-in-negligence/#fn193anc, accessed on September 25, 2022.

29 *See*, for example, the judgement of the UK Supreme Court in *Robinson v. Chief Constable of West Yorkshire Police* [2018] UKSC4.

30 *Supra* note 10.

31 Ibid.

In **Level 0**, the full-time performance by the human driver of all aspects of the dynamic driving task, even when enhanced by warning or intervention systems. Who, once again, is in charge of steering and acceleration/deceleration? Who will be held accountable for negligence, now that the answer is a human driver. Another aspect of driving a car is the monitoring of the driving environment, which is likewise done by a human driver. If a fallback execution of the dynamic driving task is available, who is the performing '*human driver*'. Is there any capability (driving mode) in the system? The answer is negative. As a result of the arguments presented by the author, the author argues that only human driver/operator is liable under the law of negligence under "*§§ 823 BGB, 823 BGB I, 823 BGB II, 276 I BGB, 276 I 2 BGB, 839 BGB, 839 I 1 BGB, and 839 I 2 BGB.*"[32]

In **Level 1** (Driver Assistance), the execution of either steering or acceleration/deceleration by a driver assistance system based on information about the driving environment, with the expectation that the '*human driver' will handle* the remaining components of the 'dynamic driving task'. Who will be held accountable for negligence, now that the answer is a human driver and system. Is there any capability (driving mode) in the system? The answer is some driving modes. As a result of the arguments presented by the author, the author believes that only human driver/operator is liable under the 'law of negligence' under *"§§ 823 BGB, 823 BGB I, 823 BGB II, 276 I BGB, 276 I 2 BGB, 839 BGB, 839 I 1 BGB, and 839 I 2 BGB."*[33]

In **Level 2** (Partial Automation), the execution of both steering and acceleration/deceleration by one or more driver assistance systems based on information about the driving environment, with the expectation that the '*human driver' will handle* the remaining components of the 'dynamic driving task'. Here the system is in charge of steering and acceleration/deceleration. Who will be held accountable for negligence, now that the answer is a system.

Another aspect of driving a car is the monitoring of the driving environment, which is likewise done by a human driver. If a fallback execution of the dynamic driving task is available, who is the performing '*human driver'*. Is there any capability (driving mode) in the system? The answer is some driving modes. As a result of the arguments presented by the author, the author believes that only human driver/operator is liable under the 'law of negligence' under *"§§ 823 BGB, 823 BGB I, 823 BGB II, 276 I BGB, 276 I 2 BGB, 839 BGB, 839 I 1 BGB, and 839 I 2 BGB."*[34]

SAE Level 3-5: Automated driving system ('system') monitors the driving environment.

In **Level 3** (Conditional Automation), the 'automated driving system's' handling of all parts of the 'dynamic driving task' in a certain driving mode, with the expectation that the human driver will respond properly to a request to intervene. Who, once again, is in charge of steering and acceleration/deceleration? Who will be held accountable for negligence, now that the answer is a *system*. Another aspect of driving a car is the monitoring of the 'driving environment', which is likewise done by a *system*. If a

[32] *See Supra* note 10, accessed on September 27, 2023.

[33] Ibid.

[34] Ibid.

fallback execution of the 'dynamic driving task' is available, who is the performing '*human driver*'. Is there any capability (driving mode) in the system? The answer is *some driving modes.* As a result of the arguments presented by the author, the author contends that the 'human driver/operator' and the manufacturer are both guilty under the 'law of negligence'.

In **Level 4** (High Automation), the 'automated driving system's' performance of all components of the 'dynamic driving task' in a certain driving mode, even if a human driver does not respond appropriately to a request to intervene. Who, once again, is in charge of steering and acceleration/deceleration? Now that the answer is a *system,* who will be held liable for negligence? Another aspect of driving a car is the monitoring of the driving environment, which is likewise done by a *system.* If a fallback execution of the 'dynamic driving task' is available, who is the performing *system.* Is there any capability (driving mode) in the system? The answer is '*some driving modes*'.

The author contends that the manufacturer is liable as a result of the arguments presented, but that a sui generis law is required to deal with cases of negligence in Germany, or that a place should be given under existing legislation to deal with 'Level 4 autonomous cars', as the existing provisions only deal with 'human drivers', not 'machines or autonomous cars'.

In Level 5 (Full Automation), full-time 'automated driving system' performance of all components of the 'dynamic driving task' under all roadway and environmental conditions that a 'human driver' can manage. Who, once again, oversees steering and acceleration/deceleration? Now that the answer is a system, who will be held liable for negligence? Another aspect of driving a car is the monitoring of the driving environment, which is likewise done by a system. If a fallback execution of the 'dynamic driving task' is available, who is the performing system. Is there any capability (driving mode) in the system? The answer is 'all driving modes'.

The author contends that the manufacturer is liable as a result of the arguments presented, but that a sui generis law is required to deal with cases of negligence in Germany, or that a place should be given under existing legislation to deal with 'Level 5 autonomous cars', as the existing provisions only deal with 'human drivers, not machines or autonomous cars'.

3.2.2 German's Strict Product Liability

'The German Federal Ministry of Transport and Digital Infrastructure' issued "*ethical principles for automated and connected vehicular traffic,*" which established strict liability for manufacturers.[35]

---

[35] While these ethical guidelines are not legally binding at this time, the German government has welcomed the report's findings and aims to help with the technology's evolution, laying out how it plans to adopt the results in its action plan.

According to "Article 7.1 of the German Federal Ministry of Transport and Digital Infrastructure 2017, in the case of automated and connected driving systems, the motorist's sole responsibility is transferred to the manufacturers and operators of technical systems, as well as entities responsible for infrastructure, policy, and legal actions."[36]

'The German Civil Code (Bürgerliches Gesetzbuch) and the Product Liability Act (Produkthaftungsgesetz)' are the two primary statutes that govern product liability in Germany.

Until 1989, tort law constituted the foundation of 'German product liability law', as stated in *"section 823(1) of the German Civil Code, 1900 which effectively states that anybody who intentionally or negligently injures the life, body, health, freedom, property, or another right of another person is liable in damages."* 'The European Product Liability Directive of 1985' served as the foundation for the 'Product Liability Act of 1989', which established strict liability.

In the event of a defect, a manufacturer may be held liable for product defects if it constitutes a breach of warranty under 'section 437 of the German Civil Code, 1900'.[37]

In the European Union, products are defined as "all movables" in 'Article 2 of the Product Liability Directive', according to which it applies only to physical goods. According to 'Article 2', this definition of product liability is well suited to the 'robot' and 'autonomous cars', but not to cloud-based AI.[38] Robot means any automatically operated machine that takes the place of human effort, even if it does not seem like a human or performs functions in a human-like manner. In a larger sense, an AV is a robotic car.

In the case of **Ransome v. Wisconsin, Elec. Power Co.,** where the Supreme Court of Wisconsin[39] held that electricity was held to be a product, and which therefore shifts towards defining software as a product rather than merely a service, with an assumption that software is indeed a product, it becomes binding on the developers of AI systems to make sure that their systems are designed free of defects, free from any 'manufacturing, warning, and instructions defects'.

The standard liability in a car crash deals with 'level 5 of the self-driving cars in Germany',[40] which were involved in an accident case during their first ride under the product liability law and secondly, under the 'old traffic law of 2017'.[41]

---

[36] Ethics Commission on Automated and Connected Driving (n 17).

[37] *See* <https://iclg.com/practice-areas/product-liability-laws-and-regulations/germany>, accessed on September 27, 2023.

[38] *Supra* n.3 at para 1.

[39] Ransome v. Wisconsin Elec. Power Co., 275 N.W.2d 641, 647–48. Wis. (1979).

[40] Winkler, K-C. (2019). *Autonomous Vehicles Regulation in Germany and the US and Its Impact on the German Car Industry* (Master Thesis, Tilburg Law School, Department of Business Law, Tilburg University, Tilburg).

[41] Ibid.

According to '§§ 2, 3 of the German Product Liability Law, 1989',[42] damage must be produced by the use of a product's defect. ProdHaftG[43] which provides for law on liability for defective products, as per '§ 2 of the Product Act', a defective part should be seen as a product only. This legal structure is only viable and applicable once the product has been made available to the general public. The data of Level 5 cars[44] is considered as a product by the prevalent viewpoints, and all of its pieces, including intangible software, are incorporated into the system. According to the 'European Parliament's declaration on Directive 85/374/EEC-1985'[45] responsibility for 'defective products', the law applies to all fully automated vehicles.[46]

3.2.2.1 Liability of AI Under the Law of Strict and Product Liability in Germany

The 'law on strict and product liability' would also be applicable in the case of 'SAE Level 0–5' because as per '§§ 2, 3 of the German Product Liability Law, 1989', the damage must be produced by the use of a product's defect, which provides for law on 'liability for defective products'. A defective part should only be considered a product. If the car is 'SAE Level 0–2', with a human driver/operator in charge of the vehicle and monitoring the environment, then '§§ 2, 3 of the German Product Liability Law' also applies. Even though the car is 'SAE Level 3–5', if the 'autonomous driving system' monitors the driving environment, this part is sufficient to hold the manufacturer liable under the 'law of product liability'.

3.2.2.2 Defences Available

The defence taken by the manufacturer could be based on the argument that the product met all standards and would not cause any damage. However, some liability exclusions are regulated in the 'Product Liability Act 2017', for instance, as per '***Section 1 of the Product Liability Act, 2017***'—if the manufacturer did not place the product in the market.

If the product's defect was not known at the time of supply, there is no liability in practise and principle. The onus is on the claimant to prove that the product was defective. The burden of proof is on the manufacturer to show that the problem was not previously known if the claimant successfully proves this under tort law under 'German Federal Court of Justice'.

'***Section 1(2) Product Liability Act***' provides for the defect liability exclusion scheme where it was not known or discoverable at the time of supply even after

[42] Ibid.

[43] *See* <https://www.gesetze-im-internet.de/prodhaftg/1.html≥, accessed on September 27,2023.

[44] Supra note 43.

[45] Ibid.

[46] Ibid.

having the technical and scientific knowledge when the manufacturer is exempt from liability for a product defect.

Conferring to '§ 1 (2) No. 1 to 5 ProdHaftG', there are in total five regulated exemptions for the manufacturer to exonerate liability. Those cases, in particular, comprise of the following:

The producer's liability obligation is excluded if

1. he did not put the product into circulation,

2. under the circumstances, it can be assumed that the defect which caused the damage did not exist at the time when the producer brings the product into circulation,

3. the product was neither manufactured by him for sale or any other form of distribution for economic purpose nor manufactured or distributed by him in the course of his business,

4. the defect is due to compliance of the product with mandatory regulations at the time when the producer put the product into circulation, or

5. the state of scientific and technical knowledge at the time when the producer brought the product to market was not such as to enable the defect to be discovered."[47]

Whereas, under '***Section 1(4) Product Liability Act, 2017***' in this respect, the manufacturer has the burden of proof. Pursuant to 'German Civil Procedure Code' under '***Sections 72–74***', the defendant can claim that the fault was due to someone else's actions. So they should show-cause notice to the Third Party if they have recourse claims against the third party in the case of being failed or unsuccessful in the legal proceedings.[48]

In Germany, under the '***Section 276 of the German Civil Code, 1900***':[49] where it provides for the strict liability, where under it disposes that the obligor is generally just responsible for their fault ('intention or negligence'). However, exceptionally there can be a "higher degree of liability," regardless of the obligor's fault.[50]

Whereas '***Section 254 of the German Civil Code, 1900***' talks about 'Contributory negligence'[51]: It discusses, in particular, to what extent the damage is caused

---

[47] (Bundesministerium der Justiz und Verbraucherschutz / Federal Ministery of justice and consumer protection, 2017).

[48] Ibid.

[49] "***Section 276 of the German Civil Code: Responsibility of the obligor.***

(1) The obligor is responsible for intention and negligence if a higher or lower degree of liability is neither laid down nor to be inferred from the other subject matter of the obligation, including but not limited to the giving of a guarantee or the assumption of a procurement risk. The provisions of sections 827 and 828 apply with the necessary modifications.

(2) A person acts negligently if he fails to exercise reasonable care.

(3) The obligor may not be released in advance from liability for intention."

[50] *See Supra* note 10, accessed on September 27, 2023.

[51] "**Section 254 of the German Civil Code: Contributory negligence**

primarily by one or the other party, and what if the harmed person's fault is limited to failing to alert the obligor to the risks of unusually extensive harm, where the obligor was not aware of the harm and should not have been, or failing to prevent or minimise the harm.[52]

Though there is no maximum limit in general, under ***'Section 10 of the Product Liability Act'***, in case of personal injury, the person is liable to pay compensation and is only liable up to a maximum amount of EUR 0.85 million.[53]

Majority of the car crashes in Germany are regulated and solved by the Road Traffic Act (StVG), 2017.[54] The German liability of car accidents on the persons involved is always based on the concept of the car driver or car owner, so '**§§ 7, 18 (StVG)** ***of the German Road Traffic Act*** (Straßenverkehrsgesetz)'[55] provides for strict liability of the keeper of the vehicle and both the parties can be held liable jointly and severally beside the obligatory third-party liability insurance of the owner/car keeper, which is an essential condition to have for authorisation of the car for the owner.[56] *Deliberately this rule was left unchanged when the 'Road Traffic Act, 2017' was enacted to the emergence of automated cars.*[57]

The manufacturer's defence may be that the product complied with all regulations and would not cause any harm, thus the onus is now on the driver of the car to prove his innocence.[58]

---

(1) Where fault on the part of the injured person contributes to the occurrence of the damage, liability in damages and the extent of compensation to be paid depends on the circumstances, in particular to what extent the damage is caused mainly by one or the other party.

(2) This also applies if the fault of the injured person is limited to failing to draw the attention of the obligor to the danger of unusually extensive damage, where the obligor neither was nor ought to have been aware of the danger or to failing to avert or reduce the damage. The provision of section 278 applies with the necessary modifications".

52 *See Supra* note 10, accessed on September 27, 2023.

53 *See* <https://iclg.com/practice-areas/product-liability-laws-and-regulations/germany>, accessed on September 27, 2023.

54 *Supra* note 40. See also (Prof. Dr. Dr. h.c. LL.M. (UCLA) Oppermann, Apl. Prof. Dr. Stender-Vorwachs, & Prof. Dr. LL.M. Beck, 2017).

55 Ibid.

56 (Gesamtschuldnerische Haftung von Fahrer, Halter und Haftpflichtversicherung bei einem Verkehrsunfall, (1989).

57 *Supra* note 40.

58 Ibid.

3.2.3 Vicarious Liability in Germany

'§ 831 BGB of the German Civil Code, 1900' provides for the Vicarious Liability[59]:

In Germany, under vicarious liability, there has to be some wrongful act done by the agent. If an agent has not done some wrongful act, applied foreseeability, then in that case principal is not liable vicariously. So, if the principal has exercised due care in the process of selecting an agent and supervised the performance of duties also by providing them specific tools for carrying out those duties, despite all such measures as applied by the principal, still the loss has occurred. Concerning liability for 'things', German civil law does not recognise harm emerging because of the utilisation of a tangible or intangible thing or theoretical thing or straight by the individual.[60]

If Artificial Intelligence is supposed to have a separate legal identity, then, in that case, vicarious liability could apply. For instance, pet owners are liable or responsible for the harm caused by their pets. Similar to AI, animals are also autonomous. **However**, the same could be done with artificial intelligence, *if AI is deemed to be having a separate legal identity, then, in that case, specific legislation would have to be drafted, and new standards or rules would have been created for business.*

Vicarious liability is an essential paradigm for addressing the algorithm harms, so much more to discuss and translate vicarious liability into legal doctrine. Generally, when a victim comes to a court seeking redresses against the harm caused by an algorithm. The doctrine says whether the victim has bad luck or whether some third party would pay damages.

Whom to Hold Accountable?

Modern algorithms can be highly complex and expensive. Algorithms that are not straightforward in this manner are designated 'black box algorithms'. Black box

[59] **"Section 831 of the German Civil Code: Liability for vicarious agents.**

> *(1) A person who uses another person to perform a task is liable to compensate for the damage that the other unlawfully inflicts on a third party when carrying out the task. Liability in damages does not apply if the principal exercises reasonable care when selecting the person deployed and, to the extent that he is to procure devices or equipment or to manage the business activity, in the procurement or management, or if the damage would have occurred even if this care had been exercised.*
>
> *(2) The same responsibility is borne by a person who assumes the performance of one of the transactions specified in subsection (1) sentence 2 for the principal by contract".*

[60] A recent judgment of the Federal Court of Justice (Bundesgerichtshof) (Judgment of 9.2.2018, Az. V ZR 311/16) introduced non-fault-based liability which is not provided for in the Civil Code for owners of the buildings by analogy with respect to Section 906 BGB (escape of imponderable (risky) substances) in a case in which a fire caused by works on the roof of one building harm/damaged the neighbouring property.

algorithms are created (rather than written) by incorporating techniques such as managing massive informational sets into deep neural networks.

There is some discussion concerning what degree of AI could be given legitimate character. It may be considered responsible for its activities like an individual or an organisation/company. It likewise would imply that the individual accountable for the AI could be legitimately answerable for the AI's activities through vicarious responsibility (similarly that the employer is liable for the activities of their workers throughout their work).

3.2.3.1 Liability of AI Under the Law of Vicarious Liability in Germany

The author has tried to analyse what this provision '§ 831 BGB of the German Civil Code, 1900'[61] means in terms of AVs. What role can this section have in determining vicarious liability if an AV is involved in an accident? A comprehensive analysis of these provisions reveals that existing provisions such as '§ 831 BGB of the German Civil Code, 1900'[62] only apply to human driver or/and car owner who are held liable for vicarious liability and subject to punitive damages under tort law. Now, because it must be viewed from the perspective of 'SAE Level 0–2', where the car is perfectly under the control of the human driver, the human driver monitors the driving environment in these scenarios. Now will look at whether the same law applies in cases of vicarious liability ranging from 'SAE Level 0 to 5'. So, according to the author, it will be applied on a regular basis whenever the scenario requires it because it is totally in the hands of the human driver/owner/user who is driving a car because the operator can monitor the driving environment. When compared to existing provisions in the law of vicarious liability, such as '§ 831 BGB of the German Civil Code, 1900'[63] with 'SAE Level 0 to 5', the outcome is even.

In **Level 0**, the full-time performance by the human driver or/and car owner of all aspects of the dynamic driving task, even when enhanced by warning or intervention systems.

Who, once again, is in charge of steering and acceleration/deceleration? Who will be held accountable for vicarious liability, now that the answer is a human driver or/and car owner.

Another aspect of driving a car is the monitoring of the driving environment, which is likewise done by a human driver or/and car owner. If a fallback execution of the dynamic driving task is available, who is the performing *human driver or/and car owner*. Is there any capability (driving mode) in the system? The answer is negative. As a result of the arguments presented by the author, the author argues that only human driver or/and car owner are liable under the law of vicarious liability under '§ 831 BGB of the German Civil Code'.[64]

---

[61] *See Supra* note 10, accessed on September 27, 2023.

[62] Ibid.

[63] Ibid.

[64] Ibid.

In **Level 1** (Driver Assistance), the execution of either steering or acceleration/deceleration by a driver assistance system based on information about the driving environment, with the expectation that the *human driver/operator will handle* the remaining components of the dynamic driving task. Who will be held accountable for vicarious liability, now that the answer is a human driver and system. Is there any capability (driving mode) in the system? The answer is some driving modes. As a result of the arguments presented by the author, the author believes that human driver or/and car owner are liable under the law of vicarious liability under '§ 831 BGB of the German Civil Code'.

In **Level 2** (Partial Automation), the execution of both steering and acceleration/deceleration by one or more driver assistance systems is based on information about the driving environment, with the expectation that the *human driver will handle* the remaining components of the dynamic driving task. Here the system is in charge of steering and acceleration/deceleration. Who will be held accountable for vicarious liability, now that the answer is a system.

Another aspect of driving a car is the monitoring of the driving environment, which is likewise done by a human driver. If a fallback execution of the dynamic driving task is available, who is the performing *human driver*. Is there any capability (driving mode) in the system? The answer is some driving modes. As a result of the arguments presented by the author, the author believes that only human driver or/and car owner are liable under the law of vicarious liability under '§ 831 BGB of the German Civil Code'.[65]

SAE Level 3-5: Automated driving system ('system') monitors the driving environment.

In **Level 3** (Conditional Automation), the automated driving system's handling of all parts of the dynamic driving task in a certain driving mode, with the expectation that the human driver will respond properly to a request to intervene. Who, once again, is in charge of steering and acceleration/deceleration? Who will be held accountable for vicarious liability, now that the answer is a *system*. Another aspect of driving a car is the monitoring of the driving environment, which is likewise done by a *system*. If a fallback execution of the dynamic driving task is available, who is the performing *human driver*. Is there any capability (driving mode) in the system? The answer is *some driving modes*. As a result of the arguments presented by the author, the author contends that the human driver or/and car owner and the manufacturer are both guilty under the 'law of vicarious liability'.

In **Level 4** (High Automation), the automated driving system's performance of all components of the dynamic driving task in a certain driving mode, even if a human driver does not respond appropriately to a request to intervene. Who, once again, is in charge of steering and acceleration/deceleration? Now that the answer is a *system*, who will be held liable for vicarious liability? Another aspect of driving a car is the monitoring of the driving environment, which is likewise done by a *system*. If a fallback execution of the dynamic driving task is available, who is the performing *system*. Is there any capability (driving mode) in the system? The answer is *some*

[65] Ibid.

driving modes. The author contends that the manufacturer is liable as a result of the arguments presented, but that a sui generis law is required to deal with cases of vicarious liability in Germany, or that a place should be given under existing legislation to deal with 'Level 4 autonomous cars', as the existing provisions only deal with human drivers, not machines or autonomous cars.

In **Level 5** (Full Automation), full-time automated driving system performance of all components of the dynamic driving task under all roadway and environmental conditions that a human driver can manage. Who, once again, oversees steering and acceleration/deceleration? Now that the answer is a *system*, who will be held liable for vicarious liability? Another aspect of driving a car is the monitoring of the driving environment, which is likewise done by a *system*. If a fallback execution of the dynamic driving task is available, who is the performing *system*. Is there any capability (driving mode) in the system? The answer is *all driving modes.* The author contends that the manufacturer is liable as a result of the arguments presented, but that a sui generis law is required to deal with cases of 'vicarious liability in Germany', or that a place should be given under existing legislation to deal with 'Level 5 autonomous cars', as the existing provisions only deal with human drivers, not machines or autonomous cars.

So, the author is of the view that it will only be used in situations where an autonomous vehicle is at 'SAE Level 0 through 3'. For 'SAE Levels 4 and 5', *sui generis law* is required to deal with the case of 'vicarious liability in Germany'.

3.3 Position in California—Law of Negligence, Strict, and Product and Vicarious Liability

3.3.1 Law of Negligence in the United States of America—California

In US tort law on negligence states that "A bad state of mind is neither necessary nor sufficient to show negligence; conduct is everything."[66]

California Negligence Law is codified in **California Civil Code, 1988—Section 1714**[67]**:**

"Everyone is responsible, not only for the result of his or her wilful acts, but also for an injury occasioned to another by his or her want of ordinary care or skill in the management of his or her property or person, except so far as the latter has, wilfully or by want of ordinary care, brought the injury upon himself or herself. The design, distribution, or marketing of firearms and ammunition is not exempt from the duty

---

[66] Dobbs D.B.: Law of Torts. West Academic Publishing (2008).

[67] *See* <http://leginfo.legislature.ca.gov/faces/codes_displaySection.xhtml?lawCode=CIV&sectionNum=1714>, accessed September 28, 2023.

to use ordinary care and skill that is required by this section. The extent of liability in these cases is defined by the Title on Compensatory Relief."[68]

The majority of car accident lawsuits centre on a driver's alleged fault.[69] **Section 282** of Restatement[70] (Second)[71] of Torts states that "negligence is conduct which falls below the standard established by law for the protection of others against unreasonable risk of harm. It excludes action that is recklessly indifferent to the interests of others."[72] As a result, negligence does not need the presence of intent.[73] Instead, a negligence claim requires a duty, a breach of that obligation, causation, and actual loss or injury.[74]

It depends on the element of causation,[75] which results in tort liability when both actual and proximate causes are present. Actual cause is "when the harm would not have occurred absent that action."[76] Proximate cause[77] is "limited to those harms that result from the risks that made the actor's conduct tortious."[78]

---

[68] Ibid.

[69] Ken LaMance, What Is Negligence in a Car Accident Lawsuit? LEGALMATCH, <https://www.legalmatch.com/law-library/article/negligence-in-a-car-accident-lawsuit.html>, accessed on April 14, 2020, ("Most car accident lawsuits are based on negligence, because negligence does not involve intentional acts by the defendant.").

[70] Restatements are secondary sources of persuasive value. They attempt to 'restate' the legal norms that constitute the common law in a certain legal area into a set of principles.

[71] The American Law Institute published the American Restatement of Torts, Second Edition. It explains the basic elements of common law tort law in the United States. The torts volumes are part of the second series of Restatements of the Law. It is divided into four volumes, the first two of which were released in 1965, the third in 1977, and the fourth in 1979.

[72] RESTATEMENT (SECOND) OF TORTS § 282 (AM. LAW INST. 1965).

[73] VICTOR E. SCHWARTZ, KATHRYN KELLY & DAVID E. PARTLETT, PROSSER, WADE, AND SCHWARTZ'S TORTS: CASES AND MATERIALS 1 (Robert C. Clark et al. eds., 13th ed. 2015).

A tort is a civil wrong, other than a breach of contract, for which the law provides a remedy. This area of law imposes duties on persons to act in a manner that will not injure other persons. A person who breaches a tort duty has committed a tort and may be liable to pay damages in a lawsuit brought by a person injured because of that tort. *See* also Peter Y. Kim, *Where We're Going, We Don't Need Drivers: Autonomous Vehicles and AI-Chaperone Liability*, 69 Cath. U. L. Rev. 341 (2020). Available at: https://scholarship.law.edu/lawreview/vol69/iss2/9, accessed on September 28, 2023.

[74] *Id.*

[75] *See* also Peter Y. Kim, *Where We're Going, We Don't Need Drivers: Autonomous Vehicles and AI-Chaperone Liability*, 69 Cath. U. L. Rev. 341 (2020). Available at: https://scholarship.law.edu/lawreview/vol69/iss2/9, accessed on September 28, 2023.

[76] RESTATEMENT (THIRD) OF TORTS, 1997: LIABILITY FOR PHYSICAL AND EMOTIONAL HARM.

§ 26 (AM. LAW INST. 2010). Actual cause can be found under Section 27, "[i]f multiple acts occur, each of which under § 26 alone would have been a factual cause of the physical harm at the same time in the absence of the other act(s), each act is regarded as a factual cause of the harm." *Id.* § 27.

[77] *Supra* note 76.

[78] *Id.* § 29.

California Statute of Limitations for Negligence

The Law of Negligence is covered quite extensively under the 'Code of Civil Procedure, 1872 in California'.[79] The limitation period under the 'California Statute of Limitation' for cases of negligence is as under:

1. For the personal injury, 2 years as per the Code of Civil Procedure **335.1,**[80]
2. For the property, it is 2 years as per the Code of Civil Procedure **338(b) and (c)**,[81] and lastly
3. For professional malpractise, it is 1 year per the Code of Civil Procedure **340.5 and 0.6.**[82]

---

79 See <https://www.google.co.in/books/edition/The_Code_of_Civil_Procedure_of_the_State/tvcEAAAAYAAJ?hl=en&gbpv=1>, accessed on September 26, 2023.

80 ***"Section 335.1:** Within two years: An action for assault, battery, or injury to, or the death of, an individual caused by the wrongful act or neglect of another*".

81 ***"Section 338:** Within three years: (b) an action for trespass upon or injury to real property.*

*(c) (1) an action for taking, detaining, or injuring goods or chattels, including an action for the specific recovery of personal property.***"**.

82 **"Section 340.5.** :In an action for injury or death against a health care provider based upon such person's alleged professional negligence, the time for the commencement of action shall be three years after the date of injury or one year after the plaintiff discovers, or using reasonable diligence should have discovered, the injury, whichever occurs first. In no event shall the time for commencement of legal action exceed three years unless tolled for any of the following: (1) upon proof of fraud, (2) intentional concealment, or (3) the presence of a foreign body, which has no therapeutic or diagnostic purpose or effect, in the person of the injured person. Actions by a minor shall be commenced within three years from the date of the alleged wrongful act except those actions by a minor under the full age of six years shall be commenced within three years or prior to his eighth birthday whichever provides a longer period. Such time limitation shall be tolled for minors for any period during which parent or guardian and defendant's insurer or health care provider have committed fraud or collusion in the failure to bring an action on behalf of the injured minor for professional negligence".

"Section 340.6.: (a) An action against an attorney for a wrongful act or omission, other than for actual fraud, arising in the performance of professional services shall be commenced within one year after the plaintiff discovers, or using reasonable diligence should have discovered. The facts constituting the wrongful act or omission, or four years from the date of the wrongful act or omission, whichever occurs first. Suppose the plaintiff is required to establish the plaintiff's factual innocence for an underlying criminal charge as an element of the plaintiff's claim. In that case, the action shall be commenced within two years after the plaintiff achieves post-conviction exoneration in the form of a final judicial disposition of the criminal case. Except for a claim for which the plaintiff is required to establish the plaintiff's factual innocence, the time for commencement of legal action shall not exceed four years except that the period shall be tolled during the time that any of the following exist.

(1) The plaintiff has not sustained actual injury.

(2) The attorney continues to represent the plaintiff regarding the specific subject matter in which the alleged wrongful act or omission occurred.

(3) The attorney willfully conceals the facts constituting the wrongful act or omission when those facts are known to the attorney, except that this subdivision shall toll only the four-year limitation.

(4) The plaintiff is under a legal or physical disability that restricts the plaintiff's ability to commence legal action.

3.3.1.1 Liability of AI Under the Law of Negligence in California

The criterion used under "Californian law is pure comparative negligence." This means that the plaintiff is entitled to compensation for all losses brought on by the defendants. Even if the plaintiff is substantially at blame, the amount of the award may nevertheless be reduced by the plaintiff's own negligence.

After analysing the provisions under the 'California Civil Code, 1988—Section 1714[83] and California Code of Civil Procedure, 1872—Sections 335.1, 338(b) and (c), 340.5 and 0.6,[84] it seems that similar to the German legal framework'. The applicability of these provisions to AVs whether or not AI liability can be determined under the existing provisions, particularly when an AV is involved in an accident? If yes, why and how?

A comprehensive analysis of these provisions reveals that existing provisions such as 'California Civil Code Section 1714'[85] only apply to human drivers or car owners who are held liable for negligence and subject to punitive damages under tort law. Now, because it must be viewed from the perspective of 'SAE Level 0–2', where the car is perfectly under the control of the human driver, the human driver monitors the driving environment in these scenarios. Now author will look at whether the same law applies in cases of negligence ranging from SAE Level 0 to 5. So, according to the author, it will be applied on a regular basis whenever the scenario requires it because it is totally in the hands of the human driver/owner/user who is driving a car because the operator can monitor the driving environment. When compared to existing provisions in the law of negligence, such as 'California Civil Code Section 1714,[86] California Code of Civil Procedure, 1872—Sections 335.1, 338(b) and (c), 340.5 and 0.6 with SAE Level 0 to 5',[87] the outcome is even.

Level 0 (No Automation), the full-time performance by the human driver of all aspects of the dynamic driving task, even when enhanced by warning or intervention systems. Who, once again, is in charge of steering and acceleration/deceleration? Who will be held accountable for negligence? Now that a human driver is the answer. Another aspect of driving a car is the monitoring of the driving environment, which is likewise done by a human driver. If a fallback execution of the dynamic driving

---

(5) A dispute between the lawyer and client concerning fees, costs, or both is pending resolution under Article 13 (commencing with Section 6200) of Chap. 4 *of Division 3 of the Business and Professions Code. As used in this paragraph, 'pending' means from the date a request for arbitration is filed until 30 days after receiving notice of the arbitrators' award or receipt of notice that the arbitration is otherwise terminated, whichever occurs first.*

(b) In an action based upon an instrument in writing, the effective date of which depends upon some act or event of the future, the period of limitations provided for by this section shall commence running upon the occurrence of that act or event".

[83] See <https://leginfo.legislature.ca.gov/faces/codes_displaySection.xhtml?sectionNum=1714.&lawCode=CIV>, accessed on September 26, 2023.

[84] See *Supra* note 80.

[85] See *Supra* note 84.

[86] Ibid.

[87] Ibid.

task is available, who is the performing *human driver*. Is there any capability (driving mode) in the system? The answer is negative. As a result of the arguments presented by the author, the author argues that only *human driver/operator* are liable under the law of negligence under 'California Civil Code Section 1714, California Code of Civil Procedure, 1872—Sections 335.1, 338(b) and (c), 340.5 and 0.6'.[88]

In **Level 1** (Driver Assistance), the execution of steering or acceleration/deceleration by a driver assistance system based on data about the driving environment, with the expectation that the human driver will handle the other components of the dynamic driving task. Who will be held accountable for negligence, now that the answer is a human driver and system. Is there any capability (driving mode) in the system? The answer is some driving modes. As a result of the arguments presented by the author, the author believes that only *human driver/operator* are liable under the law of negligence under 'California Civil Code Section 1714, California Code of Civil Procedure, 1872—Section 335.1, 338(b) and (c), 340.5 and 0.6'.[89]

In **Level 2** (Partial Automation), the use of one or more driver assistance systems to execute steering and acceleration/deceleration functions based on information about the driving environment, with the hope that the *human driver will handle* the remaining tasks involved in dynamic driving. Here the system is in charge of steering and acceleration/deceleration. Who will be held accountable for negligence, now that the answer is a *system*. Another aspect of driving a car is the monitoring of the driving environment, which is likewise done by a *human driver*. If a fallback execution of the dynamic driving task is available, who is the performing *human driver*. Is there any capability (driving mode) in the system? The answer is some driving modes. As a result of the arguments presented by the author, the author believes that only *human driver/operator* are liable under the law of negligence under 'California Civil Code, 1988 Section 1714,[90] California Code of Civil Procedure, 1872—Sections 335.1, 338(b) and (c), 340.5 and 0.6'.[91]

SAE Level 3-5: Automated driving system ('system') monitors the driving environment.

In **Level 3** (Conditional Automation), in a certain driving mode, the automated driving system will handle every aspect of the dynamic driving task with the hope that the human driver will react appropriately when asked to intervene. Who, once again, is in charge of steering and acceleration/deceleration? Who will be held accountable for negligence now that the answer is a *system*. Another aspect of driving a car is the monitoring of the driving environment, which is likewise done by a *system*. If a fallback execution of the dynamic driving task is available, who is the performing *human driver*. Is there any capability (driving mode) in the system? The answer is *some driving modes*. As a result of the arguments presented by the author, the author contends that the human driver/operator and the manufacturer are both guilty under the law of negligence.

---

[88] See *Supra* note 80.

[89] See *Supra* note 80.

[90] See *Supra* note 84.

[91] See *Supra* note 80.

In **Level 4** (High Automation), even if a human driver doesn't react adequately to a request to intervene, the automated driving system must nonetheless complete all aspects of the 'dynamic driving task' while in a certain driving mode. Again, whose responsibility is it to steer and accelerate or decelerate? Now that the answer is a *system*, who will be held liable for negligence? Another aspect of driving a car is the monitoring of the driving environment, which is likewise done by a *system*. If a fallback execution of the dynamic driving task is available, who is the performing *system*. Is there any capability (driving mode) in the system? The answer is *some driving modes*. The author contends that the manufacturer is liable as a result of the arguments presented, but that a sui generis law is required to deal with cases of negligence in California, or that a place should be given under existing legislation to deal with Level 4 autonomous cars, as the existing provisions only deal with human drivers, not machines or autonomous cars.

In **Level 5** (Full Automation), the performance of all dynamic driving task components by a fully automated driving system in all traffic and environmental circumstances that a human driver is capable of handling. Again, whose responsibility is it to steer and accelerate or decelerate? Now that the answer is a *system*, who will be held liable for negligence? Another aspect of driving a car is the monitoring of the driving environment, which is likewise done by a *system*. Who is performing *system* if there is a fallback execution of 'dynamic driving task'? Is there any capability (driving mode) in the system? The answer is *all driving modes*. The author contends that the manufacturer is liable as a result of the arguments presented, but that a sui generis law is required to deal with cases of negligence in California, or that a place should be given under existing legislation to deal with Level 5 autonomous cars, as the existing provisions only deal with human drivers, not machines or autonomous cars.

3.3.2 California's Strict Product Liability

In contrast to the German system, where liability and the general legal framework surrounding an automobile accident are characterised by *federal law*, state law is predominant in the United States. To maintain unity throughout the nation, only information regarding product manufacture liability, procedures, and methodology from all states is posted or summarised at the federal level.

However, it is not binding; only the general court practises follow it.[92] Furthermore, every state has its specifications and provisions on drivers' standards per the traffic law liability. To govern safety standards at the level of *federal structure*, the *"National Highway Traffic Safety Administration (NHTSA)"* is the functioning authority.

At the state level, it is the proper particular *'Department of Transportation'* that is in charge. When it comes to car accidents, the United States of America's legal

[92] (The American Law Institute, 2015).

system divides up responsibility between the federal and state levels as explained under NHTSA, 2017.[93]

In September 2017, NHTSA released new voluntary guidelines or regulations for the simplifying of assembling or manufacturing, testing, and deploying AVs while deterring states from carrying out clashing AV regulations. Additionally, NHTSA's safety 2.0 guidelines deal with levels 3 to 5 automation especially. The guidelines also urge automakers to introduce deliberate security and safety (self-evaluation authentications) to NHSTA, demonstrating how safety has tended in AVs. California has allowed the testing of AVs on a public road without an operator.[94]

Furthermore, while the NHTSA can approve exceptions for certain vehicles from conforming to specific norms on a yearly basis—for example, having a steering wheel or brake pedal—there appears to be a growing desire to expand these yearly exclusions to allow for more extensive testing of self-driving vehicle.[95]

Senate of California, 2017[96] positively encouraged the *'Department of Transportation'* in California while improving and maintaining the road infrastructure, investing in devices, having the ability to communicate through the V2I technology with the autonomous vehicles, *'Road Maintenance and Rehabilitation Program 2030 (d)'*.[97] In 2016, California[98] amended its legislation concerning *'Section 38,755 of the Vehicle Code'*,[99] this relates to autonomous vehicles and permits self-driving vehicles without a steering wheel or brake pedals to travel over predetermined testing routes at a maximum speed of 65 km/h.[100]

The US government[101] is reluctant to regulate autonomous cars on a federal level because it believes that this tort liability applies to AVs engaged in auto-accidents. Different states have different ways to cope up with liability issues and approaches.[102] Moreover, the *'Federal Department of Transportation (US DOT)'*,[103] known as federal authorities or the *'National Highway Traffic Safety Administration'*,[104] less effort is being made to amend and fill in the gaps in future liability federal regulation.[105]

---

93 (NHTSA, 2017).

94 Gurney, J.K. Sue My Car Not Me: Products Liability and Accidents Involving Autonomous Vehicles. J. Law Technol. Policy 2013, 2, 247–277.

95 *See* <https://www.ncsl.org/research/transportation/regulating-autonomous-vehicles.aspx>, accessed on June 26, 2021.

96 *Supra* note 40.

97 (Senate of California, 2017), See also *Supra* note 40.

98 Ibid.

99 *See* <https://leginfo.legislature.ca.gov/faces/codes_displayText.xhtml?lawCode=VEH&division=16.6.&title=&part=&chapter=&article=, accessed on September 26, 2023.

100 (Senate of California, 2018).

101 *Supra* note 40.

102 Ibid.

103 Ibid.

104 *Id.*

105 *Supra* note 40.

In California, product liability claims are based on a theory of 'strict liability', though generally, personal injury's standard claims are based on the theory of negligence, and this theory is helping make their path into 'California-strict product liability law'.[106]

Impact of software being a product or service on determining an AI's responsibility.

Now, the question is what will be the implication on the liability of AI in each case when software programmed into it is a product or a service? Given under the 'Uniform Commercial Code, 1952' *mass-produced, off-the-shelf software is a 'good'*, like self-driving cars but defining software here means—*software specifically designed for a customer is a 'service'*.

If it is a product, then strict liability will apply, where the flaws are in product design, manufacturing design, or warnings that may cause personal injury or damage to the property of others. In the case of services, negligence applies to services.

In California, to prove a product liability claim, a plaintiff has to fulfil the following ingredients:

1. The product was manufactured, sold, or distributed by the defendant;
2. The product had a manufacturing defect, was defectively designed, did not have proper instructions, or failed to warn consumers about its dangers; and
3. The defect or failure to warn consumers caused harm to the plaintiff.

If a plaintiff successfully proves these three ingredients, she or he will likely win their California products liability case. Most importantly, the plaintiff also has to prove that she or he used the product the way it was instructed or supposed to be used — or, at least how a manufacturer could have predicted consumers would use it.[107]

> California Product Liability, 1963 is defined under **§ 1714.45.** of California Code, Civil Code-CIV.[108]

---

[106] *See* <https://www.brianogradylaw.com/Articles/Strict-Product-Liability-in-California.shtml>, accessed on September 26, 2023.

[107] *See* <https://www.larryhparker.com/explaining-californias-product-liability-laws/>, accessed on June 25, 2023.

[108] "**California Product Liability, 1963: Section 1714.45.**

(a) In a product liability action, a manufacturer or seller shall not be liable if both of the following apply.

(1) The product is inherently unsafe, and the product is known to be unsafe by the ordinary consumer who consumes the product with the ordinary knowledge common to the community.

(2) The product is a common consumer product intended for personal consumption, such as sugar, castor oil, alcohol, and butter, as identified in a comment i to Section 402A of the Restatement (Second) of Torts.

(b) This section does not exempt tobacco manufacturers and their successors' manufacture or sale of tobacco products in interest from product liability actions. However, it does exempt the sale or distribution of tobacco products by any other person, including, but not limited to, retailers or distributors.

Additionally, it addresses the parties concerned about liabilities in terms of sale, product distribution, and manufacture. To apply this doctrine, it must first confirm that ***AI must qualify as a product, not as a service***. Though it has created an autonomous AI product using machine learning and algorithms, what would happen if any defects occurred in the supply chain of its product, and how would it know where any defect occurred?

This is what commentators thought that while solving the issues related to autonomous vehicles, robots, drones, and other AI-enabled systems, the product liability will become a relevant subject of issues to solve like defective products, dangerous products liability, and types of product defects.[109]

Case-law on Self-Driving Cars

Wang v. Tesla Inc.,[110]

JING WANG and WAI-LEUNG CHAN, Plaintiffs, v. TESLA, INC., Defendant.

NICHOLAS G. GARAUFIS, UNITED STATES DISTRICT JUDGE.

Facts of the case:

Plaintiff Chan got interested in buying a Tesla vehicle for his everyday commute through Long Island traffic in or around 2015. (Am. Compl., Tesla's Autopilot feature

---

(c) For purposes of this section, the term 'product liability action' means any action for injury or death caused by a product, except that the term does not include an action based on a manufacturing defect or breach of an express warranty.

(d) This section is intended to be declarative of and does not alter or amend existing California law, including Cronin v. J.B.E. Olson Corp. (1972), 8 Cal. 3d 121, and shall apply to all product liability actions pending on or commenced after, January 1, 1988.

(e) This section does not apply to, and never applied to, an action brought by a public entity to recover the value of benefits provided to individuals injured by a tobacco-related illness caused by the tortious conduct of a tobacco company or its successor in interest, including, but not limited to, an action brought pursuant to Section 14,124.71 of the Welfare and Institutions Code. In action brought by a public entity, the fact that the injured individual's claim against the defendant may be barred by a prior version of this section shall not be a defense. This subdivision does not constitute a change but is declaratory of existing law relating to tobacco products.

(f) It is the intention of the Legislature in enacting the amendments to subdivisions (a) and (b) of this section adopted at the 1997–98 Regular Session to declare that there exists no statutory bar to tobacco-related personal injury, wrongful death, or other tort claims against tobacco manufacturers and their successors in interest by California smokers or others who have suffered or incurred injuries, damages, or costs arising from the promotion, marketing, sale, or consumption of tobacco products. It is also the intention of the Legislature to clarify that those claims that were or are brought shall be determined on their merits, without the imposition of any claim of statutory bar or categorical defense.

(g) This section shall not be construed to grant immunity to a tobacco industry research organization.".

[109] *Supra* note 107.

[110] Wang v. Tesla Inc., No.1:20-cv-03040 (E.D.N.Y.Aug.31, 2020), 20-CV-3040 (NGG) (SJB). United States District Court, Eastern District of New York, Decided Jul 16, 2021.

piqued his interest, as it is designed to assist drivers with "the burdensome portions of driving," according to Tesla. Tesla vehicles equipped with Autopilot technology may steer, accelerate, and brake autonomously; match their speed to surrounding traffic; accelerate and decelerate to maintain a specified distance behind the nearest vehicle; change lanes on the highway; and detect neighbouring automobiles to avoid collisions.)

Plaintiff Chan says that he visited Tesla's website on a weekly basis before purchasing a Tesla vehicle in order to learn more about the product's capabilities. Based on his research on the Tesla website, Chan concluded that a Tesla vehicle would be ideal for his transportation needs. Plaintiff Chan went to dealerships in Syosset, New York, and Manhasset, New York, to test drive the Model S and Model X vehicles. A salesman promised Plaintiff during his visit to the Manhasset store.

The Model X, one of Tesla's Autopilot-equipped vehicles, is touted as "the safest, quickest, and most capable sport utility vehicle in history" and "the safest SUV ever," according to Tesla.

"He could take the Tesla into the HOV lane… and then close his eyes and 'relax'," he said, adding that the Autopilot option would be ideal for his commutes.

Chan acquired a Model X in Tesla's Brooklyn, New York showroom in September 2016, based on what he learnt from the company's website and through his showroom visits.

Plaintiff Chan was in an accident on the Long Island Expressway on December 13, 2017, while driving the Model X through heavy traffic. Plaintiffs claim that when a white Audi merged in front of Chan's car, the Autopilot feature failed to react, alert Chan of an approaching collision, or activate the "Automatic Emergency Breaking" function. Plaintiff Chan steered to the left, seeking to avoid a collision, but instead collided with two other cars, with only a fraction of a second to react. The Autopilot system failed to notice the oncoming collision as well, as well as its "'Automatic Emergency Breaking'" function was once again disabled. Plaintiff Chan argues he was alert the entire time and drove the vehicle in a reasonable manner. The incident caused serious damage to Plaintiffs' Model X, which was declared a total loss, as well as damage to two other vehicles; no physical injury was claimed.

Issues Involved:

1. Plaintiff Wai-Leung Chan was engaged in a car accident while driving a vehicle acquired under the name of his wife, Plaintiff Jing Wang, from Defendant Tesla, Inc. ('Tesla'). Plaintiffs sued Tesla for failure to warn, breach of express and implied warranties, deceptive and misleading business practises and false advertising, common law fraud, and negligent misrepresentation.
2. Plaintiffs claim that neither Tesla nor its representatives warned them about the limitations of the Model X and the Autopilot feature, nor did they provide proper instructions on how to operate the Model X and the Autopilot feature, either through Tesla's website or during Plaintiff Chan's visits to Tesla showrooms.

3. That alleging for the breach of warranty, negligence, and other charges based on an auto-accident death resulted in Tesla's alleging defective Autopilot characteristic/feature caused the car to crash into another car.[111]

Findings:

Tesla's Partial Motion to Dismiss is GRANTED IN PART with regard to Plaintiffs' fraud claim and DENIED IN PART with respect to Plaintiffs' punitive and exemplary damages claim. The motion by Tesla to strike certain factual statements from Plaintiffs' Amended Complaint has been denied. ***The court found Tesla (the manufacturer) accountable for negligence, strict liability, and product liability and awarded the defendant exemplary damages under tort law.***

SO IT WAS ORDERED.

3.3.2.1 In an AV Case, Proving Defect and Liability

The primary focus of a product liability claim involving an AV will be on *whether the AV's design and operation were defective.* Examining accidents where an independent vehicle disregarded a traffic[112] regulation and caused a crash will be utilised to study AV configuration flaws. Aside from feasibly predictable protections for support, the independent vehicle will be dared to be harmed and compelled in such situations. Furthermore, it's possible that the accountable party was the vehicle's manufacturer or administrator. In the second set of circumstances, it will look at the circumstances where another vehicle or person violated a traffic rule and was the primary cause of the accident.[113] This may shield the AV manufacturer from liability in many of these accidents, but it won't provide a comprehensive defence against liability in the case that the AV might have prevented or reduced the impact.[114] This will entail looking at what constitutes an AV's deformity as well as the standard of care that will be applied to AV. Finally, this section will look at the expected failure to warn difficulties and whether an AV warning could help an AV with attempting to avoid having to assume responsibility for configuration deserts.[115]

[111] *See* <https://iclg.com/practice-areas/product-liability-laws-and-regulations/2-u-s-product-liability-law-recent-developments-trends-and-future-outlook>, accessed on September 26, 2023.

[112] Marchant, G., & Bazzi, R. (2020). Autonomous vehicles and liability: what will juries do?. *BUJ Sci. & Tech. L.*, *26*, 67.

[113] Ibid.

[114] Ibid.

[115] Ibid.

A. *Design Faults: accidents in Which AV Was Assumed to Be the Cause of the Crash*[116]

In an accident where the AV[117] was clearly to blame for the collision, it will almost certainly be held entirely or largely responsible for the impact and the injuries that resulted. Whether or not AVs consistently outperform human-driven vehicles, it is extremely likely that they will occasionally become confused about what is happening and make a mistake that results[118] in an accident, especially given the nearly infinite variety of situations that such vehicles would encounter.[119] The temperament of AI frameworks is such that they could behave strangely when confronted with a situation that they haven't encountered in its prior training or learning. The AV might, for example, defy another condition and cross a centre or route divider, fail to stop at a red light or stop sign, or ram into another car or object from behind.[120] While AV armadas will learn from their mistakes and the likelihood of such catastrophes happening less frequently with each horrifying incidence, the AV producer will most likely be blamed for the majority of these incidents unless one of the accompanying guards or mitigating variables is present.[121]

1. Failure to Establish a Defect[122]

In a product liability action,[123] the plaintiff bears the burden of proving that the manufacturer's product is defective.[124] It may be difficult to pinpoint the exact mechanical or programming flaw in the AV that caused the accident, making it possible for there to be errors in an accident involving an AV.[125] The majority of AI frameworks are 'black boxes' that the customer cannot influence. Even though AI engineers are investing a lot of money into making their frameworks more visible, the majority of AI frameworks are 'black boxes', where the computer's dynamic cycle is typically beyond the grasp of humans.[126]

---

[116] *Id.*

[117] Ibid.

[118] Ibid.

[119] *Supra* note 40.

[120] Ibid.

[121] Ibid.

[122] Ibid.

[123] *Id.*

[124] *"RESTATEMENT (THIRD) OF TORTS: PRODUCTS LIABILITY § 2 cmt. D."*

[125] *See* Bryant Walker Smith, *Automated Driving and Product Liability*, 2017 MICH. ST. L. REV. 1, 2 (2017). ("requiring the plaintiff to specifically demonstrate how and why an automated driving system performed poorly and should have performed better could impose technical and financial barriers to many claims, especially those involving comparatively minor injuries"). The specification is also impacted by a design defect, in addition to the technological design. It might be less expensive to establish a flawed specification, as illustrated by AV behaviour, than it is to demonstrate that the implementation does not adhere to the specification.

[126] Will Knight, *The Dark Secret at the Heart of AI*, MIT TECH. REV. (Apr. 11, 2017), https://www.technologyreview.com/s/604087/the-dark-secret-at-the-heart-of-ai/ [https://perma.cc/3QJH-MT3J]; Andreas Holzinger, Holzinger Grp., Keynote Talk at IEEE DISA 2018 Conf.: From Machine Learning to Explainable AI (Aug. 23, 2018); David Gunning, Med. Univ. of Graz, Speech for the

However, if the AV was responsible for the accident and violated a traffic rule, the aggrieved parties will very certainly argue that the AV was at fault because of how it violated the traffic rule, which is known as '*res ipsa loquitor*'.[127] When product performance "was of a character that typically occurs as a result of product defect...," according to the Restatement, it is an adequate replacement for direct proof of defect.[128]

The AV's failure to follow transit regulations is likely to be viewed by judges and juries as significant evidence of poor execution, which would generally show a flaw.[129] This argument would be particularly persuasive in wards that genuinely employ the customer assumption test because the majority of legal hearers wouldn't anticipate that a fully functional AV should violate a traffic regulation and result in an accident.[130]

However, a manufacturer can try to make the offended party feel compelled to acknowledge a specific flaw that caused the breach. On the other hand, the manufacturer can argue that its invention was 'state of the art' when it was assembled; therefore, it could not have been anticipated to perform as well as it did.[131]

Whether or not a court accepts such a claim, the offended party's expert can most likely attest (with the benefit of hindsight) that some aspect of the AV's innovation or execution[132] could have been done better to prevent disobeying the transit law and causing the accident, and as a result, was flawed.[133]

Another claim made by the manufacturer is that, while the AV may have behaved dangerously and possibly improperly in the specific circumstance where the accident occurred, it actually outperforms a nearly identical item (such as a human-driven vehicle) in the full range of vehicle operating settings and is thus ostensibly not 'flawed' in its fundamental operation.[134]

Def. Advanced Research Projects Agency (DARPA): Explainable Artificial Intelligence (XAI) (Nov. 2017); Pat Langley et al., Dep't of Comput. Sci., Univ. of Auckland, Twenty-Ninth AAAI Conf. on Innovative Applications: Explainable Agency for Intelligent Autonomous Sys. (2017).

[127] *Supra* note 113.

[128] *"RESTATEMENT (THIRD) OF TORTS: PRODUCTS LIABILITY § 3."*

[129] *Supra* note 113.

[130] Smith, at 51–52.

[131] Stephen S. Wu, *Product Liability Issues in the U.S. And Associated Risk Management*, in AUTONOMOUS DRIVING 553, 553 (M. Maurer et al. eds., 2015); Mark A. Geistfeld, *A Roadmap for Autonomous Vehicles: State Tort Liability, Automobile Insurance, and Federal Safety Regulation*, 105 CAL. L. REV. 1611, 1616–17 (2017). The "state of art" defense is only available in some states and not others. *Id.*

[132] *Supra* note 113.

[133] *See* J.D. POWER & MILLER CANFIELD, *supra* note 67, (detailing how plaintiffs' experts were able to identify a design error in the Toyota electronic throttle control system's algorithm and suggesting that comparable complexity could apply to AV algorithms).

[134] Mark A. Geistfeld, *A Roadmap for Autonomous Vehicles: State Tort Liability, Automobile Insurance, and Federal Safety Regulation*, 105 CAL. L. REV. 1611, 1616–17 (2017).

However, product responsibility doesn't operate in this manner.[135] While the placement of the gasoline tanks on the vehicle increased the risk of side effects, GM attempted to defend their 'side seat' GM pickups by claiming that they were safer overall than test cars with fuel tanks in the back.[136] The two adjudicators and jury members ignored this argument and decided that the flaw depended only on the type of crash involved in the current case.[137]

An AV[138] will eventually come into a practically infinite number of circumstances, and it is difficult for the AV manufacturer to anticipate them all.[139] In fact, the item obligation law expects predictable damage from the use of the product even in circumstances of extreme responsibility.[140] As a result, a highly rare event, frequently referred to as a 'corner event' in the AV sector, may fail to meet this foreseeability condition.[141]

No predictable outcome, however, a guard is unlikely to provide any security to an AV engineer or manufacturer.[142] Think about the scenario where an AV runs a red light on the pretext that a green inflatable was flying in the background and the AV mistook it for a green light.[143] The manufacturer could legitimately argue that since such a common combination of circumstances was not anticipated, the accident was unforeseeable.[144] Nevertheless, a jury would probably rule that the AV designer or maker[145] should be held liable for the costs of this unfortunate (and shocking) mishap since they delivered a device that they knew could operate differently and possibly dangerously in unknown situations.[146] The absence of predictability was occasionally foreseeable.[147]

---

[135] *Supra* note 113.

[136] GM v. Moseley, 447 S.E.2d 302 (Ga. App. Ct. 1994) (jury awarded $101 million in punitive damages against GM)).

[137] Ibid.

[138] *Supra* note 113.

[139] Gary E. Marchant & Rachel A. Lindor, The Coming Collision Between Autonomous Vehicles and the Liability System, 52 SANTA CLARA L. REV. 1321, 1330 (2012).

[140] *Supra* note 135.

[141] Shai Shalev-Shwartz et al., SAFE, MULTI-AGENT, REINFORCEMENT LEARNING FOR. AUTONOMOUS DRIVING 6 (2016), https://arxiv.org/pdf/1610.03295.pdf.

[142] *Supra* note 113.

[143] Ibid.

[144] *Id.*

[145] *Id.*

[146] *See*, e.g., Larsen v. Gen. Motors Corp., 391 F.2d 495, 502 (8th Cir. 1968) *("We do agree that under the present state of the art an automobile manufacturer is under no duty to design an accident-proof or fool-proof vehicle or even one that floats on water, but such manufacturer is under a duty to use reasonable care in the design of its vehicle to avoid subjecting the user to an unreasonable risk of injury in the event of a collision. Collisions with or without fault of the user are clearly foreseeable by the manufacturer and are statistically inevitable.")*.

[147] *Supra* note 113.

2. Excuse

Much has been expounded on the alleged 'trolley problem' issue for AVs,[148] in which the AV should pick between two unfortunately various demonstrations that could harm or kill various numbers or kinds of individuals. Such episodes are supposed to be exceptional, as the more normal situation is for the AV to get away from a crash completely or have a mishap with a particular vehicle that was inescapable given the innovation, programming, and conditions right now.[149] However, in the rare instances where an AV purposely collides with a single object or vehicle in order to avoid a more horrific collision with another vehicle or group, the AV manufacturer may be able to use a justification safeguard in order to avoid liability.[150] This analysis will frequently focus on the producer's requirements and concessions, as well as the moral principles used to make such judgements, all of which are inadequately described and incapable of being reconsidered by the advice of injured parties and legitimate truth seekers.[151]

3. Assigning Liability to a Third Party

The most reliable defence is that an accident was caused by someone else when a self-driving car ignores a traffic rule and causes one.[152] The illegal traffic crime and accident may have been caused by a flaw on the part of a co-producer, an outside developer, or a data provider.[153] The manufacturer of a component integrated into a complex object, such as an AV, is often shielded from liability for failure to exercise prudence.[154] When a component manufacturer asserts that its component was adequate, it will not be held accountable for a design flaw.[155]

However, in many circumstances, proving this will be challenging, and determining what technical specification or component was accountable[156] for the error

---

[148] Ibid.

[149] *Supra* note 113.

[150] Ibid.

[151] Ibid.

[152] Ibid.

[153] *Supra* note 140.

[154] *"RESTATEMENT (THIRD) OF TORTS: PRODUCT LIABILITY § 5 cmt. b (AM. LAW INST. 1998)."*

("The component seller is required to provide instructions and warnings regarding risks associated with the use of the component product. However, when a sophisticated buyer integrates a component into another product, the component seller owes no duty to warn either the immediate buyer or ultimate consumers of dangers arising because the component is unsuited for the special purpose to which the buyer puts it.").

[155] Jones v. W + M Automation, Inc., 818 N.Y.S.2d 396, 398 (N.Y. App. Div. 2006) (Claims against manufacturers of components of workplace robotic system that injured worker dismissed when manufacturers "established as a matter of law that they manufactured only non-defective component parts, and plaintiffs failed to raise an issue of fact to defeat their motions").

[156] *Supra* note 113.

that led to the accident may be difficult for the plaintiff or the court.[157] The manufacturers of the vehicles and parts may occasionally have a reimbursement arrangement in place that separates risk in the event of an accident caused by clear-cut failure mechanisms.[158] Furthermore, some manufacturers, like as Volvo, have stated that "whenever one of its cars is in autonomous mode," they "shall accept complete liability."[159] If none of these options are applicable,[160] it is possible that the vehicle manufacturer and part manufacturer will square off in court. This is because the legal representatives of the offended parties will likely file lawsuits against both the vehicle manufacturer and the component manufacturer designer[161] (especially if the latter option is also a large company with plenty of resources) and turn the matter over to the litigants to determine who is at fault.[162] Another question is whether the AV administrator or the AV manufacturer was responsible for the incident. The level of AV being used might have an effect on this argument. The producer will actually want the ability to shift liability to the administrator if the vehicle is a '*Level 4 or 5* independent vehicle'. The main scenario is that the administrator shouldn't have operated the vehicle in independent mode if egregious circumstances existed and the vehicle was suitable for operation in the non-independent method of activity (i.e., level 4).[163]

But if the car is a '*Level 2 or 3*', the manufacturer[164] might contend that the driver was still primarily in charge of it and was responsible for it breaching the law and getting into an accident.[165] There is some legitimate point of reference for this sort of administrator obligation task. Since "those responsible for a plane under robot control have an obligation to those responsible for a plane under robot control," the court for a situation from the 1940s in which a plane on autopilot crashed found the human pilot responsible as opposed to the manufacturer of the plane with the autopilot innovation.[166]

---

[157] Marchant & Lindor, supra note 140, at 1328.

[158] Daniel A. Crane et al., *A Survey of Legal Issues Arising from the Deployment of Autonomous and Connected Vehicles*, 23 MICH. TELECOMM. & TECH. L. REV. 191, 267 (2017).

[159] Press Release, Volvo Car Group, US Urged to Establish Nationwide Federal Guidelines for Autonomous Driving (Oct. 7, 2015), https://www.media.volvocars.com/global/en-gb/media/pressreleases/167975/us-urged-to-establishnationwide-federal-guidelines-for autonomous-driving [https://perma.cc/M4JS-4P2P].Volvo would presumably need to clarify this remark to explain that they will only be liable if their vehicle is at fault—otherwise, anyone with a dented bumper can get it mended for free by colliding with a Volvo autonomous vehicle.

[160] *Supra* note 113.

[161] Ibid.

[162] Marchant & Lindor, supra note 140, at 1328–29.

[163] Even so, the AV should be able to determine when the environmental conditions are unsuitable. Existing regulation mandates that if the AV system fails or is unable to function effectively, the car must be able to enter a safe mode.

[164] Ibid.

[165] Kyle Colonna, *Autonomous Cars and Tort Liability*, 4 J. L. TECH. & INTERNET 81, 91- 102 (2012).

[166] Brouse v. United States, 83 F.Supp. 373, 374 (N.D. Ohio 1949).

The American Association for Justice ('AAJ'),[167] an expert organisation of plaintiffs' attorneys, claims that '*Level 2 and 3* AVs'[168] are inherently risky because of the 'handover problem'.[169] The question of whether it is reasonable to expect a human operator to take control of an AV operating in autonomous mode on short notice[170] in the event that something unusual occurs is raised by studies showing that when humans are asked to monitor a situation where nothing unusual typically occurs, they become complacent and distracted.[171]

According to the 'AAJ', the attempt to place the guilt on the motorist is a 'moral crumple zone'[172] that legislators, regulators, and courts should reject.[173] 'The American Association of Justice' has asked legislators and courts to hold autonomous vehicles responsible for accidents they cause.[174] In response to worries about distracted or overly complacent drivers, manufacturers of AVs with a human operator have already announced plans to include a variety of active alerts to monitor operators and provide alerts if the operator fails to maintain adequate attention, even pulling the vehicle off the road if the operator is non-responsive.[175]

More study is required to determine if the driver of a vehicle is primarily or fully legally responsible for crashes[176] when they are informed beforehand and informed in real time of their duty to manage the vehicle, as the first Tesla crashes involving vehicles on 'autopilot' have demonstrated.[177] Of course, for marketing purposes, some car manufacturers might be reluctant to imply that owners of the vehicles they sell[178] might be responsible for any accidents that happen, which explains why some producers (like Volvo) have declared that they will bear responsibility for any

---

[167] *Supra* note 113.

[168] Ibid.

[169] AMERICAN ASSOCIATION FOR JUSTICE, DRIVEN TO SAFETY: ROBOT CARS AND THE FUTURE OF LIABILITY 14 (Feb. 2017).

[170] *Supra* note 113.

[171] Robert E. Llaneras, Jeremy Salinger & Charles A. Green, *Human Factors Issues Associated with Limited Ability Autonomous Driving Systems: Drivers' Allocation of Visual Attention to the Forward Roadway,* PROCEEDINGS OF THE SEVENTH INT'L DRIVING SYMP. ON HUMAN FACTORS IN DRIVER ASSESSMENT, TRAINING AND VEHICLE DESIGN, 92, 92–98 (2013); Tracy Hresko Pearl, *Hands on the Wheel: A Call for Greater Regulation of Semi-Autonomous Cars,* 93 IND. L.J. 713, 731–37 (2018).

[172] *Supra* note 113.

[173] Ibid.

[174] *Id.*

[175] See Christopher D.D. Cabrall, et al., *How to Keep Drivers Engaged While Supervising Driving Automation? A Literature Survey and Categorisation of Six Solution Areas,* 20 THEORETICAL ISSUES IN ERGONOMICS SCI. 332, 334 (2019) (listing driver alert technologies in various automated driving systems); Geistfeld *supra-86*,(citing Tesla vehicles slowing down if driver has not passed checks to ensure attention); *Id.* (Stating GM developing active alert system for semi-autonomous vehicles).

[176] *Supra* note 113.

[177] *See* NAT'L TRANS. SAFETY BOARD, PRELIMINARY REPORT HIGHWAY HWY19FH008 (2019).

[178] *Supra* note 113.

accidents involving their AVs.[179] Furthermore, as the artificial intelligence system in a 'Level 2 or 3' vehicle[180] develops and its failure rates fall, the challenge of effective human supervision of such a sophisticated system increases.[181] A manufacturer may argue that a 'Level 4 or Level 5 AV' would be riskier because it lacks a human override option if a plaintiff asserts that a 'Level 2 or Level 3'[182] car is defective since it isn't as safe as those vehicles.[183] To put it another way, a machine-human hybrid could be a viable (and possibly safer) substitute for a fully autonomous car.[184]

B. *Design Defects: accidents in Which AV Wasn't the Cause of the Crash*[185]

The following damage will be partially the responsibility of the other at-fault party if the accident is initially caused by another vehicle or pedestrian breaking a traffic law.[186] However, the manufacturer might be partially liable if a plaintiff successfully argued that the AV's sophisticated sensor and avoidance capabilities should have been used to avoid the collision.[187] Jurors in this instance are likely to believe that an autonomous vehicle can avert an accident more effectively than a human-driven one.[188] Similar to 'crashworthiness' claims, which hold automakers accountable for preventing preventable injuries in the event of an accident, even if the vehicle was not at fault, this one focuses on the design of a vehicle's safety features.[189] A plaintiff must demonstrate that the AV was 'defective' in order to hold an AV developer or manufacturer partially responsible for a crash under product liability law.[190] Compliance or non-compliance with government regulations, industry norms, and tradition is not conclusive, but it can aid in determining whether a defect exists.[191] Comparative performance analysis is widely used to demonstrate design flaws in car

---

179 *See* Volvo Cars Press Release, supra note 96 and accompanying text.

180 *Supra* note 113.

181 Philip Koopman & Beth Osyk, *Safety Argument Considerations for Public Road Testing for Autonomous Vehicles,* SAE WCX 1, 11 (forthcoming in 2019) ("[A]s the autonomy capabilities start to mature, safe road testing will actually increase the performance demands placed upon human supervisors to remain vigilant and effective.").

182 *Supra* note 113.

183 Plaintiffs in the Toyota unexpected acceleration lawsuit claimed that the lack of a "brake override mechanism," which would have allowed a human driver to manually stop or slow the engine by disabling the automated electronic control system, rendered Toyota cars faulty.

184 Smith, *supra* note 140, at 46.

185 *Supra* note 113.

186 Smith, *supra* note 140, at 49.

187 *Id.*

188 *Id.*

189 *See*, e.g., Haberkorn v. Chrysler Corp., 533 N.W.2d 373, 379–80 (Mich. Ct. App. 1995) (determining that a vehicle manufacturer has a duty to design its product to reduce the likelihood that foreseen injuries will occur at an unacceptable risk). Mary Anne Mellow, Timothy C. Sansone & Jesse Rochman, The Legal Landscape: Crashworthiness Claims and Comparative Fault, 50 No. 12 FOR THE DEF. 38, 38 (Dec. 2008).

190 *See* Kim v. Toyota Motor Corp., 424 P.3d 290, 295 (Cal. 2018).

191 Kim v. Toyota Motor Corp. 424 P.3d 290, 298 (Cal. 2018). Section IV.A.2. talks about the role of standards in assigning liability and punitive damages.

collision situations.[192] Plaintiffs alleged that in the 'Toyota's vehicles case'[193] that Toyota unintended acceleration product liability litigation, which ultimately settled for $1.5 billion, it was claimed that Toyota's vehicles were flawed because they lacked brake override mechanisms that other manufacturers had included in their vehicles.[194]

C. Failure to Warn About Defects[195]

Another important area of product liability that AVs[196] may be subject to is failure to warn.[197] A plaintiff hurt in an AV accident could separately claim that the manufacturer's failure to provide adequate warning about the AV's limitations and risks of crashing contributed[198] to the crash and injuries, regardless of whether the legal judge or jury determines the manufacturer's failure to provide adequate warning about the AV's limitations and risks of crashing.[199]

The plaintiff would have to prove that the warning was inadequate and that the accident might have been averted with a more specific or obvious warning in order to succeed in a claim for failure to warn.[200]

One option to warn is for a *'Level 2 or 3 semi-autonomous vehicle's'* manufacturer[201] to demand active and careful driving from the driver.[202] In reality, manufacturers are currently working on active warning systems that alert the driver to take charge, continuously track their actions, and execute a fail-safe manoeuvre[203] to draw the car off the road[204] and bring it to a halt if the human driver would be unable to maintain control of the vehicle.[205] If the active warning system functioned as intended, it is difficult to see how an AV maker could be held responsible for failing to advise the driver to take control under safe circumstances. "*Instructions and warnings may be ineffective because users of the product may not be adequately reached,*

---

192 There are certain limitations to this comparison analysis. One court, for example, stated in examining the limitations of a comparable analysis in an automobile crash case that a bicycle without a light or bell is not defective simply because some bicycles have those safety features. Branham v. Ford Motor Co., 701 S.E.2d 5, 16 (S.C. 2010).

193 Kim v. Toyota Motor Corp., 424 P.3d 290, 295 (Cal. 2018).

194 Aaron Ezroj, *Product Liability After Unintended Acceleration: How Automotive Litigation Has Evolved*, 26 LOY. CONSUMER L. REV. 470, 490 (2014).

195 *Supra* note 113.

196 Ibid.

197 Ibid.

198 Ibid.

199 "*RESTATEMENT (THIRD) OF TORTS: PRODS. LIAB. § 2 cmt. i (AM. LAW INST. 1998)*".

200 *Id.*

201 *Supra* note 113.

202 *Supra* note 113.

203 Ibid.

204 Ibid.

205 See Geistfeld, supra note 135, at 1628.

may be inattentive, or may be inadequately motivated to follow the instructions or heed the warnings," according to the Restatement.[206]

If "a safer design[207] can reasonably be implemented and risks can reasonably be designed out of a product," then "adoption of the safer design is required over a warning that leaves a significant residuum of such risks."[208] Most exact accident situations involving autonomous vehicles are difficult for AV manufacturers to forecast.[209] These kinds of mishaps are more likely to occur under unanticipated circumstances that the AV operating system had never encountered during its training.[210] If a car manufacturer adequately monitors and responds rapidly to such accident circumstances, there seems to be little basis for failure to warn responsibility. There may be some limited general driving situations, like as adverse weather, odd road designs, or highway construction zones, where AV accident risks are more foreseeable.[211] If the AV manufacturer warns about such unusual circumstances, however, there appears to be little room for claims and liability if the manufacturer fails to do so.[212]

In addition to the fact that failure to warn claims are unlikely to prevail in the majority of AV accident lawsuits, manufacturer warnings may feasibly provide AV manufacturers with some liability protection in design flaw liability claims.[213] The customer expectation test in particular, according to some product liability experts, may shield audio-visual makers from accountability for design flaw.[214] A notice is sent regarding any limitations or elimination of manufacturer duty. A warning would not shield the AV manufacturer from liability for other parties, such as occupants of another vehicle struck by the AV, bystanders struck by the AV,[215] or even passengers riding in the AV, as they would only apply to the operator (who would receive the warning when purchasing the vehicle).[216] None of those people or organisations would have missed the warning.

Second, an AV manufacturer is not able to predict all possible failure modes and particular accident circumstances that an AV may experience, and cannot do so in order to issue a warning. The AV manufacturer could only issue a general warning about the potential for an unexpected failure as a result.[217] Therefore, a plaintiff's

---

206 *"RESTATEMENT (THIRD) OF TORTS: PRODS. LIAB. § 2 cmt. l (AM. LAW INST. 1998)"*.

207 *Supra* note 113.

208 *Id.*

209 Marchant & Lindor, supra note 140, at 1334.

210 *Supra* note 140.

211 Supra note 113.

212 Ibid.

213 Ibid.

214 Geistfeld, supra note 135, at 1641 ("An adequate warning about the safe use and inherent risks of a safely designed autonomous vehicle will absolve the manufacturer from liability for crashes caused by the fully functioning operating system.").

215 *Supra* note 113.

216 *"RESTATEMENT (THIRD) OF TORTS: PRODS. LIAB. § 2 cmt. i (AM. LAW INST. 1998)"*.

217 *Id.*

expert would contend that the manufacturer ought to have provided a warning on the failure mode for the specific accident at hand given the benefit of hindsight.[218] Product liability has struggled to[219] establish the necessary level of precision that product warnings must convey given the challenges of foreseeing every event scenario.[220]

Furthermore, it is well-established under the Restatement[221] that a warning will not suffice to preclude responsibility[222] if a design adjustment may have eliminated or minimised the danger warned about, which is another problem with relying on generic warnings for manufacturers.[223]

Furthermore, it is well-established under the Restatement[224] that a warning will not suffice to preclude responsibility if a design adjustment may have eliminated or minimised the danger warned about, which is another problem with relying on generic warnings for manufacturers.[225]

The fact that AVs[226] will be safer than human-driven vehicles and the widely held belief that they will be are irreconcilable with a clear warning about the risks they pose. Public perceptions of safety are necessary for both the commercial viability of AVs[227] and the favourable juror treatment of AVs.[228] These consumer and juror safety messages would be contradicted and undermined by harsh warnings that AVs are intrinsically dangerous.[229] For instance, one of the tort experts who supports using warnings to insulate AV producers from accountability cites the case of cigarettes, where package labels stating that nicotine is extremely hazardous and carcinogenic helped to protect the manufacturers from liability.[230]

In contrast to cigarettes, however, AVs won't ultimately harm public safety; therefore, the warning strategy utilised by cigarette businesses to evade responsibility would probably backfire for AV companies under the umbrella of punitive penalties.[231]

Autonomous vehicles, which are also known by the name of self-driving cars or driverless cars, come with many benefits like increased safety, lower energy usage,

---

218 *Id.*

219 *Supra* note 113.

220 *"RESTATEMENT (THIRD) OF TORTS: PRODS. LIAB. § 2 cmt. i (AM. LAW INST. 1998)"* ("It is impossible to identify anything approaching a perfect level of detail that should be communicated in product disclosures... No easy guideline exists for courts to adopt in assessing the adequacy of product warnings and instructions").

221 *Supra* note 113.

222 Ibid.

223 *See* "RESTATEMENT (THIRD) OF TORTS: PRODS. LIAB. § 2 cmt. l (AM. LAW INST. 1998)." *See* Marchant & Lindor, supra note 106, at 1334.

224 *Supra* note 113.

225 *Supra* note 113.

226 Ibid.

227 Ibid.

228 *Id.*

229 *Supra* note 113.

230 Geistfeld, *supra* note 135, at 1640.

231 *Supra* note 113.

the potential to reduce traffic, and generate free time. However, they also may lead to new liability risks. In the year 2020—high profile lawsuits emerged against the manufacturers of self-driving cars on product liability. Individuals took the risk of using AVs because California was the first state to enact legislation on autonomous cars in 2012.[232] Between 2016 and 2021, the states have amended, reviewed, and adjusted their autonomous vehicles legislation many times. Liability concerning California and Nevada law on AVs has explicitly defined the driver (operator) as liable for strict liability for any accident.[233]

However, still, the question remains the same that what if the AV does not alert the sleeping driver or regarding any other hazard to take control of that, so the question is whether the driver can sue the manufacturer or not, because it does not make sense to hold manufacturers legally liable[234] all the time simply because their product did not match their functionality or did not work as expected.[235] In California, the 'Contra Costa Transportation Authority' is approved to test the completely self-driving vehicle not furnished with a steering wheel, brake pedal, or brake pedal on certain public streets.[236]

<u>The applicability of these provisions to AVs</u>

Regulation for the self-driving car, operated on public roads in California, as per "***Section 38,750 under the Vehicle Code of California, 1993***"[237] a motor car shall not be operated in an autonomous mode on the public roads in California except as allowed under 'Sections 1651 and 38,750' and the regulation in this article.[238] "***Section 38,755 of the Autonomous Vehicles, division 16.6 of the California Vehicle Code***"[239] came into force. This section deals with driverless cars on public roads for testing and ensuring that the operator/driver should not be seated in the vehicle but still be able to control and monitor the AV simultaneously and continually along with its security features. It has all the options necessary to take over AV control manually at any point.

According to The 'AAJ (American Association for Justice)' huge exacting responsibility on manufacturers may eventually be the most reasonable way to deal with the risk issues.[240] According to a Swedish automaker, manufacturers are strictly liable for a mishap, and assuming they are not prepared for this thing, it ought not to form

---

[232] (National Conference of State Legislatures, 2012).

[233] *Supra* note 113.

[234] Ibid.

[235] Uzair, M. Who Is Liable When a Driverless Car Crashes? World Electr. Veh. J. 2021, 12, 62. https://doi.org/10.3390/ wevj12020062, pg.no. 15–16.

[236] Ibid.

[237] *Supra* note 100.

[238] Ibid.

[239] Ibid.

[240] *Supra* note 113.

AVs.[241] Expecting only manufacturers to take responsibility, or imposing an excessive amount of restrictions or strict guidelines, or taking no action, may also stifle the advancement of this technology.[242]

Author believes if the car has highly and fully autonomous functions, such as 'SAE Level 4–5', the AVs should be held strictly liable.[243]

3.3.2.2 Liability of AI Under the Law of Strict and Product Liability in California

Because California Product Liability is defined under "***Section 1714.45 of the California Civil Code, 1872,***"[244] the rule on strict and product liability would also apply in the instance of 'SAE Level 0–5'. Product Liability ***for "§ § Products 2, 3, and 5 of the Restatement (Third) of Torts."*** According to "***§ § 38,755 and 38,750 of the Autonomous Vehicles, division 16.6 of the California Vehicle Code, 1993,***"[245] which creates a legal foundation for 'product liability', damage must be caused by the use of a product's fault. Only a defective part should be considered a product. If the car is 'SAE Level 0–2', and there is a human driver/operator in charge of the vehicle and monitoring the surroundings, "*Product Liability 2, 3, and 5 of the Restatement (THIRD) of Torts*" also apply. Even if the car is 'SAE Level 3–5', if the environment is monitored by the autonomous driving system, this portion is sufficient to make them liable under 'strict and product liability laws'.[246]

3.3.3 Vicarious Liability in California

In ***California***, 'vicarious liability' is a legal doctrine that creates liability for an individual who has not caused any injury but has a special relationship with the one who did it. Vicarious liability is also referred to as 'Respondeat Superior' and imputed negligence. The 'Respondeat Superior' doctrine is *Latin* and works on the concept of "*let the master answer,*" which makes an employer liable for the acts of

---

[241] Ibid.

[242] Ibid.

[243] *Supra* note 113.

[244] The Civil Code of the State of California, as Enacted in 1872. James Henry Deering and Richard Maury Sims (1906), "The Code of Civil Procedure of the State of California", Volumes 1–147, Publisher: Bancroft-Whitney. Adopted March 11, 1872, and Amended Up to and Including 1905, with Statutory History and Citation Digest Up to and Including Volume 147 of California Reports. *See* <https://www.google.co.in/books/edition/The_Civil_Code_of_the_State_of_Californi/aL8EAAAAYAAJ?hl=en> , accessed on September 26, 2023.

[245] *Supra* note 100.

[246] *Supra* note 113.

his/her employees, which does not remove the liability of the employee; instead, it adds another liable party to it.[247]

Although negligence is a fair, straightforward concept, it gets much more complicated when vicarious liability is added. Adding several parties held liable for an accident might increase the chances of receiving more compensation.

Without this relationship, one can be held liable for the actions of another. This is what exactly happened in the case of ***Maloney v. Rath***[248] where the Supreme Court of California held that nondelegable duties exist under strict liability to ensure that affected parties are reimbursed by the person who did the injury, and the person who created the harm may be held accountable for the negligence of his agent, whether the agent was an employee or an independent contractor.

In the case of ***Collins v. Hertfordshire***,[249] HILBERY J said; "*the distinction between a contract for services and a contract of service can be summarised in this way: in one case the master can order or require what is to be done, while in other case he can not only order or require what is to be done, but how it shall be done.*"[250]

Individuals who employ independent contractors to maintain instrumentalities that pose a risk of serious bodily harm or death, or who employ contractors to provide safeguards that the individual was under a statutory or regulatory duty to provide, are liable for the contractor's negligence, according to the ***"Restatement of Torts–Sections 423 and 424"*** in this scenario, these parts suggest that a nondelegable responsibility is appropriate.

In California, the parents or the legal guardian has to sign a driving licence application for his child or any minor child for that matter whosoever is under the age of 18, as per ***"California Vehicle Code, 1993–Section 17,707"***[251] civil liability for parents and legal guardian, if the minor causes a car accident.[252]

The very next ***"California Vehicle Code, 1993 Section 17,708"***[253] makes a parent liable for all foreseeable damages any time they give express or implied permission for a minor to drive a vehicle regardless of minor is a licenced driver or not.[254] Under the ***"California Civil Code, 1872 Section 1714.1,"***[255] the statute goes on to say that

---

[247] *See* Preeti Singh, "Vicarious Liability in India", legalservicesindia.com, < http://www.legalservicesindia.com/article/1634/Vicarious-Liability-in-India.html>, ISBN: 978–81-928,510–1-3, accessed on September 29, 2023.

[248] Maloney v. Rath (1968) 69 Cal.2d 442, 71 Cal.Rptr. 897, 445 P.2d 513.

[249] Collins v. Herts C.C., [1947] 1 All E.R. 633.

[250] *Supra* note 248.

[251] ***"California Vehicle Code Section 17707*** *Any civil liability of a minor arising out of his driving a motor vehicle…is hereby imposed upon the person who signed and verified the application of the minor for a license, and the person shall be jointly and severally liable with the minor for any damages proximately resulting from the negligent or wrongful act or omission of the minor in driving a motor vehicle."*

[252] *See* <https://www.penneylaw.com/blog/car-accident/vicarious-liability-california>, accessed on September 29, 2023.

[253] *Supra* note 100.

[254] *Supra* note 253.

[255] *Supra* note 245.

the custodial parent or guardian, together with the minor, is jointly accountable for any damages resulting from the minor's wilful misbehaviour.[256]

The question now is whether all of these regulations also apply to an AI, which they do if the vehicle only operates at 'SAE Levels 0–3', where AI is only employed to assist young toddlers.[257]

"Section 38,750 of the California Vehicle Code, 1993"[258] States the Following[259]:

Manufacturers must comply with "California Vehicle Code Section 38,750(c)(1),[260]" which requires them to certify that their autonomous technology has a set of protections (for example, an alert when a fault is discovered), is conveniently accessible, and has a separate data recorder, among other things.[261]

3.3.3.1 Liability of AI Under the Law of Vicarious Liability in California

The author has tried to analyse what this provision 'Sections(§§) 423 and 424, §§17,707,17,708 and 38,750 of the California Vehicle Code, 1993'[262] and 'Sections 17 and 1714.1 of the California Civil Code, 1872'[263] mean in terms of AVs. What role can this section have in determining vicarious liability if an AV is involved in an accident? A comprehensive analysis of these provisions reveals that existing provisions such as 'Sections(§§) 423 and 424, §§17,707,17,708, and 38,750 of the California Vehicle Code, 1993'[264] and 'Sections 17 and 1714.1 of the California Civil Code, 1872'[265] only apply to human driver or/and car owner who are held liable for 'vicarious liability' and subject to punitive damages under tort law. Now, because it must be viewed from the perspective of 'SAE Level 0–2', where the car is perfectly under the control of the human driver, the human driver monitors the driving environment in these scenarios. Now author will look at whether the same law applies in cases of vicarious liability ranging from 'SAE Level 0 to 5'. So, according to the author, it will be applied on a regular basis whenever the scenario

---

256 ***"California Civil Code, 1872 Section 1714.1*** *Any act of wilful misconduct of a minor that results in injury or death to another person or of any damage to the property of another, shall be imputed (transferred) to the parent or guardian. The statute goes on to state that the custodial parent or guardian is jointly liable, along with the minor, for any damages resulting from the minor's wilful misconduct, for an amount not to exceed $25,000 for each wrongful act."*

257 *Supra* note 248.

258 *Supra* note 100.

259 *See* <https://codes.findlaw.com/ca/vehicle-code/veh-sect-38750.html>, Accessed on September 26, 2023.

260 *Supra* note 100.

261 Ibid.

262 Ibid.

263 *Supra* note 245.

264 *Supra* note 100.

265 *Supra* note 245.

requires it because it is totally in the hands of the 'human driver/owner/user' who is driving a car because the operator can monitor the driving environment.[266]

When compared to existing provisions in the 'law of vicarious liability', such as 'Sections(§§) 423 and 424, §§17,707,17,708, and 38,750 of the California Vehicle Code, 1993'[267] and 'Section 17 of the California Civil Code, 1872',[268] which talks about the master-servant relationship, one person is liable for the actions that caused liability for another person, the 'agent', for acts/actions performed or undertaken by the 'principal'. Based on a legal maxim: '*Qui facit per alium facit* per se', which is a Latin legal term that means, *"He who acts through another does the act himself"* with the 'SAE Level 0 to 5', the outcome is even.

In **Level 0**, the full-time performance by the human driver or/and car owner of all aspects of the 'dynamic driving task', even when enhanced by warning or intervention systems.[269]

Who, once again, is in charge of steering and acceleration/deceleration? Who will be held accountable for 'vicarious liability' now that the answer is a human driver or/and car owner.[270]

Another aspect of driving a car is the monitoring of the driving environment, which is likewise done by a human driver or/and car owner. If a fallback execution of the 'dynamic driving task' is available, who is the performing *human driver or/and car owner.*[271] Is there any capability (driving mode) in the system? The answer is negative. As a result of the arguments presented by the author, the author argues that only human driver or/and car owner are liable under the law of vicarious liability under 'Sections(§§)423and424, §§17,707,17,708, and 38,750 of the California Vehicle Code'[272] and 'Sections 17 and 1714.1 of the California Civil Code'.[273]

Level 1 (Driver Assistance), the execution of steering or acceleration/deceleration by a driver assistance system based on data about the driving environment, with the hope that the human operator will handle the other parts of the 'dynamic driving task'. Who will be held accountable for 'vicarious liability',[274] now that the answer is a human driver and system.[275] Is there any capability (driving mode) in the system? The answer is some driving modes. As a result of the arguments presented by the author, the author believes that human driver or/and car owner are liable under the law of 'vicarious liability' under 'Sections(§§) 423 and 424, §§17,707,17,708, and 38,750

[266] *Supra* note 100.
[267] Ibid.
[268] *Supra* note 245.
[269] *Supra* note 113.
[270] Ibid.
[271] *Supra* note 113.
[272] *Supra* note 100.
[273] *Supra* note 245.
[274] *Supra* note 248.
[275] *Supra* note 113.

of the California Vehicle Code'[276] and 'Sections 17 and 1714.1of the California Civil Code'.[277]

In **Level 2** (Partial Automation), the application of steering and acceleration/deceleration by one or more driver assistance systems in accordance with information about the driving environment, with the hope that the 'human driver' would handle the advanced settings of the dynamic driving task. Here the system is in charge of steering and acceleration/deceleration. Who will be held accountable for 'vicarious liability',[278] now that the answer is a system.[279]

Another aspect of driving a car is the monitoring of the driving environment, which is likewise done by a human driver.[280] If a fallback execution of the dynamic driving task is available, who is the performing '*human driver*'. Is there any capability (driving mode) in the system? The answer is some driving modes. As a result of the arguments presented by the author, the author believes that only human driver or/and car owner are liable under the law of vicarious liability under 'Sections(§§) 423 and 424, §§17,707,17,708, and 38,750 of the California Vehicle Code'[281] and 'Sections 17 and 1714.1 of the California Civil Code'.[282]

SAE Level 3-5: Automated driving system ('system') monitors the driving environment.

In **Level 3** (Conditional Automation), in a certain driving mode, the 'automated driving system' will handle every aspect of the 'dynamic driving task' with the hope that the human driver will react appropriately when asked to intervene. Who, once again, is in charge of steering and acceleration/deceleration? Who will be held accountable for 'vicarious liability'[283] now that the answer is a *system*. Another aspect of driving a car is the monitoring of the driving environment, which is likewise done by a *system*. If a fallback execution of the dynamic driving task is available, who is the performing '*human driver*'. Is there any capability (driving mode) in the system? The answer is *some driving modes*. As a result of the arguments presented by the author, the author contends that the human driver or/and car owner and the manufacturer are both guilty under the 'law of vicarious liability'.[284]

In **Level 4** (High Automation), in a certain driving mode, the 'automated driving system' will handle every aspect of the 'dynamic driving task' with the hope that the human driver will react appropriately when asked to intervene. Now that the answer is a *system*, who will be held liable for 'vicarious liability'? Another aspect of driving a car is the monitoring of the driving environment, which is likewise done by a *system*. If a fallback execution of the dynamic driving task is available, who

---

276 *Supra* note 100.

277 *Supra* note 245.

278 *Supra* note 248.

279 *Supra* note 113.

280 Ibid.

281 *Supra* note 100.

282 *Supra* note 248.

283 *Id.*

284 *Supra* note 113.

is the performing *system.* Is there any capability (driving mode) in the system? The answer is *some driving modes.* The author contends that the manufacturer is liable as a result of the arguments presented, but that a sui generis law is required to deal with cases of 'vicarious liability in California', or that a place should be given under existing legislation to deal with 'Level 4 autonomous cars', as the existing provisions only deal with 'human drivers, not machines or autonomous cars'.[285]

In **Level 5** (Full Automation), the performance of all 'dynamic driving task' components by a fully automated driving system in all traffic and environmental circumstances that a human driver is capable of handling.[286] Who, once again, is in charge of steering and acceleration/deceleration? Now that the answer is a *system,* who will be held liable for 'vicarious liability'? Another aspect of driving a car is the monitoring of the driving environment, which is likewise done by a *system.* If a fallback execution of the 'dynamic driving task' is available, who is the performing *system.* Is there any capability (driving mode) in the system? The answer is *all driving modes.* The author contends that the manufacturer is liable as a result of the arguments presented, but that a sui generis law is required to deal with cases of 'vicarious liability in California', or that a place should be given under existing legislation to deal with 'Level 5 autonomous cars', as the existing provisions only deal with 'human drivers, not machines or autonomous cars'.

So, the author is of the view that it will only be used in situations where an 'autonomous vehicle' is at 'SAE Level 0 through 3'. For 'SAE Levels 4 and 5', *sui generis law* is required to deal with the case of 'vicarious liability in California'.

3.4 Position in India—Law of Negligence, Strict, and Product and Vicarious Liability

3.4.1 Law of Negligence in India

Indian view on negligence in specific and the 'Indian law of torts' is based on the English common law, similar to US and Canada but unlike Germany, as approved, adopted, and modified by the courts in India on the principles of 'justice, equity, and good conscience'. As the Supreme Court of India in the case of ***Rajkot Municipal Corpn. V. Manjulben Jayantilal Nakum***[287] held that the Indian judiciary has explicitly accepted the common law principles of the law of torts as developed and evolved by the courts in England.

Negligent Torts are defined as wrongful acts caused by the negligence of another individual or group of people. These are situations that frequently occur as a result of a person failing to act with the level of caution that a person of ordinary prudence

[285] Ibid.

[286] Ibid.

[287] *See* <https://www.supremecourtcases.com>, accessed on September 28, 2023.

would. It is critical to demonstrate that there was no additional duty of care owed and that a person was negligent in exercising the level of care that a prudent person would have exercised. Negligent harm to a person's body or property is one example of such a tort. For example, under negligent torts, a person who has negligently disobeyed traffic laws and caused an accident is accountable.

It tends to be characterised in three forms:

Nonfeasance: not doing an act which it had to do.

Misfeasance: doing act wrongly.

Malfeasance: doing the wrong act.

Punishment under civil negligence case shall extend to the extent of damage caused to the plaintiff, i.e., compensation for the damages.

3.4.1.1 Liability of AI Under the Law of Negligence in India

The present research has tried to analyse whether the Indian law is adequate to determine the tortious liability in the case of Autonomous vehicles especially in the case of 'Contributory Negligence'.

Due to the lack of a driver in an autonomous vehicle, it will be difficult for the plaintiff to prove their claim under contributory negligence in India, or 'SAE Level 4–5', as this would shift some of the blame for the unfortunate event from the defendant to the plaintiff.

Being a futuristic technology, where it would have its own autonomy in its acts and decision-making capability after decades, where the legal status of AI would be decided, to hold AVs liable for their own actions and to impose 'contributory negligence liability under tort law'.

3.4.2 India's Strict Product Liability

In India, there are two main laws that control or govern motor vehicles: the 'Motor Vehicles Act, 1988' and the 'Consumer Protection Act, 2019'. Even the 'Motor Vehicle (Amendment) Act, 2019' has no discernible effect on 'autonomous or self-driving vehicles'.

Product[288] Liability focuses and warns on many aspects like '*negligent design, manufacture*, and *breach of duty*' under the common law.

---

[288] *"**Section 2(33) of the Consumer Protection Act, 2019: 'product'** means.*

any article or goods or substance or raw material or any extended cycle of such product, which may be in gaseous, liquid, or solid-state possessing intrinsic value which is capable of delivery either as wholly assembled or as a part and is produced for introduction to trade or commerce, but does not include human tissues, blood, blood products, and organs.".

'Product liability'[289] refers to a set of regulations where injured consumers can claim damages against the concerned parties whosoever involved at any step of the manufacturing, distribution, or retail process of the concerned product.

Defective Products: If anyone is harmed by an unsafe and defective product, is entitled to compensation, including 'self-driving car parts, drone parts, robot, machinery', and more.[290]

Dangerous Products and Liability: Who will bear the consequences if products fail and they are no more capable of giving the safety of using that product?[291] The only reasonable person is a manufacturer who will be held liable and bear the consequences. Forcing manufacturers to pay compensations to the claimant (plaintiff), whether it is for self-driving car seat belts that have been destroyed, defective drones, or dangerous cribs.[292]

3.4.2.1 Strict and Product Liability in India in Case of an AI

'Sections 2(33), 2(34), 2(10), 2(12), 2(36), 2(37), 2(38), 2(35) of the Consumer Protection Act, 2019', the damage must be caused by the use of a product's defect, the law on strict and product liability would apply in the all cases of 'SAE Level 0–5' even if the 'autonomous driving system' monitors the driving environment, this part is sufficient to hold the manufacturer liable under the law of 'product liability'. It establishes a legal framework for 'product liability'. Only a product should be considered if a part is defective.[293]

3.4.3 Vicarious Liability in India

> The doctrine of liability of the master for act of his servant is based on the legal maxim 'respondeat superior' which means *'let the principal be liable'* and it puts the master in the same position as he if had done the act himself.[294] It also derives validity from the maxim

---

[289] ***"Section 2(34) of the Consumer Protection Act, 2019: 'product liability'*** *means.*

the responsibility of a product manufacturer or product seller, any product or service, to compensate for any harm caused to a consumer by such defective product manufactured or sold or by a deficiency in services relating to it.".

[290] ***"Section 2(10) of the Consumer Protection Act, 2019: 'defect'*** *means.*

any fault, imperfection or shortcoming in the quality, quantity, potency, purity or standard which is required to be maintained by or under any law for the time being in force or under any contract, express or implied or as is claimed by the trader in any manner whatsoever in relation to any goods or product and the expression 'defective' shall be construed accordingly".

[291] *Supra* note 113.

[292] Ibid.

[293] *Supra* note 113.

[294] *Supra* note 248, accessed on June 30, 2023.

qui facit per alium facit per se, which means *'he who does an act through another is deemed in law to do it himself'*.[295]

Now, when it comes to distributing responsibility and risk, generally, employers are strictly held accountable for the acts of their employees for any harm caused during employment. For the liability of the master to arise, the following two essential ingredients are required, namely.

1. The tort was committed by the servant only;
2. The servant must have committed the tort in the course of employment.[296]

As a general rule, the master is only liable for the tort of his servant and not for the tort of an independent contractor. There the only servant will be alone liable for that.[297]

A car driver, for example, is a servant. He will be held liable if he irresponsibly knocks down X. However, if he hires a taxi to take him to the train station and the taxi driver hits X, he will not be liable to X because the taxi driver is not a servant, but rather an independent contractor.[298]

That will be solely the responsibility of the taxi driver.

If AI is classified as an animal, it will be subject to the 'Animals Act of 1971'. In that situation, it states that if an animal enters someone else's property and causes injury, the animal's owner is responsible. Because there is strict liability, there is no compelling reason to show negligence or purpose (for the benefit of humans or animals). It is possible that a similar lawful structure would be appropriate for a few real AI types (for example, AVs).[299]

3.4.3.1 Liability of AI Under the Law of Vicarious Liability in India

In India, 'vicarious liability for autonomous vehicles', i.e., 'SAE Level 4–5', would move from the employer-employee relationship to the owner-manufacturer one.

So, the author is of the view that it will only be used in situations where an autonomous vehicle is at 'SAE Level 0 through 3'. For 'SAE Levels 4 and 5', *sui generis law* is required to deal with the case of 'vicarious liability' in India.

Indeed, even without making another or extended legislative framework, the current legal framework is, on a fundamental level, fit for covering AI-based advances. The specific test is to cover the space of AI accurately if the current liability framework remains set up for the appraisal of prospective risk.

---

[295] Ibid.

[296] Ibid.

[297] Ibid.

[298] Ibid.

[299] Ibid.

3.5 Conclusion

If AI functions as a tool, it is termed a service; alternatively, it is regarded as a product if it is owned by persons and serves as both an operator and a tool. Services are defined as data analysis to determine the maintenance. So, the manufacturers and developers of AI must disclose the content or information the AI collects during its usage to the users or purchasers. Companies need to educate consumers about AI's capabilities, limitations, and risks, explicitly dealing with the limitations on an operating domain. That is the reason it should pass the risk-utility test, which may turn on proof that products incorporating AI performed safely as their human-dependent counterparts. As a result, the initial stage is designing, followed by developers, testing, and finally manufacturers, who reach the end-users. Testing, simulations, and field performance data across the various foreseeable misuses and uses, as well as documented design changes, to lower the foreseeable risks, would later help to demonstrate reasonable safety. It distinguished between the *things containing the software, a product, and information produced by software, is not a product.*[300]

California transportation authority's made two major changes in its policy on autonomous vehicles in September 2016, which was a turning moment in terms of the state legislature. The first change is the passage of a new bill that allows the 'Contra Costa Transportation Authority' to test a pilot project on public roads without a driver. Prior to this, public road testing was only permitted if a human driver was present and "capable of taking immediate manual control of the vehicle in the event of an autonomous technology failure or other emergency." The bill requires that testing data be provided to the government, that self-driving cars be insured for $5 million, that they not go faster than 35 miles per hour, and that there be geographical constraints.

The second change, "California's Department of Motor Vehicles' draft regulations," could potentially impact how all 'self-driving vehicles' are tested in the state by extending the privileges granted to the aforementioned pilot program. If the bill passes (it is still in the parliamentary process), car manufacturers will be able to test vehicles that the federal government deems safe on public roads without the use of licenced drivers. Rather than having a driver in the vehicle, the new proposed laws call for a test driver to have two-way communication with the vehicle.

According to a KPMG survey,[301] almost 94% of the people consider that finding the liability issues would be the most vital component to deal with in their AVs components coverage in the coming days.

One thing is without a doubt: corporations will unquestionably profit from this, and there is additionally the likelihood that individuals will be a lot more secure out and about. Some even believe that fatalities from drunk driving could be eliminated with primarily self-driving vehicles (at the highest level) that do not require human input.

---

300 *Supra* note 113.

301 Albright, J.; Bell, A.; Schneider, J.; Nyce, C. Survey results. In Automobile Insurance in the Era of Autonomous Vehicles; KPMG, USA: New York, NY, USA, June 2015.

The number of such lawsuits has recently dropped to 50. In contrast, fewer than 200 car product liability claims were decided each year against manufacturers.[302] In the case of AVs, however, the manufacturer is the most probable party to be sued, and a 'product liability' claim is virtually always brought.[303] As a result, AVs will result in a "*transition from a compensation regime for traditional driving that is mostly based on vehicular carelessness to a compensation regime for automated driving that increasingly involves product liability.*"

Furthermore, here the author is of the view that the driver should be held responsible for any accidents but they could possibly later sue the manufacturer for any defects that result in some kind of loss. In case, if the car owner did nothing wrong then the onus would lie on the manufacturer to prove that their product is not faulty, else they should be held liable. Here by manufacturer, it means companies like Tesla who are building these products. Tesla would be answerable in such cases as they are responsible for testing their features before rolling them out. Tesla could however sue their vendors if the mistake is on their end. As for the developers and designers employed by Tesla, they would just get fired and are not likely to be legally liable.

Not only will legal, civil, and driving obligations shift because of AVs, but criminal liability will as well. The criminal liabilities and moral-related issues about AVs are discussed in the next chapter.

---

[302] *See* https://www2.deloitte.com/uk/en/insights/focus/future-of-mobility/electric-vehicle-trends-2030.html, accessed on April 15, 2022.

[303] Marchant & Lindor; Smith. But *see* J.D. POWER & MILLER CANFIELD, AUTOMATED VEHICLES: LIABILITY CRASH COURSE 18 (Mar. 2018), <https://www.millercanfield.com/assets/htmldocuments/JDP_Miller%20Canfield%20MCity%20White%20Paper_2018_Final.pdf [https://perma.cc/SQ2R-TBXR>] ("It is important to note that under [the] current liability framework, a 'manufacturer' is not limited to the manufacturer of the complete automobile—everyone in the supply chain is potentially liable.").

Chapter 4
Criminal Liability of Artificial Intelligence

If he has a conscience he will suffer for his mistake.
That will be the punishment as well as the prison.
Fyodor Dostoevsky, Crime and Punishment
AI-criminal—*"criminal legal effects to electronic entities in the AVs field."*

Abstract The author will analyse various international and regional instruments pertaining to Artificial Intelligence and their monitoring bodies' case laws to find the legal remedy for victims of crime. This study will help determine how the theory of punishment will apply to artificial intelligence—which is facing a regulatory issue that has been addressed practically under the criminal justice systems of countries, namely—Germany, California, and India. This chapter also talks about the issues of actus reus and mens rea, which involves criminal liability, so how to prove mens rea of a machine to make them criminally liable for its actions. Applying an actus reus to an artificial intelligence system takes an action that results in a criminal act, or fails to take any action, when there is a duty to act. The actus reus of an offence has been committed. Lastly, it also discussed the liability issues in case of negligence—given in two situations concerning computer programs, firstly, when the software is defective and secondly, when a party is injured due to using the software. To prevail on a negligence claim, a plaintiff must show the defendant has a duty of care but breached it and caused an injury to the plaintiff as a result of that breach.

4.1 Introduction

AI's criminal liability will necessitate legal personhood of AI similar to a corporation. AI cannot be awarded legal personhood until and unless it becomes highly and fully autonomous in nature, in terms of autonomous vehicles, and in general, when it reaches the level of AGI and ASI, where AI can make decisions on its own independently. Otherwise, even for granting the status of electronic personality, or legal personality, it must meet the criteria of being independent in its own actions and

S. Fahim, *Ethico-Legal Aspect of AI-driven Driverless Cars*, Frontiers of Artificial Intelligence, Ethics and Multidisciplinary Applications,
https://doi.org/10.1007/978-981-97-6883-7_4

decisions, being able to sue and be sued, and AI is still at the stage of ANI, where it is not even capable of perceiving and making decisions without human intervention.

Criminal liability is penal because punishment is a predominant feature of criminal proceedings. It requires culpable act ***actus reus*** (an action) and the defendant's mental state ***mens rea*** (guilty mind). So the fundamental principle of penal liability is ***actus non facit reum, nisi mens sit rea:*** *"the act itself is not criminal unless accompanied by a guilty mind."* There might be some overlap between the conduct, which will later lead to *civil* and *criminal* consequences. For making anyone liable for an overt act/omission, a higher degree of fault requires punishing him/her. In criminal law, it is about the 'defendant's subjective state of mind' *what actually did the perpetrator intend or believe to do* Mens rea is quintessential for a crime and it differs between the legal systems and crimes of arrays because *mens rea* requires both "*a will direct to a certain act and knowledge as to the consequences that will follow from a particular act.*" Sometimes the guilty mind goes beyond and does some acts where the defendant does the act without foreseeing the outcome and does it, where the defendant does not intend to, willed/desired for that event to occur.[1] However, if a person commits some crime, he/she should be penalised for his/her conduct, typically in a fine or imprisonment.[2] To find an individual's guilt or blameworthiness of an act, the defendant needs to exceed in terms of private laws. However, on the contrary, with respect to a crime, a mere preponderance of probability is not only needed, but a higher burden of proof needs to be established in proving the guilt of an individual.

Now, why is it necessary to examine and decide criminal liability in the context of artificial intelligence? The question of criminal liability, as well as protection against cybercrime and hackers, are among the legal challenges posed by autonomous driving in the area of criminal law. When it comes to criminal liability for harm caused by an AV, most European states' criminal codes allow the driver (or vehicle owner) to be punished with carelessness even if the AV was in control (in autonomous mode). If no fault is proven, the manufacturer is held criminally liable. Because a vehicle manufacturer is almost always a legal entity, it is important to determine corporate criminal liability.

The chapter looks into the determination of criminal liability in the case of an AI. It is yet disputed that an AI can have the necessary mens rea to commit a crime, it is still apt to discuss the criminal liability where an AI is involved. The pertinent question remains the same: Whether criminal liability can be imposed where an Artificial Intelligence system is involved? If yes, who would be liable and who can be accused for holding the intention or mens rea to commit the crime? Can an AI be held criminally liable? For the purpose of this chapter also, autonomous vehicles have been selected, to understand the contours of criminal liability in the case of an AI system. The chapter deeply analyses the possibility of determining criminal liability under the existing legal regime of Germany, California, and India in the case

---

[1] TURNER, J. (2019). *ROBOT RULES-Regulating Artificial Intelligence*, London-UK: Palgrave Macmillan, ISBN-978-3-319-96,234-4, pp. 117–121.

[2] *Id.* at pg. 82–102.

of an AI system such as an Autonomous vehicle. The chapter looks into whether or not the existing theories of punishment are applicable to an AI system?

Further, it also looks into whether the existing legal provisions in all the three jurisdictions are adequate to determine the liability or is there a need for a sui generis legislation?

4.1.1 Whether and How Artificial Intelligent Entities May Be Held Liable Criminally?

Gabriel Hallevy[3] has classified components of crime as follows:

- Cases where actually actus reus comprises of actions, or where the actus reus be composed of a failure to act; and
- In cases of mens rea, whether it requires knowledge or being informed of or whether it only requires only negligence, *a prudent and reasonable person would have known*, or lastly, it requires strict liability where no mens rea needs to be showcased/demonstrated.

Artificial Intelligence system is of different levels and different kinds. To understand the criminal liability of an AI in a more nuanced manner, autonomous vehicles (AVs) have been selected by the author. This chapter focuses on studying and understanding the working of AVs and the legal and regulatory regime governing the functioning of AVs and also on determining that whether or not anyone can be made liable for an act of crime involving an AV. It can be generally presumed that the principles of determination of criminal liability of AV can be applicable to other kinds of artificial intelligence systems also.

In the case of an AV, criminal legal liability/legal regime arises when the unmanned vehicle is involved in a car accident. The pertinent question is whether an AI (AV in this context) can commit a crime or an accident with a criminal intention? If not, then whether an AI (AV in this context) can be used to commit a crime? In either case, on whom a criminal liability can be imposed?

- *The manufacturer who manufactured or produced the AI systems, or the programmer who programmed the AI systems, or*
- *The user who has deployed and is using the AI systems, or the maintainer who, on behalf of users, is maintaining the AI systems, or*
- *The artificial intelligence systems themselves?*

For the purpose of understanding the criminal liability in the context of an artificial system, the author has chosen autonomous vehicles mainly because it is quite evident that AV technology aims to bring revolution in the mobility ecosystem by lessening

---

[3] J.K.C. Kingston, *Artificial Intelligence and Legal Liability*, University of Brighton, BN2 4JG, UK, 21 Feb.2018, pg.5–6, available at <https://www.researchgate.net/publication/309695295>, accessed on April 20, 2023.

the number of accidents and through other benefits like '*the potential to reduce traffic, increase safety and mobility, lower energy usage, and generate free time*'.

It is worth mentioning that California had 88 accidents with autonomous vehicles in 2014, with the drivers being culpable for 81 of them. Only one of these AVs was at fault in the 62 collisions where the car was in completely autonomous mode.[4] Who will be liable when the crime is committed using an AI system such as an AV? Another question stems here: how could the law react if the criminally held liable entity is also a legal entity, i.e., auto-manufacturer?

Now the question arises, seeing all the instances, who will be held liable?

The Operator (Driver) of the car—not being attentive during the auto-mode;

The Owner of the Vehicle;

Network Provider;

Hacker;

Original Equipment Manufacturer (OEM); or someone else.

So, if it is a shared liability/responsibility, then how will it be divided?

Most importantly, if an accident causes death, especially a pedestrian death, another different set of questions would arise.

WHO WILL GO TO THE COURT?

4.2 Applying Theories of Punishment in AI[5]

In the words of ***Salmond***, "The law may be defined as the body of principles recognised and applied by the State in the administration of justice".

What results in punishing the wrongdoers if an individual neglects to do legally enforceable obligations? This hypothesis depends on the Sovereign's capacity to oversee criminal equity. Moreover, lawmakers would arguably be forced to rewrite criminal theories again because of the emergence of AI that wants. This part tries to understand whether the existing theories of punishment apply to AI.

---

[4] *See* <https://www.businessinsider.com/self-driving-car-accidents-caused-by-humans-2018-9?IR=T,>accessed on July 1, 2023.

[5] *Supra* n.1 at 121.

4.2.1 *Deterrent Theory*

This theory is based on the principle that discipline should be of such a character that it demonstrates the hindrance to both the offender and the public at large. Essentially, it demonstrates to the rest of the population the consequences of breaking the law, so that if they continue to break the law, they must face the consequences, such as disciplinary action in public places. Even if it is less useful because the majority of wrongdoings are done on the spur of the moment, the theory can directly check but not an uncontrolled activity.[6]

Moving forward with the theory of Over-Deterrence in regards to AI, to deter software programmers from creating algorithms and developing software that violates legal standards, regulations, and ethical rules through the wrongful use of an algorithm, where AI would only function as a tool in the hands of the user, software programmers are put in danger and face criminal charges, to deter them from creating such software and introducing it in a system where AI would only function as a tool in the hands of the user. Following the best practises will result in a huge number of new and intriguing AI in the future, as well as more advancement and improvement in nature and its various kinds.[7]

Interpreting the behaviour of autonomous and even intelligent machines is critical for criminal lawyers. Because there is a limitation in autonomy in terms of artificial narrow intelligence (ANI), where individuals only ask machines to do certain tasks as instructed by humans, how to deal with artificial agents' increasingly independent behaviour and questions of accountability for their activities in the legal profession is a major concern. Whether the manufacturer should be held directly liable under this theory, or the designer or developer who coded the programming, is a major concern. AI will remain a tool until it evolves into Artificial Super Intelligence with its own mind, emotions, reasoning, and powers.[8]

Currently, the responsibility and monetary weight of money-related pay for actions caused by AI to victims of threat could be placed on an insurer or a corporation, or viewed as operational risks. Furthermore, there is a cultural cost to expressing financial guilt that cannot be completely eradicated or diminished.[9]

4.2.2 *Retributive Theory*

The retributive theory's goal is to seek revenge, which is based on the tooth-for-tooth and eye-for-an-eye rule. Although the retributive theory is regarded to be a method of analysing justice, identifying the scope of the retributive motion is challenging. This notion could also be considered a means to an end. In this vein, it is asserted

[6] *Supra* n.1 at 121.

[7] Ibid.

[8] *Supra* n.1 at 121.

[9] Ibid.

that liability is a true and long-lasting consequence reserved for cases in which the intentional criminal offence is of this sort.[10]

Danaher cautions, "*.....I have noted how doctrines of command responsibility or gross negligence could be unfairly stretched so as to inappropriately blame the manufacturers and programmers. Anyone who cares about the strict requirements of retributive justice, or indeed justice more generally should be concerned about the risk of moral scapegoating.*"[11]

So the two options have been given here[12]:

1. *Firstly,* either to serve AI's actions as 'Acts of God' this would have no legal consequences/results thereof.

Or

2. *Secondly,* somehow managing to find a 'liable' human, for that matter. Unlike floods or earthquakes, then AI's acts would not likely be seen as not fortunate enough but ethically neutral natural disasters.[13]

The ultimate challenge for AI is that as it advances, it will become more difficult to hold humans responsible for its demonstration and oversight. It is thus blameworthy for its illustration, without overstating the acknowledged concepts of cause and effect out of awareness. John Danaher, a legal expert, has described the gap between humanity's assumptions that puts someone at risk of civil unrest. In light of the current situation, it is providing and establishing an entrance for a 'retributive hole' by omitting to apply criminal laws in AI. Despite the fact that it is easy to separate risk from financial benefit in the setting of private law, as demonstrated above.[14]

4.3 Essential Ingredients Required for Criminal Liability in AI System

4.3.1 Recklessness[15]

The concepts of recklessness and negligence are recognised in both criminal and civil law. It is a common/civil matter for private parties to seek compensation for injuries sustained as a result of any catastrophe. The state, on the other hand, is responsible for filing any criminal accusations or charges related to a car accident. For example,

[10] *Supra* n.1 at 121.

[11] *Id.* at 122.

[12] *Id.* at 123.

[13] *Id.* at 123–124.

[14] *Id.* at 125.

[15] Lina, D. (2018). Could AI Agents Be Held Criminally Liable: Artificial Intelligence and the Challenges for Criminal Law. *South Carolina Law Review, 69*(3), 8.

if the driver was driving while intoxicated and caused an accident, criminal charges would be documented and filed. When people are reckless, they are aware that their actions pose a major hazard or risk of causing specific damage. Nonetheless, they acted in this manner, oblivious to the consequences for others. The danger is so great that it's not even close to what a reasonable person would do if they followed the law. Driving at speed above 100 mph in a storm or when intoxicated or drugged are two instances. On the basis of real-time case studies, one can examine AI technology implementations in AV and hold the other person criminally liable for recklessness.[16]

4.3.2 *Negligence*[17]

When someone behaves in a way where they know there exists a danger of injury, they act negligently. The person acting negligently does not have to know with certainty that the actions will cause harm, only that they could. People owe others a duty to drive safely and follow the rules of the road. If someone fails to look both ways before pulling into a busy intersection and causes an accident, that is negligence. Negligence, fundamentally, spins around the liability to take proper and sensible consideration to avert damage to other people and spotlights on the predictability of the unfortunate result.[18]

Furthermore, negligence is the most appropriate model for criminal fault liability for unforeseen consequences that occur as a result of an AI agent's normal programming or use—that is, as it fulfils its tasks without fail.[19] The emphasis here is on a mindful developer or programmer who fails to take reasonable precautions to avoid a disagreeable result that could occur during the usual execution of the Al expert and that the developer or vendor should have anticipated. In these situations, the Al component behaves appropriately and commits a harm in order to fulfil its obligation. A cleaning machine, for example, could pulverise valuable items while mistaking them for dirt.[20] In such circumstances, the most important question to ask is whether the developer or user might have predicted it and been in a position to prevent it. It can examine AI technology implementations in AV based on recent instances and hold the other person criminally accountable for wrongdoing.[21] As an example,

Tesla Model S caused its first demise in Florida while in autopilot mode. On May 7, 2016, a mishap occurred wherein Tesla's autopilot sensors neglected to perceive a white semi-truck going across the interstate. The driver, Joshua Brown, put the car in autopilot mode, anticipating driving itself while on the parkway. Sadly, the AV neglected to recognise the 18-wheeler truck that went across the roadway. Thus, it

---

[16] Ibid.

[17] *Supra* note 15.

[18] *Id.* at 16.

[19] Ibid.

[20] Gless et al., *supra*, at 423 (discussing negligence that results in bodily injury).

[21] *Supra* note 15.

endeavoured to pass through it at max throttle. The Tesla driver died as a result of the injuries sustained in the crash.

4.3.3 *Intention*[22]

Direct Liability: This model provides two ingredients of a crime to an AI system.

a. Act, which is physical, i.e., Actus reus, and
b. Intent, which is mental, i.e., Mens rea.

An actus reus can be assigned to an AI system very easily. For instance, if a system acts in a way that leads to criminal activity or fails to intervene in a situation where it has a duty to act, the actus reus of the offence has been established. What is tough to establish in an offence is mens rea, much harder to prove, perhaps because of its nature, it demands the three levels of mens rea, which has become essential to prove the legal liability, as even under the case of strict liability offences also no intent (guilty mind) is required to commit a crime, indeed possible to hold *AI programs* liable criminally. For instance, in Self-driving cars, if the car speeds up then it will come under the purview of a strict liability offence.

As legal scholar Hallevy[23] explained a scenario, when a self-driving car exceeds the speed limit on the road, the AI program is immediately charged with rash and reckless driving, as well as a breach of the road traffic rules for breaking the law while driving the car on the spur of the moment. In Western countries, criminal law is defined by its ability to respond to misbehaviour, which is referred to as a proof. It is a widely accepted principle of modern criminal law that only acts, not considerations, convictions, or objectives, which can lead to criminal liability.

4.3.4 *Respondeat Superior?*[24]

Perpetrator-Via-Another: humans' vicarious Criminal Liability

The idea of *'vicarious liability'* (or, in fitting to the current topic terms, of *respondent superior*—"let the master answer") in criminal law[25] works in a similar way to private law and is subject to the same constraints as private law. One significant distinction is that private law vicarious liability does not focus on the principal's mens rea; rather, the inquiry concerns the principal-agent relationship. In criminal law, on the

---

[22] Ibid.

[23] Hallevy, G. (2010) *'I, Robot—I, Criminal'—When Science Fiction Becomes Reality: Legal Liability of AI Robots Committing Criminal Offences.* Syracuse Science and Technology Law Reporter, 22 (Spring), p. 1.

[24] *Supra* note 15.

[25] *Supra* note 1.

other hand, the principal must normally have the appropriate mens rea to commit the offence.[26]

If the mens rea requirement is simply showing the principal was reckless as to harm (rather than intending harm), the prosecutor may not have a difficult time overcoming this barrier. It is also applicable in strict liability offences.[27] If an AI engineer designs an AI system for making toast, and that machine subsequently burns down a house, killing everyone within, on the grounds that "all the bread would be toasted," the programmer may face criminal charges.[28] Legal scholar Gabriel Hallevy describes this as "natural-probable-consequence" liability, and it "seems legally suitable for situations in which an AI entity committed an offence, while the programmer or user had no knowledge of it, had not intended it, and had not participated in it."[29] Likewise, *AI programs* could also be held here as innocent agents. Going by this model, either it will hold the *users* or the *software programmer/system developer* criminally legally liable for an offence as an offender/perpetrator-via-another.[30]

4.4 Regulation of AVs Internationally and the Existing Legal Regime in Germany, California, and India

Whether the existing legal doctrines and the application of these legal provisions can be extended to the new, emerging, and sophisticated AI technologies or not? Whether it applies to all kinds of AI or only autonomous AI or/and the damage/harm made by AI, and if so, how?

The chapter attempts to first look into the determination of criminal liability of an AI under the existing legislation in countries such as Germany, California, and India and then further analyse its applications in the fields of autonomous vehicles.

---

[26] *See id.* at 414 (discussing damages caused by Al agents); see generally Sophia H. Duffy & Jamie Patrick Hopkins, *Sit, Stay, Drive: The Future of Autonomous Car Liability*, 16 SMU SCI. & TECH. L. REV. 453 (2013) (explaining how implementing a stringent liability regime for autonomous vehicles will fairly determine culpability without unreasonably impeding innovation); Kyle Graham, *Of Frightened Horses and Autonomous Vehicles: Tort Law and Its Assimilation of Innovations,* 52 SANTA CLARA L. REV. 1241 (2012) (discussing how difficult it is to foresee how innovation and liability will interact in the context of autonomous vehicles); Gary E. Marchant & Rachel A. Lindor, *The Coming Collision Between Autonomous Vehicles and the Liability System*, 52 SANTA CLARA L. REV. 1321 (2012) examining how reducing the amount of vehicle accidents with driverless vehicles will still cause manufacturers liability issues; Matthew U. Scherer, *Regulating Artificial Intelligence Systems: Risks, Challenges, Competencies, and Strategies,* 29 HARV. J.L. & TECH. 354 (2016) (arguing against direct regulation of autonomous vehicles in favour of the adoption of a tort system).

[27] *Supra* note 1.

[28] Ibid.

[29] *Supra* note 15.

[30] Morrisey v. State, 620 A.2d 207 (Del.1993); Conyers v. State, 367 Md. 571, 790 A.2d 15 (2002); State v. Fuller, 346 S.C. 477, 552 S.E.2d 282 (2001); Gallimore v. Commonwealth, 246 Va. 441, 436 S.E.2d 421 (1993).

International Regulation and the Law in Germany, the US, and India on self-driving Cars

After analysing the overall legal frameworks of Germany, the US (California), and India, the chances and potential outcomes, opportunities, and risks of autonomous driving will be briefly discussed in relation to the entirety of German industry, the traffic system, and the participants in the AV development. The popularity of AVs has given rise to new issues and changes that have an impact on the interaction and regulation of that innovation/technology because the guideline affects technology or the other way around.

International United Nations Treaties on Traffic

To begin, one must look to an international agreement, specifically the 'Vienna Convention on Road Traffic of 1968', to which Germany has been a party since 1979. The Convention is concerned with international traffic, and it establishes consistent norms for driving on public roadways. The arrangements are successful for the whole European Union and afterwards likewise called agreements of the 'United Nations Economic Commission for Europe (UNECE)'.[31] The UN Regulations[32] annexed to the "Agreement concerning the adoption of uniform technical prescriptions for wheeled vehicles, equipment and parts that can be fitted and/or used on wheeled vehicles, and the conditions for reciprocal recognition of approvals granted on the basis of these prescriptions" of March 20, 1958[33]; and the 'UN Global Technical Regulations'[34] developed in the framework of the "Agreement concerning the establishing of global technical regulations for wheeled vehicles, equipment, and parts which can be fitted and/or be used on wheeled vehicles" of 25th June 1998.[35]

National law can potentially allow driverless vehicles in theory if international laws permit it. In the case of self-driving cars, the rules are still uncertain. The most recent agreement of 3rd September 2019,[36] the 'UN Economic Commission for Europe's Framework Document' on Automated/Autonomous Vehicles (which is not a binding Convention), it appears that a person/operator who can take over the driving function is still required to drive the car when autonomous mode requests to do so to avoid the criminal liability.[37]

The Vienna Convention on Road Traffic[38]

---

[31] (UNECE, 2019).

[32] Magnus, U. (2019). Autonomously driving cars and the law in Germany. *Wiadomości Ubezpieczeniowe*, (4), 13-24. *See* <https://piu.org.pl/wp-content/uploads/2020/03/WU2019-0402 *Magnus.pdf*>.

[33] Ibid.

[34] Ibid.

[35] Ibid.

[36] www.unece.org/fileadmin/DAM/trans/doc/2019/wp29/ECE-TRANS-WP29-2019-34-rev.1e.pdf.

[37] *See* "4. (c) of the cited Framework Document".

[38] *Supra* note 32.

The "*Convention of Vienna of 1968 is a multilateral, global, UN-perceived/ recognised*" and started concession to norms concerning road traffic. Its starting point lies in a definitive aim of fitting road traffic rules, specialised road norms, and traffic signs to work with portability throughout the planet.[39]

Originally, Article 8 of the Convention[40] just states: "(1) Every moving vehicle or combination of vehicles must have a driver. ... (5) Every driver shall at all times be able to control his vehicle or to guide his animals." Furthermore, Art. 13 (1)[41] states that: "Every driver of a vehicle shall in all circumstances have his vehicle under control so as to be able to exercise due and proper care and to be at all times in a position to perform all manoeuvres required of him. ...." Driving a self-driving car appears to be prohibited by this regulation, which applies to all Contracting States.[42]

Since March 23 in 2016, Article 8,[43] which characterises the need and capacities to add a new paragraph (5bis) was added to Art. 8 of the Convention. Germany embraced this new provision and executed it into their national enactment/legislation as per *'Article 59 (2) Grundgesetz (GG)'*.[44]

'A new paragraph (5bis) of the Convention's Article 8'[45] discusses:

"*Vehicle systems which influence the way vehicles are driven shall be deemed to be in conformity with paragraph 5 of this Article and with paragraph 1 of Article 13, when they are in conformity with the conditions of construction, fitting and utilization according to international legal instruments concerning wheeled vehicles, equipment and parts which can be fitted and/or be used on wheeled vehicles.*[46]

Vehicle systems which influence the way vehicles are driven and are not in conformity with the aforementioned conditions of construction, fitting and utilization, shall be deemed to be in conformity with paragraph 5 of this Article and with paragraph 1 of Article 13,[47] *when such systems can be overridden or switched off by the driver.*"[48]

The amendments to 'Germany's Road Traffic Act, 2017'[49] that were recently enacted take into account the change in the 'Convention on Road Traffic'.

---

39 (Bundestag/ German Parliament, 1977).

40 *Supra* note 32.

41 Ibid.

42 Ibid.

43 Ibid.

44 Grundgesetz/ Basic Law, (Bundesrepublik Deutschland / Federal State of Germany, 1949).

45 *Supra* note 32.

46 Ibid.

47 *Supra* note 32.

48 The UN Regulations annexed to the "Agreement concerning the adoption of uniform technical prescriptions for wheeled vehicles, equipment, and parts that can be fitted and/or used on wheeled vehicles, and the conditions for reciprocal recognition of approvals granted on the basis of these prescriptions" of March 20, 1958; and the UN Global Technical Regulations developed in the framework of the "Agreement concerning the establishing of global technical regulations for wheeled vehicles, equipment, and parts which can be fitted and/or be used on wheeled vehicles" of 25th June 1998.

49 *Supra* note 32.

However, several countries have not ratified the 'Vienna Agreement',[50] and as a result, it has not been fully implemented. It is ratified by 78 nations. Few nations have endorsed or ratified the agreement to maintain their autonomy and freedom to determine their own legal or judicial decisions regarding traffic and road regulations. The 'Road Traffic Convention' is not binding on the United States of America because it was not signed.[51] Interestingly, Germany has signed it, whereas India has not. India has not yet signed an umbrella UN Agreement under which licences issued by the signing member nations would be valid across all countries.

As Eva Molnar-director of the transport division of 'UN Economic Commission for Europe (UNECE)' said "India was a contracting part to the '1948 UN Convention on road traffic', but it is yet to sign the 1968 agreement on it." This means that other nations are not legally bound to accept the International Driving Licences issued by the Indian Government. Once India signs the agreement, it has to follow certain standards.

The Convention and Autonomous Cars

"The German Road Traffic Act (Straßenverkehrsgesetz, 'StVG') was amended in 2017"[52] to allow the use of vehicles equipped with 'Level 3' automatic steering systems on public roads. These automated systems allow the driver to take a break from driving while the car is being driven by the automated steering system.[53] However, 'Level 3' is confined to specific conditions, and the driver must be able to regain control when the system requests it.[54]

In February 2021, the 'German Federal Government' took a step further by adopting a proposed bill that included 'Level 4 autonomous driving' as a public transport option.[55] 'Level 4' refers to completely automated driving, in which the 'vehicle's driving system' is capable of managing all driving functions without the need for human intervention. In adverse driving conditions, however, a human driver may be required to assume control of the car. Germany would be the first country in the world to allow 'Level 4'-capable vehicles to operate on public roads.[56]

Despite not signing the 'Vienna Agreement', the US adopted the simultaneousness on specialised standardisation in 1998, specifically after the US changed its self-authorisation/affirmation framework for automobile underwriting. The USA didn't support it, and the states voluntarily tried to agree with it, but the agreement hasn't yet passed muster with the US experts.[57]

---

[50] Ibid.

[51] (Franz, 2016).

[52] *See* <https://www.globalcompliancenews.com/2021/03/30/germany-german-government-introduces-bill-for-level-4-highly-automated-driving-23032021/>, accessed on September 28, 2023.

[53] *Supra* note 32.

[54] *Supra* note 52.

[55] Ibid.

[56] Ibid.

[57] *Supra* note 32.

According to *'Article 5 of the Vienna Convention on Road Traffic, 2017'* autonomous frameworks integrated into moving vehicles that abide by the agreement establishing the foundation of global technical standards for wheeled vehicles are covered. These frameworks are therefore legally recognised and allowed to assist and support the driver of a vehicle.[58] Such an understanding, however, does not clearly forbid or mention automated vehicles or any other sort of driving development. It merely conveys the essential characteristics of wheeled vehicles, such as the presence of brakes, a steering wheel, a seat belt, or headlights.[59] The arrangement's No. 79 prohibits AVs from running on highways or city roads because this Section is clearly prohibited, prohibiting self-driving controlling frameworks, even those on a closed parking lot. Those frameworks are required for self-driving cars.[60]

4.5 Determination of Criminal Liability in Germany[61]

Offences in Relation to Use of Motor Vehicles Which Are Punishable Under German Criminal Code[62]

- Negligent manslaughter under **Section 222** of the German Criminal Code,1871.[63]
- Causing bodily harm by negligence under **Section 229** of the German Criminal Code.[64]
- Endangering road traffic under **Section 315 c** of the German Criminal Code.[65]

---

[58] Ibid.

[59] Ibid.

[60] Wissenschaftliche Dienste Deutscher Bundestag/Scientific commission of the German Parliament, 2018.

[61] *See* <https://www.gesetze-im-internet.de/englisch_stgb/englisch_stgb.pdf>, accessed on September 25, 2023.

[62] Ibid.

[63] "***Section 222: Negligent manslaughter***

Whosoever through negligence causes the death of a person shall be liable to imprisonment not exceeding five years or a fine".

[64] "***Section 229: Causing bodily harm by negligence***

Whosoever by negligence causes bodily harm to another shall be liable to imprisonment not exceeding three years or a fine".

[65] "***Section 315 c: Endangering Road traffic***

(1) Whoever, in road traffic,

1. drives a vehicle although they are not in a condition to drive the vehicle safely

(a) due to having consumed alcoholic drinks or other intoxicating substances or.

(b) due to mental or physical deficiencies, or

2. in gross violation of road traffic regulations and carelessly

(a) does not observe the right of way,

- Driving under the influence of drink or drugs under **Section 316** of the German Criminal Code.[66]

Introduction of self-driving cars in mainstream traffic

When automated vehicles can be allowed to public traffic is one of the main focuses of the recent German reform. The new '§ 1a StVG, 2017'[67] is a lengthy and complicated provision that reads as follows in English:

"§1a StVG Motor vehicles with highly or fully automated driving function[68]

(1) *the operation of a motor vehicle with a highly or fully automated driving function is permissible if the function is used as intended.*
(2) *Motor vehicles with a high or fully automated driving function within the meaning of this act are those which have technical equipment,*

1. *Which can control the respective motor vehicle after activation to accomplish the driving task—including longitudinal and lateral guidance (vehicle control),*
2. *Which can comply with the traffic regulations addressed to the driver during highly or fully automated vehicle control,*
3. *Which can be manually overridden or deactivated by the driver at any time,*

(b) overtakes improperly or otherwise drives improperly in the process of overtaking,

(c) drives improperly in the vicinity of pedestrian crossings,

(d) drives too fast in places with poor visibility, at road crossings, junctions, or railway crossings,

(e) fails to keep to the right-hand side of the road in places with poor visibility,

(f) turns, drive backward or contrary to the direction of traffic, or attempts to do so on a motorway or a main road or

(g) fails to make vehicles that have stopped or broken down recognizable at a sufficient distance. However, this is required to ensure traffic safety, endangers the life or limb of another person or property of significant value belonging to another, incurs a penalty of imprisonment for a term not exceeding five years or a fine.

(2) In the cases under subsection (1) no. 1, the attempt is punishable.

(3) Whoever, in the cases under subsection (1),

1. causes the danger by negligence or

2. acts negligently and causes the danger by negligence incurs a penalty of imprisonment for a term not exceeding two years or a fine."

66 **"*Section 316: Driving under the influence of drink or drugs***

(1) Whoever drives a vehicle in traffic (sections 315 to 315e) although they are not in a condition to drive the vehicle safely due to having consumed alcoholic drinks or other intoxicating substances incurs a penalty of imprisonment for a term not exceeding one year or a fine unless the offence is subject to a penalty under section 315a or *315c.*

(2) Whoever commits the offence negligently also incurs the penalty specified in subsection (1)".

67 *Supra* note 32.

68 Ibid.

4. *Which can recognize the need for the driver to control the vehicle himself,*
5. *which is capable of visually, acoustically, tactilely, or otherwise perceptibly indicating to the driver the need for personal control of the vehicle with sufficient time before delivery of the vehicle control to the driver; and.*
6. *Which indicates a use contrary to the system description.*

The manufacturer of such a motor vehicle must declare in the system description that the vehicle complies with the requirements of sentence 1.

(3) *The above paragraphs shall only apply to vehicles registered in accordance with § 1 paragraph 1, which comply with the requirements set out in paragraph 2 sentence 1 and whose highly automated or fully automated driving functions*

1. *Are described in and comply with international regulations applicable within the scope of this Act, or*
2. *have been granted type-approval pursuant to Article 20 of Directive 2007/46/EC of the European Parliament and of the Council of 5th September 2007 establishing a framework for the approval of motor vehicles and their trailers, and of systems, components and separate technical units intended for such vehicles (Framework Directive) (OJ L 263, 9.10.2007, p. 1).*

(4) *A driver is also the person who activates a highly or fully automatic driving function within the meaning of paragraph 2 and uses it for vehicle control, even if he does not control the vehicle himself within the scope of the intended use of this function.*"

This is pertinent to the issue of whether even a fully autonomous car must always be accompanied by a person who is capable of driving. Paragraphs (2) Nos. 4 and 5[69] of the provision are relevant in this case. These paragraphs clearly show that any self-driving vehicle must have a human driver. However, the paragraph raises some concerns regarding this necessity. If a person only activates the vehicle but does not operate it, he or she is classified as a driver under this clause. It's unclear whether this definition's phrasing covers a circumstance in which a parent drives a car full of tiny children to school but stays at home. On the other hand, the legislator did not intend a natural-probable-consequence liability. As a result, the use of fully autonomous vehicles on German roads is now restricted, except for experimental purposes.[70]

The Road Traffic Act, 2017[71]

In 2017, Germany had invested in their legislative framework regarding what kind of technology is recognised officially and thus provides legal certainty to the vehicle industry to make sure that everyone who is travelling in a vehicle is safe. Germany

---

[69] *Supra* note 32.

[70] *See* the Reasoning of the Draft of the new provisions, BR-Drucks. 69/17, p. 7; also Ch. Armbrüster, ZRP 2017, p. 83.

[71] *Supra* note 32. *See also* https://bmdv.bund.de/blaetterkatalog/catalogs/327056/pdf/complete.pdf, accessed on September 28, 2023.

has amended its law by inserting a new section, that is, "*§ 1 a-c StVG, into the Road Traffic Act, 2017*"[72] which enhances the regulation of autonomous vehicles. Furthermore, solving the civil liability problem and providing legal certainty, The German government works to reduce the lack of faith/hope that potential users have in AV technology.[73]

In both precedent-based/civil law and common law frameworks, the investigation into criminal obligation begins at the fundamental dimension of acting that is the idea is reflected in actus reus in the main framework and incorporated into the '**German Tatbestandsmifj3igkeit**' 0 in the most noticeable agent locale of the last mentioned (which means "satisfaction of the components of the offence," while Tat itself signifies 'act').[74]

A performance must be controllable by the performer and 'socially pertinent'—that is, it must pass on social relevance—according to criminal law author in Germany. For instance, a display that refers to or is directed towards someone other than oneself, as liberal scholars would urge based on John Stuart Mill's popular interpretation of the Harm Principle, which states that power must be utilised regardless of the harm it causes to others.[75] It is important to highlight that when a perpetrator uses goods, equipment, or machines to achieve the desired result, the wrongdoing is considered the perpetrator's activities. For example, the '**German Criminal Code'** unequivocally states under **Section 25** that a principal is someone who "carries out the offence himself or through another."[76] Against this setting, artificial intelligence brings up some amazingly fascinating issues. Most importantly, it makes the person to think about whether Al operators/agents are acting in a way which is prohibited under criminal law.[77]

Determination of Criminal Liability of AI in Germany

Whether these provisions cover AVs also. The present research has tried to analyse whether these provisions under the German law are adequate to determine the criminal liability in the case of autonomous vehicles? The applicability of these provisions to AVs.[78]

A comprehensive analysis of these provisions reveals that existing provisions such as 'Section 222-*Negligent manslaughter*, Section 229-*Causing bodily harm by negligence*, Section 315 c-*Endangering road traffic*, and Section 316-*Driving under the influence of drink or drugs only applies to human drivers or car owners'* who

---

[72] Ibid.

[73] Ibid.

[74] *Id.*

[75] *See* JOHN STUART MILL, ON LIBERTY 17 (1859) ("That the only purpose for which power can be rightfully exercised over any member of a civilised community, against his will, is to prevent harm to others.").

[76] MICHAEL BOHLANDER, THE GERMAN CRIMINAL CODE: A MODERN ENGLISH TRANSLATION 43 (Hart Publ'g 1st ed. 2008).

[77] Ibid.

[78] *Supra* note 32.

are held liable for negligence and subject to punishment under criminal law. In these circumstances, the human driver monitors the driving environment since it must be regarded from the perspective of 'SAE Level 0–2', where the car is perfectly under the control of the human driver whether the same law applies in negligence situations ranging from 'SAE Level 0 to 2' and 'SAE Level 3–5'. When comparing existing provisions in the criminal law of negligence connected to traditional driving, such as 'Sections (222, 229, 315 c, and 316)', to 'SAE Level 0 to 5', autonomous driving, the outcome is as follows:

Section 222: Negligent manslaughter—Whoever causes the death of another person by negligence suffers a penalty of up to five years in jail or a fine. In this context, Whoever, who is considered as a natural and legal person in this context, in the category of 'SAE Level 0–3' is adequately regulated and governed by the existing provisions. However, in the case of highly and fully autonomous system, i.e., 'SAE Levels 4 and 5' the existing provisions and framework to impose liability of any kind are not adequate; in 'SAE Level 0–3', there is a presence of human intervention to control the AI; whereas in 'SAE Level 4–5' no human intervention is present.

CONCLUSION —There is a gap in the legislation that does not specifically cover the highly and fully autonomous system.

PROPOSAL—That a proper law be put in place to regulate 'SAE Levels 4 and 5'.

Section 229-Causing bodily harm by negligence—Whoever, who is considered as a natural and legal person in this context, in the category of 'SAE Level 0–3' is adequately regulated and governed by the existing provisions. However, in the case of highly and fully autonomous system, i.e., 'SAE Levels 4 and 5' the exciting provisions and framework to impose liability of any kind are not adequate; in 'SAE Level 0–3', there is a presence of human intervention to control the AI; whereas in 'SAE Level 4–5' no human intervention is present.

As a result, the author observed that there is a gap in the legislation that does not specifically cover the highly and fully autonomous system. The author proposed that a proper law be put in place to address the current issue, namely 'SAE Levels 4 and 5'.

Section 315c-Endangering road traffic—Whoever, in road traffic drives a vehicle while intoxicated or unable to drive safely due to the consumption of alcoholic drinks or other intoxicating substances, or due to mental or physical deficiencies, or in gross violation of road traffic regulations, and causes bodily harm to another by negligence faces a penalty of imprisonment for a term not exceeding three years or a fine. In this context, whoever is considered a natural and legal person is true to 'SAE Level 0–3' but not to a highly and fully autonomous system, because autonomous systems are independent in their actions and reasoning, whereas in 'SAE Level 0–3', humans control and monitor the "AI agent/tool/machine on their own, and human intervention is present to control the AI agent/tool/machine." As a result, the author observed that there is a gap in the legislation that does not specifically cover the highly and fully autonomous system. The author proposed that a proper law be put in place to address the current issue, namely 'SAE Levels 4 and 5'.

"*Section 316-Driving under the influence of drink or drugs only applies to human drivers or car owners*"—Unless the offence is punishable under 'Section 315a or 315c', whoever drives a vehicle in traffic while intoxicated ('Sections 315 to 315e') faces a punishment of imprisonment for a period not exceeding one year or a fine. In this context, Whoever, who is considered as a natural and legal person in this context, in the category of 'SAE Level 0–3' is adequately regulated and governed by the existing provisions. However, in the case of highly and fully autonomous system, i.e., 'SAE Levels 4 and 5' the existing provisions and framework to impose liability of any kind are not adequate; in 'SAE Level 0–3', there is a presence of human intervention to control the AI; whereas in 'SAE Level 4–5' no human intervention is present.

CONCLUSION —There is a gap in the legislation that does not specifically cover the highly and fully autonomous system.

PROPOSAL—That a proper law be put in place to regulate 'SAE Levels 4 and 5'.

In **Level 0**, the full-time performance by the human driver of all aspects of the 'dynamic driving task', even when enhanced by warning or intervention systems. Who, once again, is in charge of steering and acceleration/deceleration? Who will be held accountable for negligence, now that the answer is a *human driver*. Another aspect of driving a car is the monitoring of the driving environment, which is likewise done by a *human driver*. If a fallback execution of the dynamic driving task is available, who is the performing *human driver*. Is there any capability (driving mode) in the system? The answer is negative. As a result of the author's reasoning, the author believes that SAE Level 0 is true to traditional driving, and thus the same sections will apply to 'SAE Level 0', namely 'Sections 222: Negligent manslaughter, Section 229: Causing bodily harm by negligence, Section 315 c: Endangering road traffic, and Section 316: Driving under the influence of drink or drugs'.

In **Level 1** (Driver Assistance), the application of steering and acceleration/deceleration by one or more driver assistance systems in accordance with information about the driving environment, with the hope that the human driver would handle the advanced settings of the dynamic driving task. Who will be held accountable for negligence, now that the answer is a human driver and system. Is there any capability (driving mode) in the system? The answer is some driving modes. As a result of the author's reasoning, the author believes that SAE Level 1 is true to traditional driving, and thus the same sections will apply to 'SAE Level 1', namely 'Sections 222: Negligent manslaughter, Section 229: Causing bodily harm by negligence, Section 315 c: Endangering Road Traffic, and Section 316: Driving under the influence of drink or drugs'.

In **Level 2** (Partial Automation), in a certain driving mode, the automated driving system will handle every aspect of the 'dynamic driving task' with the hope that the human driver will react appropriately when asked to intervene. Who, once again, oversees steering and acceleration/deceleration? Here the system oversees steering and acceleration/deceleration. Who will be held accountable for 'negligence', now that the answer is a system.

Another aspect of driving a car is the monitoring of the driving environment, which is likewise done by a human driver. If a fallback execution of the 'dynamic driving task' is available, who is the performing *human driver*. Is there any capability (driving mode) in the system? The answer is some driving modes. As a result of the author's reasoning, the author believes that 'SAE Level 2' is true to traditional driving, and thus the same sections will apply to 'SAE Level 2', namely 'Sections 222: Negligent Manslaughter-Whoever causes a person's death by negligence faces a penalty of up to five years in prison or a fine'. Whoever is considered as a natural and legal person in this context, which stands true to SAE Level 0–3 but not to a highly and fully autonomous system, because here autonomous system is independent in its actions and reasoning but in 'SAE Level 0–3', it is humans who is controlling and monitoring on its own, human intervention is present to control the 'AI agent/tool/machine'. As a result, the author observed that there is a gap in the legislation that does not specifically cover the highly and fully autonomous system. The author proposed that a proper law be put in place to address the current issue, namely 'SAE Levels 4 and 5'.

"*SAE Level 3–5: Automated driving system ('system') monitors the driving environment*":

In **Level 3** (Conditional Automation), in a certain driving mode, the 'automated driving system' will handle every aspect of the 'dynamic driving task' with the hope that the human driver will react appropriately when asked to intervene. Who, once again, is in charge of steering and acceleration/deceleration? Who will be held accountable for negligence now that the answer is a *system*. Another aspect of driving a car is the monitoring of the driving environment, which is likewise done by a *system*. If a fallback execution of the dynamic driving task is available, who is the performing *human driver*. Is there any capability (driving mode) in the system? The answer is *some driving modes*. The author contends that the human driver/operator and the manufacturer are both guilty under the law of negligence. As a result of the author's reasoning, the author believes that 'SAE Level 3' is partially true to traditional driving, with the expectation that the human driver will respond properly to a request to intervene and thus the same sections will apply to 'SAE Level 3', namely 'Sections 222: Negligent manslaughter, Section 229: Causing bodily harm by negligence, Section 315 c: Endangering road traffic, and Section 316: Driving under the influence of drink or drugs'.

In **Level 4** (High Automation), the performance of all 'dynamic driving task' components by a fully automated driving system in all traffic and environmental circumstances that a human driver is capable of handling. Who, once again, is in charge of steering and acceleration/deceleration? Now that the answer is a *system*, who will be held liable for negligence? Another aspect of driving a car is the monitoring of the driving environment, which is likewise done by a *system*. If a fallback execution of the 'dynamic driving task' is available, who is the performing *system*.

Is there any capability (driving mode) in the system? The answer is *some driving modes.*

The author contends that the manufacturer is liable as a result of the arguments presented, but that a sui generis law is needed in Germany to deal with cases of 'highly autonomous car negligence', or that a place should be made in existing legislation to deal with 'Level 4 autonomous cars', because the existing provisions only deal with human drivers, not machines or autonomous cars.

In **Level 5** (Full Automation), performance by a fully 'automated driving system' of all aspects of the 'dynamic driving task' in all traffic and environmental situations that a human driver is capable of controlling. Again, whose responsibility is it to steer and accelerate or decelerate? Now that the answer is a *system*, who will be held liable for negligence? Another aspect of driving a car is the monitoring of the driving environment, which is likewise done by a *system.* If a fallback execution of the 'dynamic driving task' is available, who is the performing *system.* Is there any capability (driving mode) in the system? The answer is *all driving modes.*

The author contends that the manufacturer is liable as a result of the arguments presented, but that a sui generis law is needed in Germany to deal with cases of 'fully autonomous car negligence', or that a place should be made in existing legislation to deal with 'Level 5 autonomous cars', because the existing provisions only deal with human drivers, not machines or autonomous cars.

4.6 Determination of Criminal Liability in California

The Model Penal Code in the United States,[79] for example, defines criminal responsibility as follows: "An individual isn't blameworthy of an offence unless his liability is based on direct, which includes a willful demonstration or the exclusion to play out a demonstration of which he is physically skilled," while a demonstration is defined as 'substantial development' (regardless of whether deliberate or not) under 'General Definitions'.[80]

Furthermore, the demonstration need is often regarded as the most striking, if not the most important, exception to the rule that substantive criminal law in the United.[81]

Nevada set the bar in 2011 for states that legalise and regulate the use of autonomous vehicles. Thirty-three states had familiar legislation relating to the subject enacted in 2017; twenty of them have recently approved substantial legislation, and a further five have seen significant official requests submitted.[82]

---

[79] "*MODEL PENAL CODE § 2.0*" (AM. LAW INST. 1962).

[80] *Id* § 1.13.

[81] MARKUS D. Dubber & TATJANA HORNLE, CRIMINAL LAW: A COMPARATIVE APPROACH 197 (Oxford Univ. Press 2014).

[82] *See Self-Driving Vehicles*, NAT'L CONF. STATE LEGISLATURES, http://www.ncsl.org/research/transportation/autonomous-vehicles-self-driving-vehicles-enacted-legislation.aspx#E

In the United States, almost forty-one states have considered AV legislation.[83] Out of forty-one states, twenty-two states have agreed and approved the regulations related to AVs, and the governors of ten states have issued executive orders. California has been permitted to test AVs on public roads without an operator.[84] Californian law distinguishes between OEMs and autonomous vehicle manufacturers but does not expressly cover OEMs from the liability relating to AVs.

The California Legislature delegated the work of regulation of autonomous cars to the 'Department of Motor Vehicles', which is charged with administering licencing requirements, adopting safety and performance standards, and adopting any regulation applicable to the operation of autonomous cars in the absence of a driver inside. Level 5 AVs are already in use in various states of the USA like Arizona, Florida, Michigan, and Pennsylvania.[85]

Another section which is newly added to the list under '**Section 38,750–38,751 of Autonomous Vehicle defines under the Vehicle Code of California, 1959'.**[86]

While analysing and determining this section criminal liability for the driver, owner, manufacturer, or developer, it is believed that this section identifies all of the constituent technologies involved as well as a definition of an operator. This section outlines the roles and responsibilities of everyone involved in the use of autonomous vehicles on the road.

(a) This section defines the following concepts related to AVs[87]:

Autonomous technology means it is "*technology that has the capability to drive a vehicle without the active physical control or monitoring by a human operator*."

---

nacted%/o20Autonomous%2OVehicle%20Legislation (last visited Feb. 20, 2019), for these figures as well as further information on actions taken by the fifty states regarding autonomous vehicles.

[83] Gurney, J.K. Sue My Car Not Me: Products Liability and Accidents Involving Autonomous Vehicles. J. Law Technol. Policy **2013**, 2,247–277.

[84] Adeel, L.; Frank, D.; Onyiah, I. Self-Driving Vehicles, and Policy Implications: Current Status of Autonomous Vehicle Development and Minnesota Policy Implications. Minn. J. Law Sci. Technol. **2015**, 16, 45–105.

[85] James, M.; Nidhi, K.; Karlyn, D.; Stanley, P.; Oluwatobi, A. Autonomous Vehicle Technology: A Guide for Policy Makers; Rand Corporation: Santa Monica, CA, USA, 2016.

[86] "*Division 16.6 was added by Stats. 2012, Ch. 570, Sec.2-Autonomous Vehicles [38750–38755]*", available at <http://leginfo.legislature.ca.gov/faces/codes_displayText.xhtml?lawCode=VEH&division=16.6.&title=&part=&chapter=&article_=_>, accessed on April 30, 2020.

[87] "***Section 38,750—Autonomous Vehicle***

Sub-section(c) (D) The autonomous vehicle shall allow the operator to take control in multiple manners, including, without limitation, through the use of the brake, the accelerator pedal, or the steering wheel, and it shall alert the operator that the autonomous technology has been disengaged.

Sub-section(c) (G) The autonomous vehicle has a separate mechanism, in addition to, and separate from, any other mechanism required by law, to capture and store the autonomous technology sensor data for at least 30 s before a collision occurs between the autonomous vehicle and another vehicle, object, or natural person while the vehicle is operating in autonomous mode. The autonomous technology sensor data shall be captured and stored in a read-only format so that the data is retained until extracted from the mechanism by an external device capable of downloading and storing the data. The data shall be preserved for three years after the date of the collision.

How does it define Autonomous vehicles in this section? So it means "*any vehicle equipped with autonomous technology that has been integrated into that vehicle.*"

Sub-Clause(B) states that "*An autonomous vehicle does not include a vehicle that is equipped with one or more collision avoidance systems, including, but not limited to, electronic blind spot assistance, automated emergency braking systems, park assist, adaptive cruise control, lane keep assist, lane departure warning, traffic jam and queuing assist, or other similar systems that enhance safety or provide driver assistance, but are not capable, collectively or singularly, of driving the vehicle without the active control or monitoring of a human operator.*"

Sub-clause (4) defines the term—'operator' of an autonomous vehicle "*as the person seated in the driver's seat, or, if there is no person in the driver's seat, causes the autonomous technology to engage.*"

Sub-clause (5) defines manufacturer of autonomous technology "*is the person as defined in Section 470 that originally manufactures a vehicle and equips autonomous technology on the originally completed vehicle or, in the case of a vehicle not originally equipped with autonomous technology by the vehicle manufacturer, the person that modifies the vehicle by installing autonomous technology to convert it to an autonomous vehicle after the vehicle was originally manufactured.*"

Sub-section (b) states that "*an autonomous vehicle may be operated on public roads for testing purposes by a driver who possesses the proper class of license for the type of vehicle being operated if all of the following requirements are met:*

(1) *The autonomous vehicle is being operated on roads in this state solely by employees, contractors, or other persons designated by the autonomous technology manufacturer.*
(2) *The driver shall be seated in the driver's seat, monitoring the safe operation of the autonomous vehicle, and capable of taking over immediate manual control of the autonomous vehicle in the event of an autonomous technology failure or another emergency.*"

Sub-section (c) of (A): "*The autonomous vehicle has a mechanism to engage and disengage the autonomous technology that is easily accessible to the operator.*"

Sub-section (c) of (B): "*The autonomous vehicle has a visual indicator inside the cabin to indicate when the autonomous technology is engaged.*"

Sub-clause (C) "*The autonomous vehicle has a system to safely alert the operator if an autonomous technology failure is detected while the autonomous technology is engaged, and when an alert is given, the system shall do either of the following:*

(i) *Require the operator to take control of the autonomous vehicle.*

Sub-section (h): The manufacturer of the autonomous technology installed on a vehicle shall provide a written disclosure to the purchaser of an autonomous vehicle that describes what information is collected by the autonomous technology equipped on the vehicle. The department may promulgate regulations to assess a fee upon a manufacturer that applies under subdivision (c) to operate autonomous vehicles on public roads in an amount necessary to recover all costs reasonably incurred by the department".

(ii) *If the operator does not or is unable to take control of the autonomous vehicle, the autonomous vehicle shall be capable of coming to a complete stop.*"[88]

Moreover, **'Section 38,755 of the Vehicle Code of California'** states that "authorized to conduct a pilot project for the testing of autonomous vehicles that do not have a driver seated in the driver's seat and are not equipped with a steering wheel, a brake pedal, or an accelerator."[89]

The following are the criminal liability provisions in relation to the use of AVs in the State of California:

Section 38,750:Autonomous Vehicle—In this context, the operator is considered a natural and legal person is true to 'SAE Level 0–3' but not to a highly and fully autonomous system, because autonomous systems are independent in their actions and reasoning, whereas in SAE Level 0–3, humans control and monitor the AI agent/tool/machine on their own, and human intervention is present to control the AI agent/tool/machine.[90]

As a result, the author observed that there is a gap in the legislation that does not specifically cover the highly and fully autonomous system. The author proposed that a proper law be put in place to address the current issue, namely 'SAE Levels 4 and 5'.

'Section 38755 Vehicle Code of California' talks about "*authorized to conduct a pilot project for the testing of autonomous vehicles that do not have a driver seated in the driver's seat and are not equipped with a steering wheel, a brake pedal, or an accelerator*." As a result, the author observed that there is a gap in the legislation that does not specifically cover the highly and fully autonomous system. The author proposed that a proper law be put in place to address the current issue, namely 'SAE Levels 4 and 5'.

Offences in Relation to Use of Motor Vehicles which are punishable under 'California Criminal Code, 1872'.[91]

2. Vehicular under section 192 sub-section 2(C) of the California Penal Code, 1872.

---

88 *Supra* note 86.

89 Ibid.

90 *Supra* note 86.

91 ***"Section 192 sub-section 2(c)—Vehicular***

(1) Except as provided in subdivision (a) of Section 191.5, driving a vehicle in the commission of an unlawful act, not amounting to a felony, and with gross negligence; or driving a vehicle in the commission of a lawful act which might produce death, unlawfully, and with gross negligence.

(2) Driving a vehicle in the commission of an unlawful act, not amounting to a felony, but without gross negligence; driving a vehicle in the commission of a lawful act that might produce death, unlawfully, but without gross negligence.

(3) Driving a vehicle in connection with a violation of paragraph (3) of subdivision (a) of Section 550, where the vehicular collision or vehicular accident was knowingly caused for financial gain and proximately resulted in the death of any person. This paragraph does not prevent the prosecution of a defendant for the crime of murder.

Whether the legal regime in the State of California is adequate to fix the criminal liability in case of an AV or a dedication legislation to determine the liability in case of use of AVs is still needed?

4.6.1 Determination of Criminal Liability in California

A comprehensive analysis of this provision reveals existing provisions such as Vehicular under 'section 192 sub-section 2(c) of the California Penal Code, 1872', who are held liable for rash, reckless, and negligence driving and subject to punishment under criminal law. In this circumstance, the human driver monitors the driving environment since it must be regarded from the perspective of 'SAE Level 0–2', where the car is perfectly under the control of the human driver.

The author will now investigate whether the same law applies in negligence situations ranging from 'SAE Level 0 to 2' and 'SAE Level 3–5'. When comparing existing provisions in the criminal law of negligence connected to traditional driving, such as Section 192 sub-section 2(c), to SAE Level 0 to 5, autonomous driving, the outcome is as follows:

'Section 192 (c) (1): negligence driving'—"driving a vehicle in the commission of an unlawful act, not amounting to felony, and with gross negligence; or driving a vehicle in the commission of a lawful act which might produce death, in an unlawful manner, and with gross negligence." In this context, driving a vehicle is considered a natural and legal person is true to 'SAE Level 0-3' but not to a highly and fully autonomous system, because autonomous systems are independent in their actions and reasoning, whereas in 'SAE Level 0-3', humans control and monitor the AI agent/tool/machine on their own, and human intervention is present to control the AI agent/tool/machine. As a result, the author observed that there is a gap in the legislation that does not specifically cover the highly and fully autonomous system. The author proposed that a proper law be put in place to address the current issue, namely 'SAE Levels 4 and 5'.

In **Level 0**, the full-time performance by the human driver of all aspects of the dynamic driving task, even when enhanced by warning or intervention systems. Who, once again, is in charge of steering and acceleration/deceleration? Who will be held accountable for negligence, now that the answer is a *human driver*. Another aspect of driving a car is the monitoring of the driving environment, which is likewise done by a *human driver*. If a fallback execution of the 'dynamic driving task' is available, who is the performing *human driver*. Is there any capability (driving mode) in the

---

(d) This section shall not be construed as making any homicide in the driving of a vehicle punishable that is not a proximate result of the commission of an unlawful act, not amounting to a felony, or of the commission of a lawful act which might produce death, unlawfully.

(e) 'Gross negligence', as used in this section, does not prohibit or preclude a charge of murder under Section 188 upon facts exhibiting wantonness and a conscious disregard for life to support a finding of implied malice, or upon facts showing malice".

system? The answer is negative. As a result of the author's reasoning, the author believes that 'SAE Level 0' is true to traditional driving, and thus the same section will apply to 'SAE Level 0', namely 'Section 192 (c) (1)'.

In **Level 1** (Driver Assistance), the execution of steering or acceleration/deceleration by a driver assistance system based on data about the driving environment, with the hope that the human driver will handle the other parts of the 'dynamic driving task'. Who will be held accountable for negligence, now that the answer is a human driver and system. Is there any capability (driving mode) in the system? The answer is some driving modes. As a result of the author's reasoning, the author believes that 'SAE Level 1' is true to traditional driving, and thus the same section will apply to 'SAE Level 1', namely 'Section 192 (c) (1)'.

In **Level 2** (Partial Automation), the use of one or more driver assistance systems to execute steering and acceleration/deceleration functions based on information about the driving environment, with the hope that the human driver will handle the remaining tasks involved in dynamic driving. Here the system is in charge of steering and acceleration/deceleration. Who will be held accountable for negligence, now that the answer is a system.

Another aspect of driving a car is the monitoring of the driving environment, which is likewise done by a human driver. If a fallback execution of the dynamic driving task is available, who is the performing *human driver*. Is there any capability (driving mode) in the system? The answer is some driving modes. As a result of the author's reasoning, the author believes that 'SAE Level 2' is true to traditional driving, and thus the same section will apply to 'SAE Level 2', namely 'Section 192 (c) (1)'.

SAE Level 3–5: automated driving system ('system') monitors the driving environment.

In **Level 3** (Conditional Automation), in a certain driving mode, the automated driving system will handle every aspect of the dynamic driving task with the hope that the human driver will react appropriately when asked to intervene. Who, once again, is in charge of steering and acceleration/deceleration? Who will be held accountable for negligence now that the answer is a *system*. Another aspect of driving a car is the monitoring of the driving environment, which is likewise done by a *system*. If a fallback execution of the dynamic driving task is available, who is the performing *human driver*. Is there any capability (driving mode) in the system? The answer is *some driving modes*. The author contends that the human driver/operator and the manufacturer are both guilty under the law of negligence. As a result of the author's reasoning, the author believes that SAE Level 3 is partially true to traditional driving, with the expectation that the human driver will respond properly to a request to intervene and thus the same section will apply to 'SAE Level 3', namely 'Section 192 (c) (1)'.

In **Level 4** (High Automation), even if a human driver doesn't react adequately to a request to intervene, the automated driving system must nonetheless complete all aspects of the dynamic driving task while in a certain driving mode. Who, once again, is in charge of steering and acceleration/deceleration? Now that the answer is a *system*, who will be held liable for negligence? Another aspect of driving a car is the monitoring of the driving environment, which is likewise done by a *system*. If a fallback execution of the 'dynamic driving task' is available, who is the performing *system*. Is there any capability (driving mode) in the system? The answer is *some driving modes.*

The author contends that the manufacturer is liable as a result of the arguments presented, but that a sui generis law is needed in California to deal with cases of highly autonomous car negligence, or that a place should be made in existing legislation to deal with Level 4 autonomous cars, because the existing provisions only deal with human drivers, not machines or autonomous cars.

In **Level 5** (Full Automation), the performance of all dynamic driving task components by a fully automated driving system in all traffic and environmental circumstances that a human driver is capable of handling. Again, whose responsibility is it to steer and accelerate or decelerate? Now that the answer is a *system*, who will be held liable for negligence? Another aspect of driving a car is the monitoring of the driving environment, which is likewise done by a *system*. If a fallback execution of the dynamic driving task is available, who is the performing *system*. Is there any capability (driving mode) in the system? The answer is *all driving modes.*

The author contends that the manufacturer is liable as a result of the arguments presented, but that a sui generis law is needed in California to deal with cases of fully autonomous car negligence, or that a place should be made in existing legislation to deal with Level 5 autonomous cars, because the existing provisions only deal with human drivers, not machines or autonomous cars.

Another landmark case is that of Umeda v. tesla Inc.

Umeda v. tesla Inc.[92]

TOMOMI UMEDA, an individual, and MIYU UMEDA, an individual, and Successor-in-Interest to Yoshihiro Umeda, deceased, Plaintiffs-Appellants, v. TESLA, INC., Defendant-Appellate.[93]

BERZON, BEA, and NGUYEN, Circuit Judges.

Facts of the case:

Tomomi Umeda and Miyu Umeda (collectively, 'the Umedas') sued Tesla, Inc. in the Northern District of California after their family member Yoshihiro Umeda was killed by a Tesla Model X in Autopilot mode. The district court granted Tesla's move to dismiss the case on the grounds of forum non -conveniens. The Umedas filed an appeal.[94]

---

92 Umeda v. Tesla inc., No.20-CV-02926-SVK, 2020 WL 5,653,496(N.D.Cal. Sept.23, 2020).

***Supra* note 94.**

93 Ibid.

94 **Umeda v. Tesla, Inc.,** No. 21–15,286, United States Court of Appeals, Ninth Circuit, Decided on Jan 3, 2022.

Issues Involved:

1. A forum non-conveniens dismissal for abuse of discretion, giving the district court's decision 'substantial deference'. A defendant must show that 1) there is an adequate alternative forum, 2) the balance of private interest elements support dismissal, and 3) the balance of public interest factors favour dismissal to merit dismissal. Carijano v. Occidental Petroleum Corp., 643 F.3d 1216, 1224 (9th Cir. 2011).
2. Plaintiffs claim that the Court "did not fully consider the unique circumstances of this action" and "did not grant any consideration to the fact that this is not a case involving a Tesla driver versus Tesla the manufacturer," but rather "involves a pedestrian" who was killed "by a sleeping driver whose dozing was enabled by software that Tesla developed and installed in its vehicles."
3. Plaintiffs say that this case involves "product liability issues," and that "any evidence of Tesla vehicle driver negligence is neither relevant nor necessary to the 'efficient resolution of Plaintiff' actual claims."
4. Plaintiffs' move for reconsideration is denied because the Court finds that the requirements for setting aside the Order under 'Rule 60(b)' have not been met.[95]

Findings:

Such factors were judged by the district court to be present in this case. Although "relevant evidence is located in both California and Japan," the court noted that "[m]ost of the evidence referenced by Plaintiffs concerns the design of Autopilot and is in the ownership of Tesla," suggesting that Tesla might provide it in a Japanese court.[96]

In addition, the district court's dismissal was contingent on Tesla's willingness to allow the Umedas to depose the company under Federal Rule of Civil Procedure 30(b) (6).[97]

The requirements of a party's notice of deposition or subpoena sent to an organisation, that is, where 'the deponent' named is "a public or private company, a partnership, an association, a governmental agency, or other body" are described in this 'Rule. 30(b)(6) of the Federal Rules of Civil Procedure'.[98]

Finally, the district court evaluated whether a Japanese court's judgement might be enforced. The Umedas do not, and could not, allege that the district court neglected to examine this element. Tesla's dismissal was contingent on its "agreement[ment] to the enforcement of any Japanese judgement achieved by Plaintiffs in Japan, California, and elsewhere in the United States where Tesla has assets," according to the district court.[99]

---

[95] Ibid.

[96] Ibid.

[97] Ibid.

[98] Ibid.

[99] Ibid.

Despite the fact that this panel may have reached a different conclusion in the first instance, it cannot be inferred that the district court abused its discretion in assessing the private interest elements and dismissing them for forum non-convenience.[100]

It has been alleged that wrongful death, negligence, strict liability, and other claims based on an auto-accident and death resulted when Tesla's allegedly defective Autopilot features caused the car to accelerate into a group of pedestrians. An appeal has been filed against the same; the appeal filed number is *No.21–15,286 (9*th *Cir. Feb.18, 2021).*[101]

Plaintiffs have not shown that the Court erred in concluding that this matter incorporates both *product liability and negligence claims* and that both forums are interested in it.

Judgement:

Plaintiffs' move for reconsideration is denied because the Court finds that the requirements for setting aside the Order under Federal Rule of Civil Procedure 60(b) have not been met. Plaintiffs' move for reconsideration under Rules 59(e) and 60(b) is refused for the reasons stated above. ***The court found Tesla (the manufacturer) accountable for both product liability and negligence claims.***[102]

4.7 Determination of Criminal Liability in India

Though by "**Section 2** of the **Bharatiya Nyaya Sanhita, 2023**, ***'every person'*** is liable to punishment under the **Bharatiya Nyaya Sanhita, 2023** so the word *'person'* includes ***a company or association*** under '**Section 2(26)** of **BNS**'." Thus, a ***corporation*** is liable to punishment under the Sanhita.

Whether by this logic that Bharatiya Nyaya Sanhita, 2023 is applicable to ***every person***, it would be applicable to AI-*AVs* also? Perhaps, due to the fact that AVs are utilised to relieve the driver, corporate criminal liability is also essential to fix the liability of the manufacturer. What should the law do if the criminally responsible entity (automaker) is also a legal company?[103]

Offences in Relation to Use of Motor Vehicles which are punishable under Bharatiya Nyaya Sanhita, 2023.

1. Rash Driving or Riding on Public Way under 'Section 281 of Bharatiya Nyaya Sanhita, 2023'.[104]

---

[100] Ibid.

[101] *See* <https://iclg.com/practice-areas/product-liability-laws-and-regulations/2-U-S-product-liability-law-recent-developments-trends-and-future-outlook>, accessed on June 25, 2023.

[102] *Supra* note 94.

[103] *See* <https://www.mdpi.com/2032-6653/12/2/62/htm>, accessed on September 25, 2023.

[104] "***Section 281 BNS:*** *states that whoever drives any vehicle or rides on any public way in manner so rash and negligent as to endanger human life or to be likely to cause hurt or injury to any other person shall be punished with imprisonment of either description for a term which may extend*

2. Causing Death by Negligence under 'Section 106 of Bharatiya Nyaya Sanhita, 2023'.[105]
3. Act Endangering Life or Personal Safety of Others under 'Section 125 of Bharatiya Nyaya Sanhita, 2023'.[106]
4. Causing Hurt by Act Endangering Life or Personal Safety of Others under 'Section 125 (a) of Bharatiya Nyaya Sanhita, 2023'.[107]
5. Causing Grievous Hurt by Act Endangering Life or Personal Safety of Others under 'Section 125(b) of Bharatiya Nyaya Sanhita, 2023'.[108]

4.7.1 Determination of Criminal Liability of AI in India

Whether these provisions cover AVs also The present research has tried to analyse whether these provisions under the Indian law are adequate to determine the criminal liability in the case of autonomous vehicles? The applicability of these provisions to AVs.

---

to six months or with fine which may extend to one thousand rupees or with both. The offence is cognizable and bailable and triable by the Magistrate having territorial jurisdiction over the area wherein such offence has been committed".

[105] "***Section 106 BNS:*** *dealing with causing death by negligence, whoever causes the death of any person by doing any rash or negligent act not amounting to culpable homicide shall be punished with imprisonment of either description for a term which may extend to five years or with fine or both. The offence under this section is cognizable and bailable and triable by the Magistrate of the first class. This section has been couched in* general *terms, based on the main ingredients of 'rash and negligent act' which would; naturally, include the act of 'rash and negligent driving*".

[106] "***Section 125 BNS:*** *deals with Act Endangering Life or Personal Safety of Others. It is provided in the act that whoever does any act so rashly or negligently as to endanger human life of the personal safety of others shall be punished with imprisonment of either description for a term which may extend to three months, or with fine which may extend to Rs. 2500/-, or with both. The offence under this section, as under section 281, is an offence independent of its consequences, and if consequences also follow, the offence would become aggravated and taken account of under* **sections 125 and 125(a)**. *The offence under section 125 is cognizable and bailable and triable by the Magistrate having territorial jurisdiction over the area wherein such offence has been committed*".

[107] "***Section 125(a) BNS:*** *deals with cases causing hurt act endangering life or personal safety of others. It is as stated below: whoever causes hurt to any person by doing any act so rashly or negligently as to endanger human life or the personal safety of others, shall be punished with imprisonment of either description for a term which may extend to six months, or with fine which may extend to five thousand rupees, or with both. The offence under section 125(a) is cognizable and bailable and triable by the Magistrate having territorial jurisdiction over the area wherein such offence has been committed*".

[108] "***Section 125(b) BNS:*** *deals with cases causing grievous hurt by acts endangering life or personal safety of others and it states that whoever causes grievous hurt to any person by doing any act so rashly or negligence as to endanger human life, or the personal safety of others, shall be punished with imprisonment of either description for a term which may extend to three years, or with fine which may extend to ten thousand rupees, or with both. The offence under section 125(b) is cognizable and bailable and triable by the Magistrate having territorial jurisdiction over the area wherein such offence has been committed*".

A comprehensive analysis of these provisions reveals existing provisions such as Rash Driving or Riding on Public Way under 'Section 281 of Bharatiya Nyaya Sanhita, 2023'.[109] Causing Death by Negligence under 'Section 106 of Bharatiya Nyaya Sanhita, 2023'.[110] Act Endangering Life or Personal Safety of Others' under 'Section 125 of Bharatiya Nyaya Sanhita, 2023'.[111] Causing Hurt by Act Endangering Life or Personal Safety of Others under 'Section 125(a) of Bharatiya Nyaya Sanhita, 2023'.[112] Causing Grievous Hurt by Act Endangering Life or Personal Safety of Others under 'Section 125(b) of Bharatiya Nyaya Sanhita, 2023'[113]who are held liable for negligence and subject to punishment under criminal law. In these circumstances, the human driver monitors the driving environment since it must be regarded from the perspective of 'SAE Level 0–2', where the car is perfectly under the control of the human driver. The author will now investigate whether the same law applies in negligence situations ranging from 'SAE Level 0 to 2' and 'SAE Level 3–5'.

When comparing existing provisions in the criminal law of negligence connected to traditional driving, such as 'Sections (281, 106, 125, 125(a), 125(b)) BNS, 2023',[114] to 'SAE Level 0 to 5', autonomous driving, the outcome is as follows:

Section 281: Negligent manslaughter—Whoever drives a vehicle or rides on a public route in such a reckless and careless manner as to threaten human life or to be likely to cause harm or injury to another person shall be punished with either imprisonment for a term of up to six months or a fine of up to one thousand rupees, or both.[115] In this context, whoever is considered a natural and legal person is true to SAE Level 0–3 but not to a highly and fully autonomous system, because autonomous systems are independent in their actions and reasoning, whereas in SAE Level 0–3, humans control and monitor the 'AI agent/tool/machine' on their own, and human intervention is present to control the 'AI agent/tool/machine'. As a result, the author observed that there is a gap in the legislation that does not specifically cover the highly and fully autonomous system. The author proposed that a proper law be put in place to address the current issue, namely 'SAE Levels 4 and 5'.

Section 106[116]*-Causing bodily harm by negligence*—Whoever causes the death of another person by committing any rash or negligent conduct that does not amount to culpable homicide is punishable by imprisonment of any sort for a time up to five years and shall also be liable to fine. In this context, whoever is considered a natural and legal person is true to 'SAE Level 0–3' but not to a highly and fully autonomous system, because autonomous systems are independent in their actions

[109] *See* <https://www.mha.gov.in/sites/default/files/250883_english_01042024.pdf>, accessed on July 1, 2024.

[110] Ibid.

[111] Ibid.

[112] Ibid.

[113] Ibid.

[114] Ibid.

[115] Ibid.

[116] Ibid.

and reasoning, whereas in 'SAE Level 0–3', humans control and monitor the 'AI agent/tool/machine' on their own, and human intervention is present to control the 'AI agent/tool/machine'. As a result, the author observed that there is a gap in the legislation that does not specifically cover the highly and fully autonomous system. The author proposed that a proper law be put in place to address the current issue, namely 'SAE Levels 4 and 5'.

Section 125-Endangering road traffic—Whoever does an act so rashly or negligently as to harm human life or the personal safety of others shall be punished with imprisonment of either sort for a term up to three months, or a fine up to Rs. 2500/-, or both.[117] In this context, whoever is considered a natural and legal person is true to 'SAE Level 0–3' but not to a highly and fully autonomous system, because autonomous systems are independent in their actions and reasoning, whereas in 'SAE Level 0–3', humans control and monitor the 'AI agent/tool/machine' on their own, and human intervention is present to control the 'AI agent/tool/machine'. As a result, the author observed that there is a gap in the legislation that does not specifically cover the highly and fully autonomous system. The author proposed that a proper law be put in place to address the current issue, namely 'SAE Levels 4 and 5'.

"*Section 125 (a)*[118]*-Driving under the influence of drink or drugs only applies to human drivers or car owners*"—Whoever causes harm to another person by acting rashly or negligently in such a way as to endanger human life or the personal safety of others is punishable by imprisonment of either description for a time up to six months, or a fine up to five thousand rupees, or both.[119] In this context, whoever is considered a natural and legal person is true to 'SAE Level 0–3' but not to a highly and fully autonomous system, because autonomous systems are independent in their actions and reasoning, whereas in 'SAE Level 0–3', humans control and monitor the 'AI agent/tool/machine' on their own, and human intervention is present to control the 'AI agent/tool/machine'. As a result, the author observed that there is a gap in the legislation that does not specifically cover the highly and fully autonomous system. The author proposed that a proper law be put in place to address the current issue, namely 'SAE Levels 4 and 5'.

"*Section 125(b)*[120]*-Driving under the influence of drink or drugs only applies to human drivers or car owners*"—Whoever causes serious harm to another by acting rashly or negligently in such a way as to endanger human life or the personal safety of others shall be punished with imprisonment of either sort for a time up to three years, or a fine up to ten thousand rupees, or both. In this context, whoever is considered a natural and legal person is true to 'SAE Level 0–3' but not to a highly and fully autonomous system, because autonomous systems are independent in their actions and reasoning, whereas in 'SAE Level 0–3', humans control and monitor the 'AI

[117] Ibid.
[118] Ibid.
[119] Ibid.
[120] Ibid.

agent/tool/machine' on their own, and human intervention is present to control the 'AI agent/tool/machine'. As a result, the author observed that there is a gap in the legislation that does not specifically cover the highly and fully autonomous system. The author proposed that a proper law be put in place to address the current issue, namely 'SAE Levels 4 and 5'.

In **Level 0**, the full-time performance by the human driver of all aspects of the dynamic driving task, even when enhanced by warning or intervention systems. Who, once again, is in charge of steering and acceleration/deceleration? Who will be held accountable for negligence, now that the answer is a *human driver*. Another aspect of driving a car is the monitoring of the driving environment, which is likewise done by a *human driver*. If a fallback execution of the dynamic driving task is available, who is the performing *human driver*. Is there any capability (driving mode) in the system? The answer is negative. As a result of the author's reasoning, the author believes that SAE Level 0 is true to traditional driving, and thus the same sections will apply to SAE Level 0, namely 'Sections (281, 106, 125, 125(a), 125(b))BNS, 2023'.[121]

In **Level 1** (Driver Assistance), the execution of steering or acceleration/deceleration by a driver assistance system is based on data from the driving environment, with the hope that the human driver will handle the other elements of the dynamic driving task. Who will be held accountable for negligence, now that the answer is a human driver and system. Is there any capability (driving mode) in the system? The answer is some driving modes. As a result of the author's reasoning, the author believes that 'SAE Level 1' is true to traditional driving, and thus the same sections will apply to 'SAE Level 1', namely 'Sections (281, 106, 125, 125(a), 125(b)) BNS, 2023'.[122]

In **Level 2**(Partial Automation), the application of steering and acceleration/deceleration by one or more 'driver assistance systems' in accordance with information about the driving environment, with the hope that the human driver would handle the remaining elements of the 'dynamic driving task'. Here the system is in charge of steering and acceleration/deceleration. Who will be held accountable for negligence, now that the answer is a system.

Another aspect of driving a car is the monitoring of the driving environment, which is likewise done by a human driver. If a fallback execution of the dynamic driving task is available, who is the performing *human driver*. Is there any capability (driving mode) in the system? The answer is some driving modes. As a result of the author's reasoning, the author believes that 'SAE Level 2' is true to traditional driving, and thus the same sections will apply to 'SAE Level 2', namely 'Sections (281, 106, 125, 125(a), 125(b)) BNS, 2023'.[123]

[121] Ibid.

[122] Ibid.

[123] Ibid.

SAE Level 3–5: automated driving system ('system') monitors the driving environment.

In **Level 3** (Conditional Automation), in a certain driving mode, the automated driving system will handle every aspect of the dynamic driving task with the hope that the human driver will react appropriately when asked to intervene. Who, once again, is in charge of steering and acceleration/deceleration? Who will be held accountable for negligence now that the answer is a *system*. Another aspect of driving a car is the monitoring of the driving environment, which is likewise done by a *system*. If a fallback execution of the dynamic driving task is available, who is the performing *human driver*. Is there any capability (driving mode) in the system? The answer is *some driving modes*. The author contends that the human driver/operator and the manufacturer are both guilty under the law of negligence. As a result of the author's reasoning, the author believes that SAE Level 3 is partially true to traditional driving, with the expectation that the human driver will respond properly to a request to intervene and thus the same sections will apply to SAE Level 3, namely 'Sections (281, 106, 125, 125(a), 125(b)) BNS, 2023'.[124]

In **Level 4** (High Automation), the automated driving system's performance of all components of the dynamic driving task in a certain driving mode, even if a human driver does not respond appropriately to a request to intervene. Who, once again, is in charge of steering and acceleration/deceleration? Now that the answer is a *system*, who will be held liable for negligence? Another aspect of driving a car is the monitoring of the driving environment, which is likewise done by a *system*. If a fallback execution of the 'dynamic driving task' is available, who is the performing *system*. Is there any capability (driving mode) in the system? The answer is *some driving modes*.

The author contends that the manufacturer is liable as a result of the arguments presented, but that a sui generis law is needed in Germany to deal with cases of highly autonomous car negligence, or that a place should be made in existing legislation to deal with Level 4 autonomous cars, because the existing provisions only deal with human drivers, not machines or autonomous cars.

In **Level 5** (Full Automation), the performance of all 'dynamic driving task' components by a fully automated driving system in all traffic and environmental circumstances that a human driver is capable of handling. Again, whose responsibility is it to steer and accelerate or decelerate? Now that the answer is a *system*, who will be held liable for negligence? Another aspect of driving a car is the monitoring of the driving environment, which is likewise done by a *system*. If a fallback execution of the dynamic driving task is available, who is the performing *system*. Is there any capability (driving mode) in the system? The answer is *all driving modes*.

The author contends that the manufacturer is liable as a result of the arguments presented, but that a sui generis law is needed in Germany to deal with cases of fully autonomous car negligence, or that a place should be made in existing legislation to

[124] Ibid.

deal with Level 5 autonomous cars, because the existing provisions only deal with human drivers, not machines or autonomous cars.

Grant of Compensation

Hearing of Accused Necessary under '**Section 395(1) of Bharatiya Nagrik Suraksha Sanhita, 2023**'[125] deals with a situation when a court imposes a fine or sentence of which fine also forms a part. It is the court's discretion to order as to how the whole or any part of the fine recovered from being applied. It is a statutory requirement that a fine is imposed for bringing in the application of 'Section 395(1)'. '**Section 395 (5)**[126] provides for the situation where the court imposes the compensation/damages in any subsequent civil suit relating to the same/similar matter'; while awarding compensation/damages, the court is required to take into account any sum paid or recovered as compensation/damages under '**Section 395** of the **Bharatiya Nagrik Suraksha Sanhita, 2023**'.[127]

In what circumstances will the producer be subject to liability? In what circumstances will an individual be subject to liability? It will extensively paint an individual as 'operator' for risk purposes, in any event, when those individuals have not controlled the AI or settled on choices that prompted a mishap. Courts and Statutes impose risk to the individual or Courts and statutes place a risk on the person or people who hurt others, as well as the organisation or organisations that harm them. Furthermore, in the rare 'Act of God' events, the current concept of risk allows an individual who made a decision that resulted in harm. The evolution of AI laws will quickly recognise that risk should extend beyond individual AI insurance: if such protection was set up for when the self-driving vehicle itself is at risk, it would eliminate the need to improperly allot responsibility to the manufacturer, the human 'operator', or an outsider. The fact that AI surgeons, development labourers, and pilots are all in high demand bodes well.

Having said that, there is a corresponding need for more modest AI-gadgets, where obligation may not be as obvious for more basic AI-gadgets. This does not speak well in situations where risk isn't as obvious. When an Al specialist's 'action' (or 'oversight') results in a positive outcome, a request for crediting criminal risk arises. The facts of each case, as set forth below, will have a significant bearing on how and whether criminal guilt should be credited. Procedures and concepts that are frequently employed in criminal law may offer the remedy in each of these situations. Nevertheless, the focus will shift to how legal experts, administrators, judges, and professionals will change, improve, or choose to firmly grasp their current understandings of these ideas.[128]

---

[125] See <https://www.livelaw.in/pdf_upload/bharatiya-nagarik-suraksha-sanhita-511325.pdf>, accessed on July 4, 2024.

[126] Ibid.

[127] Ibid.

[128] *Id.* at 14.

4.8 Defences for AV Litigation

When litigation in this area arises, the AV manufacturers resort to the following five categories of defences.[129]

1. **Seek to Assign Liability to the Driver and/or Injured Party.**
2. **Claim the Accident Was Unavoidable.**
3. **Deny the Existence of a Defect.**
4. **Rely on Industry Standards.**
5. **Use Another Defence.**[130]

1. ***Assigning the liability on the Driver and/or an Injured Party*, in this case, AV manufacturers**[131] are in profits from the post-accident investigations either explicitly or implicitly relative to the assigned fault among the involved parties.[132] For example, the police report regarding the non-fatal AV crash with the motorcyclist in California presumed that the motorcyclist was liable for the mishap since he endeavoured to pass the AV before it was protected to do so much.[133]

Also, police expressed the transporter (truck driver) in Las Vegas was at fault for manoeuvring into Google's AV bus.[134]

Manufacturers should decide whether to blame the driver and the casualty in fatal accidents, notwithstanding the risk of unwanted media and probable negative jury reactions.[135] Producers could make a defence for basically fractional risk by the people involved in each of the three fatal incidents. For example, the National Highway Traffic Safety Administration (NHTSA) located the driver responsible for the Florida accident, which included the semi-truck.[136]

2. ***Claim the Accident Was Unavoidable*,** in this case, either the human driver or automated system could have claimed that an accident was unavoidable

---

[129] *See* Patrick H. Reilly and Elsa M. Bullard (2018), "5 Defenses for Autonomous Vehicles Litigation", Faegre Drinker: Delaware, USA (September 04); accessible at https://www.faegredrinker.com/en/insights/publications/2018/9/5-defenses-for-autonomous-vehicles-litigation;, accessed on September 27, 2023.

[130] Ibid.

[131] Ibid.

[132] Ibid.

[133] Samuel Gibbs, *Self-Driving Bus Involved In Crash Less Than Two Hours After Las Vegas Launch, THE GUARDIAN* (Nov.2017), https://www.theguardian.com/technology/2017/nov/09/self-driving-bus-crashes-two-hours-after-las-vegas-launch-truck-autonomous-vehicle.

[134] NHTSA, *Special Crash Investigations: On-Site Automated Driver Assistance System Crash Investigation of the 2015 Tesla Model S 70D*, at 25, Jan. 2018), https://crashstats.nhtsa.dot.gov/Api/Public/ViewPublication/812481.

[135] *Supra* note 129.

[136] RJ Vogt, *GM Settles First-Known Suit Over Self-Driving Car Crash, LAW 360* (June 1, 2018), https://www.law360.com/productliability/articles/1049776/gm-settles-first-known-suit-over-self-driving-car-crash?nl_pk=3d8c97a2-7cc2-441b-b37f-56ef00851488&utm_source=newsletter&utm_medium=email&utm_campaign=productliability.

under the given circumstances. Therefore, it leads to collision—another potential defence.[137] Legal Scholar Bryant Walker Smith made a hypothesis. He laid down how it could determine that an automated driving system was at fault for not functioning properly when it was being controlled and appropriately regulated under the given circumstances by the human driver or a comparable automated driving system. So, to date, no court or regulator has established the standard of reasonableness for operating an autonomous vehicle.[138]

Advanced AVs technology permits greater accuracy in assessments.[139] The investigators have gathered data from onboard event data recorders (EDRs) to observe how a vehicle behaved at the time of the collision, and what precisely the systems were being used leading up to/during the collision, and to further analyse those systems whether it functioned adequately or not? More data will be available to assess the liability in an accident due to an increase in AVs.[140]

3. ***Denies the Existence of a Defect*, 'National Highway Traffic Safety Administration (NHTSA)'** explicitly[141] asserted that there was no design defect of any sort in the autonomous vehicle. In the case of the Florida accident, for example, NHTSA[142] investigated to find out the reason for its collision and came to the conclusion that the autopilot function was structured or designed only to prevent Tesla cars from rear-ending other vehicles, instead of handling situations where vehicles crossed the road from intersecting roadways.[143] Since it has been seen that the self-driving system was not intended to handle the situations of the collision, NHTSA lastly concluded that there was no design defect or the performance of AV.[144]

---

[137] Bryant Smith, *Automated Driving and Product Liability*, 2017 *MICH. ST. L. REV.* 1, 6 (2017).

[138] *Supra* note 129.

[139] Ibid.

[140] Tina Bellon, *Fatal U.S. Self-Driving Auto Accident Raises Novel Legal Questions*, *REUTERS* (March 20, 2020), https://www.reuters.com/article/us-autos-selfdriving-uber-liability-anal/fatal-u-s-self-driving-auto-accident-raises-novel-legal-questions-idUSKBN1GW2SP; see also https://www.nhtsa.gov/research-data/event-data-recorder (defining EDR).

[141] *Supra* note 129.

[142] Ibid.

[143] NHTSA, *Special Crash Investigations: On-Site Automated Driver Assistance System Crash Investigation ofthe2015TeslaModelS70D* (Jan.2018), https://crashstats.nhtsa.dot.gov/Api/Public/ViewPublication/812481

[144] *Supra* note 129.

Courts are of the view that "*an automobile manufacturer is under no duty to design an accident-proof or fool-proof vehicle.*" Therefore, the manufacturer should rely on this setting principle, but this defence gets weakened when any accident circumstances are regular in occurrence.[145] Taking an example of the truck-crossing the highway was a legal manoeuvre or uncommon. Courts perhaps should devise a balancing test to make the manufacturer liable or determine the manufacturer's liability.[146]

4. ***Rely on Industry Standard*, as an 'industry standard' is developing, NHTSA**[147] has published specific guidelines, but it lacks a regulatory framework. Manufacturers are hesitant to share their aspects of businesses because most of the technology is a trade secret.[148] Now the earliest cases of AV negligence would likely to on experts—asserting what is 'reasonable', with an idea of 'industry standards', which is developing slowly with the help of case laws, government regulations, AV manufacturer practises, and procedures involved.[149]
5. ***Use another Defence*, if a manufacturer/manufacturer organisation using AVs**[150] has compelled analysts or 'safety drivers' to sign waivers or similar agreements before driving AVs, this could provide liability protection to manufacturers.[151] In a well-drafted agreement, the driver would agree to observe specified safety procedures and refund and keep the Company harmless from the consequences of violating the requirements.[152] Abuse or danger-related safeguards could also be used by AV makers. Author points out that manufacturers are powerless to prevent a motorist from anticipating the dangers of operating a car with new and unproven technology. Manufacturers[153] have a better chance of effectively combating abuse or presumption of hazard by highlighting a driver's

---

145 Ibid.

146 *Larsen v. General Motors Corp.*, 391 F. 2d 495, 502 (8th Cir. 1968).

147 *Supra* note 129.

148 Ibid.

149 NHTSA, *Automated Driving Systems 2.0: A Vision for Safety* (Sept. 2017), https://www.nhtsa.gov/sites/nhtsa.dot.gov/files/documents/13069a-ads2.0_090617_v9a_tag.pdf.

150 *Supra* note 129.

151 Ibid.

152 Stephen S. Wu, *Product Liability Issues in the US and Associated Risk Management, in AUTONOMES FAHREN* 587 (2015).

153 *Supra* note 129.

lead/conduct if there is proof that a driver has manhandled or changed the sensors or control frameworks,[154] especially if such activities are in opposition to the organisation's express client instructions. Producers may benefit from a 'state-of-the-art' precaution to a plan imperfection guarantee because this technology is new and evolving.[155]

Manufacturers could argue that they couldn't have produced a better safe plan at the time of the transaction because such plans were not technologically feasible at the time.[156] Respondents or defendants can invoke the economic loss argument if the only damage done is to the actual AV. This express product liability defence bars—'product liability' civil actions where the harms are entirely or solely financial, and not for bodily injury, harm, or property damage other than the AV.[157]

4.9 Conclusion

Similarly, cybercrime is a new important problem that must be addressed by the application of criminal codes, regulatory standards, and technical standards.[158]

Prone to Hacking—Autonomous automobiles, which track and analyse the owner's details in real time, could be the next big target for hackers. This could lead to the acquisition of personal information.

The majority of potential crimes that may develop as a result of the usage of autonomous cars are crimes against life and health (particularly unintended offences such as causing another's death, bodily injury or disease, or putting another at risk). In terms of intent, it's also worth considering whether a fully automated system may conduct an intentional crime. However, a relatively recent phenomenon, cybercrime, must not be overlooked. Because AVs are managed by a type of software facility that can be the target of a variety of hacker assaults, it is critical to provide proper safety

---

[154] Ibid.

[155] *Id.*

[156] *Supra* note 129.

[157] *Id.*

[158] Muhammad Uzair (2021), "Who Is Liable When a Driverless Car Crashes?", *World Electric Vehicle Journal*, 12(**2**): 62, MDPI journals; doi https://doi.org/10.3390/wevj12020062; accessed on September 27, 2023.

to vehicle users. On the one hand, there is the criminal component of cybercrime protection provided by criminal regulations, and on the other hand, there is the development of adequate security systems governed by technological norms and standards.

Not only will legal, civil, driving, and criminal liability shift as a result of AVs, but ethical issues will as well. The next chapter covers the ethical considerations surrounding AVs.

Chapter 5
Ethical Issues Related to Artificial Intelligence in Autonomous Cars

Abstract This chapter critically analyses the options which are available to humans when it comes to coding ethics into machines, and excluding any biasness into it—how ethically and morally will it sound logical and rational, so based on determinative parameters, a person using a technology, whereby that technology does not pose an increased risk of harm upon others—should still be required to abide by the duties to proper functions like monitor, select, operate and maintain technology in use, which upon failing to make them liable for breach of those duties—if it is at fault. Lastly, it talks about setting up the limits or parameters like what parameters should it set when it comes to practising ethics, should it be geographic-specific (country-specific), or it should be ethical from the perspective of developer/programmer or from the perspective of the users—who will use AI system.

5.1 Introduction to AI Ethics

Autonomous vehicles (AVs) are vehicles that can sense their surroundings and operate with little or no human intervention. While the concept of self-driving cars has been known since the 1920s, technology has only recently advanced to the point where AVs are now being seen on public roads.

In the functioning of AI, ethical norms such as privacy, surveillance, biasness, unfairness, and discrimination are violated. Automobiles, drones, and robots all use AI that has these implications and ethical effects. A violation of the code or policies will occur if the ethical guidelines are not followed. Still, it is not a crime (civil or criminal) because a violation of ethics is not a crime in the eyes of the law. AI is a futuristic technology which violates ethical standards. As a result, there is a need for clear standards, a code, or a soft law governing AI ethics. This chapter investigates different ethical dilemmas and their ramifications.

Why is it necessary to follow ethical rules when it comes to the operation or programming of AI? How would it affect the people who are a part of this complete ecosystem, including the common man and customers, if it is not followed?

S. Fahim, *Ethico-Legal Aspect of AI-driven Driverless Cars*, Frontiers of Artificial Intelligence, Ethics and Multidisciplinary Applications,
https://doi.org/10.1007/978-981-97-6883-7_5

AI systems are undeniably powerful tools. Furthermore, like all powerful tools, AI must take great care in its development and deployment. The first step in this process is to build systems that can be trusted. AI will require a framework of best practises that incorporates appropriate values and ensures ethical behaviour, including alignment with social norms and contracts, algorithmic responsibility, and explanation capabilities. It also includes compliance with existing legislation and policy, assurance of the integrity of the data, algorithms, and systems, and protection of privacy and personal information through inclusion which has the ability to participate in areas of life that are meaningful to everyone, be it political, economic, cultural, or social. Inclusion in AI is the ability to imagine and achieve a good life in every meaningful area, from research to open data and skills development. Every initiative canters on using AI for social development and inclusive growth from indigenous rights and gender equality from cleaner water to energy conservation. AI technologies have a lesser-known list of potential benefits and opportunities for future inclusion.

Boddington[1] says. *"AI is raising all of those questions. It's almost impossible to say what AI ethics is about in general because there are so many applications. But one key issue is what happens when AI replaces or supplements human agency, a question which goes to the heart of our understandings of ethics."*[2]

Nevertheless, AI makes this problematic. Because of the 'black box' problem, which is any artificial intelligence system (AI) whose inputs and activities are hidden from the user or another interested party is considered to be an AI system. In general, a black box is an impenetrable mechanism.

Boddington[3] suggests *"If you can't guarantee that you can control it, at least you could have as much transparency as possible in terms of telling people how much you know and how much you don't know and what the risks are."*

Boddington defines ethics as "Ethics concerns how we justify ourselves to others. So transparency is a key ethical virtue."

This chapter focuses on different ethical issues which arise in the functioning of an AI. The limitations of this research study are to understand the ethical issues with respect to the functioning of the AVs in particular and a few other issues of AI will be discussed in general.

5.1.1 AVs Ethics in Context of Autonomous Cars

Ethics is defined as the moral principles governing the behaviour or actions of an individual or a group. Ethics are the rules which help us determine what is right and what is wrong. The ethics of AI lies in the ethical quality of the predictions,

---

[1] Paula Boddington, Myth and the EU study on Civil Law Rules in Robotics (January 12, 2017).

[2] Boddington, P. (2017). Towards a code of ethics for artificial intelligence (pp. 27–37). Cham: Springer. See <https://futureoflife.org/2017/07/31/towards-a-code-of-ethics-in-artificial-intelligence>, accessed on September 29, 2023.

[3] Supra note 2.

ethical quality of an end outcome drawn out of that, and the ethical quality of the impact on humans. Harm is caused when a prognosis or an end outcome negatively impacts an individual's ability to establish their rightful personhood (identify) or access resources.

From a technical perspective, it may turn into biasness based on an over-evaluation of the actual capabilities of the most advanced robots. If taken from a legal and ethical perspective, creating a legal personality for an AI is inappropriate, whatever the legal status model suggests. AI's legal status cannot be derived from the Natural Person model because then the AI would hold human rights, such as the right to its integrity, remuneration, citizenship, and dignity, so forth, thus, directly confronting Human rights. That would contradict the 'Charter of Fundamental Rights of the European Union and the Convention for the Protection of Human Rights and Fundamental Freedoms'.

i. ***Ethical responsibility***

Who is legally accountable for automaton crashes, and how (if at all) should victims be paid when vehicles driven by an algorithm cause injury? If the courts are unable to settle this issue, automaton manufacturers may face unanticipated fees, discouraging investment. However, if victims are not adequately compensated, the public is unlikely to trust or accept autonomous vehicles. In unclear situations, or 'no-win' situations, 'SAE Level 4–5' self-driving automobile will need to make decisions. However, in the absence of legal guidance, whatever ethical approach or philosophy should AVs be designed to follow? As *'Lin* et al.*'* point out, a variety of strategies can result in a range of results, including the frequency of deadly collisions.[4]

Furthermore, what needs to be looked into is what are the different ethical issues, *namely* privacy, responsibility, safety, transparency, and security, and who should decide on the autonomous vehicle's ethics: drivers, passengers, manufacturers, or politicians? Engineers, drivers, or the autonomous driving system itself? According to Loh and Loh,[5] on the other hand, Millar[6] thinks that the technology's user, in this instance, the user of an autonomous vehicle ought to possess the liberty to select the ethical or conduct norms that the AVs should follow.[7] He contends that if engineers designed cars without first consulting the driver or disclosing to the user how the vehicle will operate, there would be a moral uproar. He cites doctors as an example to show how they lack the moral standing to decide on major end-of-life care decisions without the informed agreement of their patients.[8]

---

[4] Supra note 2.

[5] Supra note 2.

[6] Ibid.

[7] See <https://www.europarl.europa.eu/RegData/etudes/STUD/2020/634452/EPRS_STU(2020)634452_EN.pdf, accessed on October 2, 2023.

[8] Ibid.

Developmental in Ethical dilemmas

The EU Parliament paper[9] mentions the Open Roboethics initiative[10] which had conducted a poll in 2014, people were questioned about how they believed an autonomous vehicle with them as a passenger should respond if a child crossed in front of it on a busy highway.[10] The car would not have enough time to brake in time to save the child, and instead would swerve into the tunnel's walls, killing the passenger. This is a variation on the famous 'trolley dilemma', in which one must choose between diverting a runaway trolley away from a path that would harm multiple people and diverting it away from a path that would only harm one person.[11]

It would be impractical to ask for the passenger's opinion in every case. Millar,[12] on the other hand, proposes a 'setup' approach in which upon purchasing a new car, users have the option to select their ethics settings. However, if a user configured their vehicle to constantly avoid automobile collisions by veering towards bikes, this may be considered deliberate damage. This would shift responsibility away from manufacturers and raise the user's accountability and obligation.[13]

5.1.2 *Reliance on the Scope of AI System in Terms of Ethics*

I. ***Trust and AI***

On the one hand, AVs aim to save lives. However, if there were to be a catastrophic accident, who would be morally responsible for those unethical digital choices? would be deciphered with the help of a black box.

Codes are used to operate autonomous vehicles to offer them reasonable and impartial choices and responses inside milliseconds due to their sensory perception, hence, letting lose the people's consideration on the driving process. Though AV is driving smoother and will keep away from moronic, human, or misrepresenting driving conduct to arrive at the objective securely. The self-driving vehicles will confront unavoidable crashes likewise, which will then, at that point, be covered and executed by the code. Initially, the self-driving car issue creates an ethical dilemma in which a person must choose which route a car should go on. The leader is aware that there are two persons or a youngster on one path while there is only one person or an elderly person on the other. This model serves as an example of utilitarian decision-making. But it shouldn't be forgotten that individuals regularly deliver and create the code that gives these impartial directives. As a result, this work cannot avoid an

[9] Ibid.

[10] Ibid.

[11] Ibid.

[12] Ibid.

[13] Ibid.

inevitable ethical conundrum and raises a number of questions and problems relating to radical emotional decisions made by individuals and carried out by codes.[14]

The decisions humans make and incorporate into the coding of AVs further add to the ethical dilemma. As an illustration, consider an autonomous vehicle moving through a metropolis.

Motorcars are approaching from the left. On the right hand vehicles are left along the road.

Out of nowhere, a passer-by is strolling into the path of the vehicle.

To arrive at a conclusion, code the three alternative events[15]:

(1) The vehicle can attempt to back off yet calculates that even with a crisis slowing down; it will not stop before the passer-by. Instead, it will collide with the person on foot who will bite the dust because of the mishap. The tenants of the AV will get under a considerably less extreme crash. The result will be one dead individual. However, the self-driving model distinguishes two different choices.
(2) When the next one comes, the car can reverse and turn into the oncoming traffic. The two occupants will be killed or suffer serious injuries when the AV collides with another car. The outcome may be around two fatalities, assuming one fatality per car.
(3) The third possible scenario is that the self-driving car impacts the departing vehicles as it is moving to the side.[16] Due to the heavy strike, the incident will very certainly result in fatalities for anyone inside the vehicles. If there is only one person in the AV, the outcome will be about one dead person. Alternative no. two (2)[17] will not be executed through the code because, in this way, more than two individuals will bite the dust. However, whether elective decision one (1) or three (3) will happen is up to the product designer[18] 'coding the AI system'.[20]

Thus, this individual[19] chooses by coding the vehicle programming how the vehicle ought to respond in a particular future case.[20] Now, the case above is a basic one, with only three prospects. Even though it is a straightforward case, the choice the coder needs to program is deadly for one of the members in that occurrence. This way, the product designer must be conscientious, watchful, and capable of coding such crisis plans before they entirely have happened.

In this manner, artificial intelligence consciousness can identify comparative scenarios and provide solutions to previously unknown crises, even if they have not been fully trained. Though, a human driver in a non-autonomous vehicle additionally has the obligation of a lethal/fatal accident. The ethical dilemma at hand is

---

[14] Supra note 2.

[15] (Li, Zhang, Wang, Li, & Liao, 2018).

[16] Winkler, K-C. (2019). Autonomous Vehicles Regulation in Germany and the US and Its Impact on the German Car Industry (Master Thesis, Tilburg Law School, Tilburg University, Tilburg). See < https://arno.uvt.nl/show.cgi?fid=149595>, accessed on October 1, 2023.

[17] Ibid.

[18] Supra note 16.

[19] Ibid.

[20] Ibid.

that, rather than a programmer ahead of the decision point at any time that it would be necessary, this task is shifting away from the driver, who is allegedly in a better position to evaluate and make a decision on the situation.[21]

To this end, companies like IBM have made great strides, both internally and with other AI stakeholders. In 2016, IBM published one of the first corporate white papers on the ethics of AI: Learning to trust artificial intelligence systems—Accountability, compliance, and ethics in the age of intelligent machines.

Moreover, IBM has built up the Principles for Transparency and Trust in the Cognitive Era. This report is valuable for any business or association engaged with the improvement of AI frameworks and applications. The centre of these standards includes the following:

- It trusts AI's motivation is to augment human knowledge.
- It will be straightforward about when and where AI is connected and about the data and training that went into its proposals.
- It trusts our customers' information, and bits of knowledge are theirs.
- It is focused on helping students, workers, and citizens obtain the abilities to draw in securely, safely, and adequately with intellectual frameworks and to do the new sorts of work that will develop in a cognitive economy.

Certain that if everyone works together and AI is carefully developed, it will vastly improve the various frameworks that support life on this planet.

ii. ***Humans: The Ethical Loop***

It is generally acknowledged that modern AI systems are immoral. Sentience and sapience are the two fixed requirements that are typically considered as pertinent to the ethical level, either taken independently or in combination (or personhood). These could be described as follows: **Sentience**: It means the ability to have an extraordinary experience, like feeling pain and suffering.

Sapience: A set of abilities associated with higher intelligence/quotients, such as self-awareness and being a reason-giving agent.

This analogy has one thing in common: a lot of animals have a lot of experience, hence they have ethical standing. However, it consistently overlooks the analysis of the fact that only humans possess sapience, which elevates them above all other non-human creatures in terms of ethics.[22] According to the paradigm of ethical status, an AI system[23] would have some ethical status if it had the ability to exist. Imagine that people with severe mental impairment are often mistakenly referred to as 'marginal humans' because they fall short of the sapience requirements. On the

---

[21] (Beck, 2017), (Prof. Dr. Hilgendorf, 2017).

[22] Winkler, K-C. (2019). Autonomous Vehicles Regulation in Germany and the US and Its Impact on the German Car Industry (Master Thesis, Tilburg Law School, Tilburg University, Tilburg). One perspective on ethical status suggests that it is not on a spectrum, but rather some beings have more significant interests than others. For example, it could be argued that saving a human is more important than saving a bird, as the human has a greater stake in preserving their life.

[23] Ibid.

other hand,[24] some non-human creatures, such as big apes, may have at least some of the characteristics of sapience.[25] In line with the aforementioned illustration, many but not many contest the complete ethical standing of so-called 'marginal humans'. Some argue that there may be additional criteria an object must have in order to qualify as a carrier of ethical level, such as belonging to a species that typically possesses sentience or sapience[26] or having a close relationship with another being that also possesses ethical status. For the current discussion, let's focus on the criteria of sapience and sentience.[27]

This perspective suggests that an AI system[28] would have moral status if it has the ability to experience sensations and feelings such as pain. Even without advanced cognitive abilities or language, a sentient AI system is not merely an inanimate object; it is more comparable to a living being. Just as it is wrong to cause unnecessary harm to a mouse without a valid moral reason, the same would apply to any sentient AI system. If an AI system possesses sapience and sentience similar to that of an average adult human, it would have the same ethical status as a human being. At present, AI systems do not meet ethical standards because they lack sapience or sentience until they reach SAE Level 4–5.[29]

5.2 Ethical Issues Involved in the Deployment of AI in Case of Autonomous Vehicles.

AVs Ethical Issues Involved

I. ***Impact on Employment and Livelihood***

As we know, Artificial Intelligence algorithms play a huge role in this modern society.

AI has been replacing humans in all the sectors and hence it's causing unemployment and affecting the livelihood of humans. According to different research methodologies, for instance, artificial intelligence will replace between 9 per cent and 47 per cent of employment, depending on whether the entire occupation is automated or simply a single task. Over the course of the next ten years, AI could eliminate 375 million jobs and displace up to one billion employment globally. By 2030, artificial intelligence (AI) could generate $15.7 trillion in economic output, 58 million new jobs, and help employees use their creativity more.[30]

---

[24] Adler, R., Bunte, A., Burton, S., Großmann, J., Jaschke, A., Kleen, P., ... & Tcholtchev, N. V. (2022). Deutsche Normungsroadmap Künstliche Intelligenz. See < https://www.dke.de/resource/blob/2017010/99bc6d952073ca88f52c0ae4a8c351a8/nr-ki-english--download-data.pdf >, accessed on October 1, 2023.

[25] Ibid.

[26] Supra note 24.

[27] Supra note 24.

[28] Supra note 24.

[29] Supra note 24.

[30] See https://www.zippia.com/advice/ai-job-loss-statistics/, accessed on October 2, 2023.

As with the digital and internet revolutions, one key issue is that of job loss. In the industrial revolution, factories replaced legions of workers who performed identical paintings by hand, giving way to the quicker and more fantastic green automation techniques. Within the internet revolution, online ventures, including Amazon.com, eBay, and even smaller "e-tailors," are nevertheless edging out brick-and-mortar retailers, who have a good deal better overhead and running fees, of which labour is one of the largest.

Certain occupations, most notably bus, taxi, and truck drivers, are expected to be jeopardised as AVs become more common.

Truck drivers in the medium term face the highest risk since long-distance truckers are at the forefront of AV technology.[31] *'A self-driving truck'* completed the first commercial beer delivery in 2016 across a 120-mile route without the assistance of a person.[34] The first fully autonomous voyage in a self-driving truck took place in 2017, with the AV travelling seven miles without a single human on board.[32]

In the long run, as more buses become driverless, bus drivers are likely to lose their employment. Several cities throughout the world, including Edinburgh,[33] New York,[34] and Singapore, have declared intentions to use self-driving shuttles in the future.[35]

The Las Vegas shuttle had a difficult start when it was involved in an accident on its first day of operation, but this ambition has already become a reality in some places,[36] and tourists in the small Swiss town of Neuhausen Rheinfall may already ride a AVs bus to see the local waterfalls.[37] In the longer term, self-driving buses will most likely be limited to routes with 100% dedicated bus lanes.

Nonetheless, in the United States, tensions have already arisen between organised labour and city officials as a result of the advancement of self-driving shuttles.[38] In 2017, the Transport Workers Union of America created a coalition to prevent autonomous buses from being introduced to Ohio's roadways.[39] Fully autonomous taxis will most likely be a long way off until AV technology has been thoroughly tested and proven at levels 4 and 5. Nonetheless, with plans to implement self-driving taxis in London by 2021[40] and an automated taxi service now operational in Arizona,[41] it's easy to see why taxi drivers are concerned.

---

[31] Supra note 7.

[32] Ibid.

[33] Ibid.

[34] Ibid. Isaac, 2016.

[35] Supra note 7.

[36] Ibid.

[37] Ibid.

[38] Ibid'.

[39] Ibid.

[40] Ibid.

[41] Sage, 2019.

Manual labour and duplicate tasks are among the jobs most at risk of being automated by artificial intelligence. Bookkeeping, proofreading, retail and courier services, security guards, and even doctors are all examples.[42]

Soft abilities such as creativity, common sense, judgement, and communication are less likely to be mechanised by artificial intelligence. Writers, lawyers, scientists, graphic designers, and software engineers are just a few examples.[43]

It's anticipated that roughly 42% of the employment lost during the COVID-19 pandemic will be gone for good because of AI. While there are definitely other variables at play in the disappearance of these employment, AI's impact on the issue cannot be overlooked.[44]

Because technology cannot become sick and is typically less expensive than human employees, the pandemic has prompted a shift away from people to technology.

In terms of the future, computers are poised to take over 47% of U.S. occupations, with those in data collecting and processing being the most vulnerable. AI, on the other hand, is unlikely to have a significant impact on vocations that need social interaction or a certain set of skills.[48]

ii. ***Control and the Ethical Use[45]—or Misuse—of Artificial Intelligence[46]***

With more sophisticated and complex new AI, comes the possibility of more sophisticated and complex misuse.[47] Individual[48] information can be used maliciously or for profit, systems can be hacked, and technology can be exploited. This is related to informed use and public awareness: as it approaches a fresh era of AI, utilising modern systems and technologies[49] arising that have never been deployed before, citizens must be informed about the risks that may arise from their use or misuse.[50]

'*The Institute of Electrical and Electronics Engineers*(IEEE)'[51] The proposal introduces new methods for educating the public about ethics and security concerns. One example is the inclusion of a 'data privacy' warning on smart devices that gather personal data. The aim is to provide education in ways that are scalable and effective. It also involves educating government officials, legislators, and law enforcement agencies about these issues so they can collaborate with citizens. This collaboration

---

[42] See https://www.zippia.com/advice/ai-job-loss-statistics/, accessed on September 29, 2023.

[43] Ibid.

[44] Ibid.

[45] Supra note 7.

[46] See, https://standards.ieee.org/wp-content/uploads/import/governance/iccom/IC16-002-Global_Initiative_for_Ethical_Considerations_in_the_Design_of_Autonomous_Systems.pdf, accessed on September 29, 2023.

[47] Supra note 7.

[48] Ibid.

[49] Ibid.

[50] Ibid.

[51] Supra note 7. 'Artificial intelligence ethics: Concerns and proactivity' The European.

could resemble police officers giving safety lectures in schools, with the goal of reducing fear and confusion.[52]

Manipulation of behaviour and data are two further difficulties. Humans must maintain control over AI while also combating subversion. Many experts see the development of AI as a potential challenge. They believe that AI should be predictable, reliable, and subject to validation and testing. Additionally, AI should serve humanity rather than exploit people and should be regularly reviewed by human experts.[53]

For example: A trio of attacks against Tesla cars were announced in 2019 by Tencent, a well-known Chinese technology corporation, along with a video showing them in action.[54]

iii. ***Environmental damage and long-term viability***

Artificial intelligence (AI) must be produced, managed, and implemented in a way that is environmentally friendly. This is also related to the concept of well-being; one of the most well-known aspects of well-being is environmental, which includes issues such as *air quality, biodiversity, climate change, soil and water quality, and so on.* According to the IEEE[59], AI must neither harm nor accelerate the degradation of Earth's natural systems and must contribute to sustainable stewardship, preservation, and/or restoration of Earth's natural systems. According to the UNI Global Union, AI must prioritise people and the environment, aiming to conserve and even improve our planet's biodiversity and ecosystems. The Foundation for Responsible Robotics cites a variety of potential AI applications in the next years, ranging from agricultural and farming to climate change monitoring and endangered species preservation.

According to the Foundation, this necessitates appropriate, educated regulations to govern AI and automation in order to limit risk and enable continued innovation and progress.

Autonomous vehicles (AVs) are vehicles that can sense their surroundings and operate with little or no human intervention. Although the idea of autonomous vehicles (AVs) has been around since the 1920s, it is only recently that technology has improved to the point that AVs are now commonplace on public roads.

Lower-level automation is well-known and available on the market, although higher-level AVs are still being developed and tested. However, when it progresses through the levels and gives the automated system more responsibility than the human driver, a variety of ethical difficulties arise.

iv. ***Ethical Concerns with AVs***

John Havens says, "We can't design these tools" and says, "We know people act this way, so, this is how we're going to kill them."[55]

---

[52] Supra note 7.

[53] Ibid.

[54] Ibid. Tencent Keen Security Lab (2019), "Experimental Security Research of Tesla Autopilot"; available at https://keenlab.tencent.com/en/whitepapers/Experimental_Security_Research_of_Tesla_Autopilot.pdf.

[55] Supra note 24.

The ethics of testing on public roadways and public safety:

In most nations, such as California, Arizona(U.S.A), Germany, France, and China cars with 'assisted driving' functions are now legal. Some Tesla models, for example, include an Autopilot feature that allows level 2 automation. On public roads, drivers are authorised to employ assisted driving functions as long as they maintain control of the vehicle at all times in a vehicle. Many of these assisted driving technologies, nevertheless, have not yet undergone independent safety testing, and as a result, they could endanger drivers and other road users. In Germany, the Ethics Commission on Automated Driving published a report indicating that all AV driving systems should be subject to official regulation and monitoring and that it is the duty of the public sector to assure the safety of AV systems deployed and licenced on public roads.[61]

Furthermore, according to some reports, the autonomous vehicle industry is about to enter its most dangerous stage because neither the human drivers nor the cars are truly autonomous. Following the first pedestrian accident involving an autonomous vehicle, the dangers this poses have gained considerable attention. In May 2018, a level 3 autonomous vehicle (AV) being tested by Uber collided with 49-year-old Elaine Herzberg as she walked her bicycle across a street late at night in Arizona. Prosecutors ruled that Uber was "not criminally liable," according to the preliminary report of the US National Transportation Safety Board.[56] All aspects of the self-driving system were operating normally at the time of the crash, according to the report, which made no conclusions about the reason. Uber stated that the driver is expected to intervene and take action in instances requiring emergency braking, prompting some observers to criticise the company's use of the terms 'self-driving cars' and 'autopilot' to deceive consumers. Following the collision, several condemned the practise of testing autonomous vehicles on roads as hazardous and unethical, causing Uber to pause its self-driving program momentarily.

Human safety—both public and passenger—is quickly becoming a major concern with self-driving automobiles. Nissan, Toyota, Tesla, Uber, and Volkswagen are among the major businesses developing autonomous vehicles capable of learning, inferring, planning, and making judgements in complicated, unpredictable environments without direct human supervision.

Self-driving cars could have a lot of advantages: statistics show that it is almost always safer in a car driven by a computer than one in a car driven by a human. They could also help to relieve *"traffic congestion in cities, cut pollution, shorten travel and commute times, and allow individuals to be more productive with their time. It will not, however, put an end to traffic accidents."* Even if a self-driving car has the most advanced software and hardware, there is still the possibility of an accident. The challenge of how such vehicles should be designed when selecting whose safety to prioritise arises whenever an autonomous vehicle encounters something unexpected, such as a child coming from behind a parked car.

Supra note 7.

[56] Supra note 24.

The safety of passengers and other road users may need to be prioritised by self-driving automobiles. When there isn't enough time to stop, the only choice is for the automobile to veer into a brick wall, endangering the passenger in the process. In this scenario, a car is driving around a corner where a group of schoolchildren is playing. Should the car put the passengers' or the child's safety first?

Applying Public health ethics in the use of AVs:

The introduction of autonomous vehicles, as well as their potential proliferation, presents the classic dilemma of balancing private manufacturers' freedom to develop with the government's responsibility to protect public health.[57]

Beyond their potential to improve safety, autonomous vehicles[58] raise a number of public health concerns, ranging from concerns about increased automobile use and less use of healthier alternatives like biking or walking, to concerns that focusing on autonomous vehicles will divert attention and funding away from efforts to improve mass transit.[59] There are also difficulties of accessibility, particularly for the poor, disabled, and those living in rural environments.[60] The impact of self-driving cars on traffic, pollution, and the built environment.[61]

Many issues affect public health beyond accident prevention, and public health leaders, with their considerable skills as an author, data analysts, policy advocates, and community catalysts, have much to contribute to discussions about health impacts, equity, social justice, and public health values.[62]

The algorithms[63] being developed for autonomous vehicles in scenarios of forced choice, such as whether to hit a parked car or a pedestrian on an ice-covered road, is a very crucial ethical issue for autonomous vehicles.[64] For better involvement of public health leaders from the outset, during the design phase, and to describe how public health values can influence talks and ultimately decisions.[65] Public health leaders can help develop guidelines that foster equity and safety across the population by reflecting on the ethical and social implications of autonomous vehicles and working collaboratively with designers, manufacturers, companies like Uber and nuTonomy, city health departments, the public, and policymakers[66] on the local, state, and federal levels.[67]

---

[57] Supra note 16.

[58] Ibid.

[59] Ibid.

[60] See, https://www.ncbi.nlm.nih.gov/pmc/articles/PMC5343691/#__sec1title, accessed on September 30, 2023.

[61] Supra note 24. Ethics Commision, 2017.

[62] Kass NE. An ethics framework for public health. Am J Public Health. 2001;91(11):1776–1782.

[63] Ibid.

[64] Ibid.

[65] Ibid.

[66] Ibid.

[67] Supra note 60.

As the standard Code of Ethics for Public Health[74] suggests, public health advocates can preserve public health while advocating for individual and community rights by assisting in the establishment of policies and priorities through "systems that offer a chance for community engagement."[68] Public health thought leaders can make sure that communities have the information they need to make informed decisions about whether and how autonomous vehicles will operate on their roads, and that manufacturers testing and deploying autonomous vehicles obtain "community consent for their implementation."[69] Finally, public health officials can endeavour to empower the disenfranchised by adopting and honouring "different community values, beliefs, and traditions," as well as partnering "in ways that promote public trust."[70]

v. ***Accident investigation procedures and technology***

Lower-level automation is already well-established and available on the market, while higher-level AVs are still being developed and tested. However, when it progresses through the levels and gives the automated system more responsibility than the human driver, a variety of ethical difficulties arise. Several significant incidents, including a number of fatalities involving level 2 AVs, have already occurred:

Case Study: Autonomous Vehicles

- Gao Yaning, 23, was killed after his Tesla Model S collided with the back of a road sweeping tractor on a highway in Hebei, China, in January 2016. The family believes Autopilot was activated at the time of the collision, and Tesla is accused of misrepresenting the system's capabilities. According to Tesla, the vehicle's damage rendered it impossible to establish whether Autopilot was activated and, if so, whether it was malfunctioning. A third-party assessor is evaluating data from the car as part of a civil case investigating the crash.[71]
- Joshua Brown, 40, was killed in May 2016 when his Tesla Model S collided with a truck in Florida while Autopilot was enabled. The driver, not Tesla, was judged to be at blame, according to a National Highway and Transportation Safety Administration inquiry (Gibbs, 2016). The National Highway Traffic Safety Administration later determined that both Autopilot and the motorist's over-reliance on Tesla's driver assistance systems were to blame.[72]
- Wei Huang was killed in March 2018 when his Tesla Model X collided with a highway safety barrier in California, USA. The severity of the collision, according

---

[68] Ibid.

[69] Supra note 24.

[70] Supra note 24.

[71] Supra note 24.

Thomas JC, Sage M, Dillenberg J, Guillory VJ. A code of ethics for public health. Am J Public Health. 2002;92(7):1057–1059.

[72] Supra note 24.

to Tesla, was 'unprecedented'. The National Transportation Safety Board eventually issued a report blaming the disaster on a navigation error made by Autopilot. The victim's family has filed a lawsuit against Tesla.[73]

Unfortunately, efforts to examine these events have been hampered by the lack of standards, methods, or regulatory frameworks for examining accidents involving autonomous vehicles. Furthermore, due to the proprietary data logging systems now installed in AVs, accident investigators rely significantly on manufacturers' assistance to give key data on the events leading up to an accident.[74]

One approach is to equip all future AVs with industry-standard event data recorders, or 'ethical black boxes', which impartial accident investigators might access. This would be similar to the aviation accident investigation model presently in place.[75] ***iv. Near-miss collisions***.

There is currently no system in place to collect near-miss accidents in a systematic manner. While it's likely that manufacturers are currently gathering this information, they aren't obligated to do so or to share it. The sole current exception is California, which compels all businesses testing AVs on public roads to determine how often human drivers had to take over the vehicle due to safety concerns (known as 'disengagement').

In 2018, the number of disengagements by AV maker ranged from one per 11,017 miles driven by Waymo AVs to one per 1.15 miles travelled by Apple AVs.[76] The need of keeping human safety drivers engaged is underscored by data on these disengagements. However, others have criticised the Californian data gathering procedure, stating that its vague phrasing and lack of stringent criteria allow businesses to avoid reporting certain instances that could be classified as near-misses.

Without access to this kind of information, policymakers cannot account for the quantity and impact of near-miss occurrences or evaluate the actions made by manufacturers because of these near-misses. Lessons could be drawn from the approach taken in aviation disaster investigations, where each near-miss is painstakingly documented and subjected to a separate examination. Policymakers demand thorough records on all accidents and near-misses in order to inform legislation.

v. ***The quality of urban environment***

AVs have the ability to change the urban environment in the long run. Pedestrians, cyclists, and locals may suffer as a result of some of these modifications. Additional infrastructure will almost certainly be required as driving becomes more autonomous (e.g., "AVs-only lanes"). Urban design might be greatly affected by automation, with changes affecting everything from parking and traffic to green spaces and lobbies.[77] The deployment of AVs will also necessitate a considerable expansion of 5G network

[73] O'Kane, 2018.

[74] Stilgoe and Winfield, 2018.

[75] Sample, 2017.

[76] (Hawkins, 2019).

[77] Marshall and Davies, 2018.

coverage, which will have repercussions for urban development.[78] Specifically for marginalised groups from both rural and urban areas, Member States should implement policies to promote and increase diversity and inclusivity in AI development teams and training data sets that reflect their populations. These policies should also ensure equal access to AI technologies and their benefits. It is understandable why taxi drivers in Arizona, USA, are concerned.[79]

Environmental effects of self-driving cars should also be taken into account. Even while self-driving automobiles have the potential to significantly reduce fuel usage and emissions, these savings might be negated by the ease and allure of long-distance driving.[80]

vi. ***Algorithmic Bias***

Bias is a phenomenon that occurs when an algorithm produces results that are discriminatory due to the built-in biases created by the programmer.

In simple words, bias means showing partiality to one person or a group of people; it is the programmer's data into the model that matters. Suppose it feeds insufficient data that contain implicit racial, gender, or ideological biases. The machine gets trained based on this, and the resulting model is more likely to fail because the bad data bias in AI systems could erode the trust between humans and machines that learn.

For example: ***Amazon's automated hiring tool—Gender Bias***

Amazon tried building an AI tool to help to recruit, but it showed bias against women. Finally, it found that AI was unfavourable towards female candidates because it had calmed through male-dominated resumes to accrue its data.

Algorithmic Racial Bias

Bias in automated facial recognition and the associate data sets. The progression of AI technologies has just started to introduce novel social and moral duties inquiries.[81] When it thinks of creating a thinking machine, it pops up with lots of ethical and social issues related to ensuring such devices that do not harm humans and other morally relevant beings, and most importantly, the moral status of the machines themselves.[82]

An illustration of machine learning ethics and other AI algorithms with specific domain knowledge will help you comprehend the subtleties of racist AI. Imagine John recommending the approval of mortgage applications using a machine learning algorithm. John may be sued by a rejected applicant who claims that the algorithm treats mortgage applicants unfairly because of their race. In reply, the organisation says this is impossible because the algorithm is blinded deliberately to the applicants.

---

[78] Khosravi, 2018.

[79] Sage, 2019.

[80] Worland, 2016.

[81] Robot Ethics: The Ethical and Social Implications of Robotics / [ed] Patrick Lin, Keith Abney and George A. Bekey, CAMBRIDGE: MIT Press, 2012, p. 169–186.

[82] Ibid.

Honestly, that was part of the organisation's rationale for implementing the system. Even the statistics show that the organisation's approval rate for black applicants has been gradually dropping. So, submitting the ten qualified genuine applicants (as determined by a separate panel of human judges) shows that the algorithm accepts mostly white applicants and rejects black applicants or accepting male over female applicants.[83] Now, what could be possibly being happening and how it disposes of AI inclination through AI or the AI itself in the area of ethics:

"***AI frameworks are made by people who can be one-sided and judgmental, so it's critical to maintain a strategic distance from algorithms that carry on in impeding ways e.g., racially profiling while foreseeing future lawbreakers***."

Undoubtedly, as the utilisation of AI and mechanical technology by law implementation becomes more inescapable all through society, always contacting upon the lives of residents, it turns out to be progressively significant for law authorisation to guarantee that the utilisation of these advances is moral. For example, in the case of:

Google AI Team Demands Ousted Black Author Be Rehired and Promoted on December 17, 2020.

Timnit Gebru, a former Google author, who studies AI ethics and was one of Google's few Black research scientists, claims she was fired unexpectedly after a disagreement over an academic publication and months of speaking out about the tech giant's need for more women and people of colour.

According to a copy of the message received from Google's Ethical AI team, Gebru's former colleagues urge that she be rehired and promoted, among other things, in a letter written to CEO Sundar Pichai.[84]

vii. ***Mass Surveillance and Privacy***

Data Protection: Now, the ultimate question that arises here is, *whether and how violation of ethical norm regarding privacy and data is happening through AI-enabled technology?*

It is evident that the manufacturers collect a substantial amount of data from AVs. As these vehicles grow more widespread on our roads, the question arises: to what degree are these data infringing on drivers' and passengers' privacy and data protection rights? If AI breaches an individual's privacy /data or even gathers data through mass surveillance, it is a grave violation of ethical norm.

Data management and privacy concerns have already emerged, with some expressing concern about the possibility for AV data to be used for advertising purposes. Tesla has also been chastised for using AV data records in an unethical manner. Following a crash, the Guardian discovered many instances when the firm

---

[83] Ibid.

[84] Seehttps://www.bloomberg.com/news/articles/2020-12-16/google-ai-researchers-lay-out-demands-escalatinginternal-fight, accessed on October 3, 2023.

shared drivers' sensitive data with the media without their permission[85] using their consent, to demonstrate that their technology was not to blame.

Tesla, on the other hand, does not let customers access their own data logs.[86] According to the *'German Ethics Commission on Automated Driving'*, one option is to ensure that all Autonomous Vehicle drivers have full data sovereignty. This would provide individual's control over how their information is used.[87] Privacy and data breaches are not allowed and are given protection under the laws of various countries.

5.3 Impact of AI Autonomy Over Human Autonomy

Different degrees of decisive autonomy[88] can be found in AI applications and the computer systems that implement them. The German Federal Government's Data Ethics Commission, 2018[89] divides autonomy into three categories: *algorithmically based, algorithmically driven, and algorithmically determined systems.*

AI applications that are *algorithmically based* function as pure help systems with no autonomous decision-making ability. However, human decisions are based on (partial) results and (partial) information calculated by them.

Algorithm-driven

AI applications influence human judgements by calculating results. As a result, humans' actual decision-making capabilities and, as a result, their self-determination options are limited.

AI applications that are *algorithmically decided* make decisions independently and so have a high degree of autonomy. Because of the high level of automation, no human decision is made in individual cases, and automated choices are not reviewed by humans.

- **Germany**

Data Protection: Now, the ultimate question that arises here is *whether and how violation of ethical norm regarding privacy and data is happening through AI-enabled technology?*

According to the *"European General Data Protection Regulation (GDPR), Art. 2 No. 1 GDPR states that the data collected by the car manufacturers are subject*

---

[85] Lin, 2014.

[86] (Thielman, 2017).

[87] Ethics Commission, 2017.

[88] W. Wahlster, "Künstliche Intelligenz als Grundlage autonomer Systeme". Informatik-Spektrum, 40, pp. 409, 418, 2017.

[89] Datenethikkommission der Bundesregierung, Gutachten der Datenethikkommission. Berlin: BMI, 2019. [Online]. Available at: https://www.bmi.bund.de/SharedDocs/downloads/DE/publikationen/themen/itdigitalpolitik/gutachten-datenethikkommission.pdf?__blob=publicationFile&v=6, accessed on October 1, 2023. [97] (European Parliament, 2016).

to an existing regulation, as the data is suitable to identify an individual, the client (personal data, Art. 4 (1) GDPR)."

"This Regulation applies to the processing of personal data wholly or partly by automated means and to the processing other than by automated means of personal data which form part of a filing system or are intended to form part of a filing system."[97]

Additionally, under this rule, manufacturers are permitted to gather, use, and share data with[90] the government if necessary in an emergency circumstance. Europe has a European and national embraced information/data regulation, which has gotten the information assurance issue exceptionally complete and comprehensive since 2018. However, the issue has not yet been resolved because many automotive companies can circumvent the law by obtaining information and data while remaining anonymous. The question remains as to whether this information is not more the property of each client or client as opposed to the free data set provided by automobile manufacturers.

In any event, the vehicle manufacturers may collect information on the user or buyer even if no confirmation is given. The enforcement of the law is also a key concern. Let's say the company fails to follow the guidelines. Because of the lack of good surveillance in that situation, authorities will have a difficult time detecting it. As a result, due to a lack of clarity or transparency, implementation is frequently absent. The EU has a legal and regulatory framework that focuses on improving an exhaustive AI Strategy, including its guidelines. They include two key developments—the European Parliament's Resolution of February 2017 on Civil Laws for Robotics and the General Data Protection Regulation (GDPR).

According to the *'German Ethics Commission on Automated Driving, 2017'*[98], one option is to ensure that the personal data of all AV drivers is secure. This would provide individuals control over how their information is used.[91]

The German government agreed on a draft act on January 25, 2017, that would allow drivers to hand over control of their vehicles to highly or totally automated driving systems and allow those vehicles to be deployed on public roads. Completely autonomous driving, in which the car is completely controlled by the driving system and there are no drivers present, only passengers, would be prohibited. The data collected by the vehicle and put together or gathered by the producers' servers could imply very detailed information about the vehicle and its users.[92]

'Highly automated driving systems' are defined as systems that do not require the driver's constant attention. If the driver is required to take over the driving functions, the system will notify him or her.

---

[90] February 2017.

[91] Ethics Commission, 2017.

[92] See <https://www.loc.gov/item/global-legal-monitor/2017-02-09/germany-government-proposes-automateddriving-act/, accessed on October 1, 2023.

'Fully automated driving systems' are defined as vehicles that do not require the driver's attention. At all times, the driving system is capable of establishing a "minimal risk situation."[93]

Under § 1a of the Draft Act, 2017—if the system is employed for its intended purpose, the driver would be able to delegate driving activities to a highly or entirely automated driving system that complies with international requirements (e.g., those set down in the Vienna Convention on Road Traffic or European Union legislation).[94]

Under § 1b, if the automated driving system told him to, or if the driver realised or should have realised that the conditions for using an automated driving system were no longer met, such as if a tyre was damaged, the driver would be obligated to take over the driving functions from the automated driving system without undue delay.[95]

Under § 63a, in the car, a 'black box' would record whether the vehicle was being driven by the driver or by the driving system. It would also keep track of when the car requested the driver to take control or when the autonomous driving system malfunctioned. Upon request, the records would have to be made available to the authorities.[96]

SAP, based in Walldorf, Germany, makes AI software for around 400,000 firms globally to manage data on everything. It is currently helping the firm develop a series of AI guidelines ranging from respect for United Nations human rights principles to data protection.

Steer the development and deployment of our AI software to help the world run better and improve people's lives. However, the firm wants to address transparency, safety, and privacy in the wake of increasingly alarming warnings about out-of-control AI.

The current AI system has widely accepted that it has no moral status. If it wants, perhaps it may change, copy, terminate, delete, or use computer programs as we please, at least as far as the programs are concerned. The ethical constraints to which humans are subject to dealing with AI systems are deep-rooted in our responsibilities to other beings, not even in any responsibilities to the system itself. Europe's biggest software maker has drafted SAP, to help craft its first 'ethics code' for research into AI. The code aims to prevent the technology from being abused, either by violating people's rights or inheriting ingrained prejudice from its creators.

- **California**

Data Protection: The California State Assembly and State Senate confirmed in 2018 a data protection Act ('California Online Privacy Protection Act, CalOPPA, 2003').[97] This Act is for residents of California given them the right to know the data, like what data it will collect from them, whether it will sell that to someone else or will that

[93] Ibid.

[94] Ibid.

[95] Ibid.

[96] Ibid.

[97] (Colbert, 2018) [106] (California's for Privacy, 2019).

get disclosed to whom, and so on. Additionally, the Act guards against the sale and disclosure of personal information, and businesses are willing to confirm the right to object to this by including a 'No' button on their websites. This regulation will be applicable to any business with profits that exceed $25 million in gross income, has data on more than 50,000 people, or generates more than half of its yearly revenue from the sale of data.[106]

The California Consumer Privacy Act (CCPA) is a new consumer privacy law that came into effect on January 1, 2020. Following the CCPA's approval, about 15 other states introduced their own CCPA-style privacy legislation, and federal legislation comparable to the CCPA is being examined. However, only Nevada has established new consumer privacy legislation, which includes a "do not sell my personal information" right, which means to assist customers in exercising their right to opt out, which is important in the case of AVs since every user's deidentified data is saved and could be utilised in another way by the company in addition to the state's existing internet privacy law, which went into effect on October 1, 2019.[98]

Among the many differences between the CCPA and existing U.S. privacy legislation, the new law's definition of personal information is exceptionally broad, including data elements that were never considered personal information under any previous U.S. legislation. Furthermore, the CCPA gives Californians new privacy rights, such as the right to know what personal information a business has acquired about them, as well as the details on how the company uses and distributes the data, and the right to have such information deleted.[108]

The CCPA will apply to a wide range of enterprises that handle personal information about California residents, requiring them to comply with a slew of new standards governing the acquisition, use, and sharing of personal data. Most AVs manufacturers will need to update their privacy notice disclosures, implement mechanisms for responding to consumer rights requests, adhere to data monetisation rules, and re-evaluate their partnerships with vendors who handle personal information on their behalf because AI would collect data of the car[99]

The extent and territorial reach of each, as well as definitions relating to protected information, levels of detail, and an opt-out right for sales of personal information, are key differences between the CCPA and the General Data Protection Regulation (GDPR) of the European Union. In other circumstances, the CCPA only considers data that was submitted by a consumer, which differs from GDPR's definition of personal information. The GDPR, on the other hand, does not make this difference and applies to all personal data, regardless of its source. In the case of sensitive personal data, this does not apply if the information was clearly made public by the data subject themselves, as allowed by Art. 9(2),e). As a result, GDPR's definition is substantially broader than the CCPA's.[110] Personal data might also include online identities and information from online or social media profiles.

---

[98] See,https://www.bakerlaw.com/webfiles/Privacy/2019/Briefs/California-Consumer-Privacy-Act-FAQs.pdf, accessed on October 1, 2023.

[99] Ibid.

[110] Ibid.

The 'Drivers' Privacy Protection Act, 1994'[100] is one of three[101] potential acts which could cover the administration of information gathered by one driving the car, i.e., the driver.[102]

The DPPA was enacted in 1994 in reaction to the state DMV's practises of selling or revealing drivers' personal information, which resulted in certain unfavourable outcomes. For example, actress Rebecca Schaeffer was assassinated by an enraged fan who hired a private investigator to track down Schaeffer's address, which the investigator discovered from the DMV. Congress enacted the DPPA in response to concerns that personal information acquired by state DMVs was being leased or sold, resulting in a loss of privacy.[103]

Personal information from a motor vehicle record is protected under the DPPA. The federal statute defines 'personal information as "information that identifies an individual," which includes a person's photograph, social security number, driver's licence number, name, address(but not the five-digit zip code), phone number, and medical or disability information. Personal information does not include details about car accidents, traffic violations, or the status of a driver. "Any record pertaining to a motor vehicle operator's permit, motor vehicle title, motor vehicle registration, or identification card issued by a department of motor vehicles" is defined as "any record pertaining to a motor vehicle operator's permit, motor vehicle title, motor vehicle registration, or identification card issued by a department of motor vehicles." The legality of a driver's licence as a 'motor vehicle record' has been questioned. The majority of courts have ruled that extracting data from a physical driver's licence is not legal.[104]

The other two[105] plausible acts are named the 'Electronic Communications Privacy Act (ECPA)[106] and the Federal Communications Act (FCA)'.[118] Initially, the 'Driver Privacy Protection Act, 1994'[107] applies to the State Department of engine vehicles and its representatives.[120]

Furthermore, the ECPA primarily prohibits any attempt to obstruct communication in an unlawful manner. Specifically, 'US Code § 2511 (2)'[108] refers to electronic communication services, not the creative industry. Aside from that, the Act's extension[109] only applies to correspondence between two buyers and its interference, not to raw data obtained by the organisation. The producer[110] must ensure that

---

[100] Supra note 7.

[101] Ibid.

[102] Ibid.

[103] See <https://www.ohiobar.org/public-resources/commonly-asked-law-questions-results/courts-andlawyers/know-about-drivers-privacy-protection-act/>, accessed on October 1, 2023.

[104] Ibid.

[105] Supra note 7.

[106] Ibid.

[107] Ibid.

[108] Ibid.

[109] Ibid.

[110] Ibid.

information is protected from outside intervention or impediment.[111] Finally, the 'Federal Communication Act' is to protect the security of the consumer information that media telecommunication transporters acquire.[112] The classification of a vehicle manufacturer as a media transmission transporter is still up in the air.

The law, on the other hand, was designed to eliminate the need to contact suppliers or administrators.[113]

Although there is explicit data security at the federal level, individual states may give their citizens access to extra legislation. On the other hand, state law for data assurance is rare and straightforward.[127]

- **India**

The Data Protection Bill establishes the concept of a data fiduciary, which is analogous to the GDPR's concept of a data controller. The 'data fiduciary' is the entity that determines the purpose or means of processing the data principal's personal data. The state, corporate entities, and individuals can all be data fiduciaries. The 'data principal', on the other hand, is the natural person whose personal data is collected. The DP Bill defines data processing broadly to include most data-related actions such as data storage, adaption, retrieval, distribution, and erasure or destruction.[128]

In Justice K.S. Puttaswamy (Retd.) & Anr. vs. Union of India & Ors., 2017[114]

The right to privacy is a constitutionally protected right in India, according to a nine-judge bench of the Supreme Court of India, and it is ancillary to other liberties provided by the Indian Constitution. Observers also anticipate the Indian government establishing a data protection regime to safeguard individual privacy and has recognised privacy including informational privacy to be a fundamental right under the right to life.[115]

The Digital Personal Data Protection Act, 2023

An analysis in context of ethical issues involved in the deployment of AI is as follows:

AI privacy considerations are different from ordinary data privacy considerations. To develop appropriate policies that protect privacy without limiting advancements in AI technology is one of the difficulties in preserving privacy in artificial intelligence. As well as the nature of the data itself and how it is used to develop the AI capabilities, the data contexts at issue include the scanning mechanisms that allow the AI tools to learn about their settings. The remedy or approach for an ethical violation, such as a data breach, should be the appointment of an ethical officer who will look into

---

111 Ibid.

112 Ibid.

113 (US. Government, 2012).

114 2017(10) SCALE 1.

115 See <https://globalfreedomofexpression.columbia.edu/cases/puttaswamy-vindia/#:~:text=Case%20Summary%20and%20Outcome,guaranteed%20by%20the%20Indian%20Constitution., accessed on October 1, 2023.

the training of data sets and uphold privacy, fairness, and transparency in preserving personal data.

Sandbox Provision[116]

The DP Bill gives the DPA the authority to form a sandbox to stimulate innovation in artificial intelligence, machine learning, and other new technologies that benefit the public good. Certain sections of the DP Bill, such as the restriction on personal data keeping, will not apply to entities included in the sandbox. Any data fiduciary with a DPA-certified privacy by design policy will be eligible to apply for inclusion in the sandbox. When asking for participation in the sandbox, the data fiduciary must include information such as I the sandbox's term (not to exceed 12 months), (ii) the creative use of technology and its positive benefits, and (iii) the data principals who will be involved in the proposed processing. The DPA must guarantee that safeguards are in place for the duration of the sandbox's participation, which is set at 36 months.[117] Now the question is whether or not the IT rules allow data collection by AI-enabled system.

Given the DP Act's key provisions relating to data principals' rights, obligations of data fiduciaries, grounds for which personal data can be processed, data breach reporting requirements, classification of significant data fiduciaries, and an enhanced penalty regime, this update provides a brief overview of previously stated 'automated means' which has been defined broadly to include any technology capable of processing personal data automatically or otherwise. Only those types of processing that can be done without the use of a computer should be included. This means that only small businesses that do not use such equipment for data processing can benefit from the exemption for certain types of processing of personal data.[118]

5.4 Conclusion

To name a few international conventions—the *"Universal Declaration of Human Rights (1948),*[119] *the instruments of the international human rights framework, the Discrimination (Employment and Occupation) Convention (1958), the International Convention on the Elimination of All Forms of Racial Discrimination (1965), the International Covenant on Civil and Political Rights (1966), the International Covenant on Economic, Social, and Cultural Rights (1966), the Convention on the Elimination of All Forms of Discrimination Against Women (1979), the Convention on the Rights of the Child (1989), and the Convention on the Rights of Persons with*

---

[116] See <https://trilegal.com/wp-content/uploads/2021/12/The-Data-Protection-Bill-2021.pdf>, accessed on October 1, 2023.

[117] Ibid.

[118] See <https://trilegal.com/wp-content/uploads/2021/12/The-Data-Protection-Bill-2021.pdf>, accessed on April 12, 2023. (US. Government, 2012).

[119] See< https://unesdoc.unesco.org/ark:/48223/pf0000381137?3=null&queryId=c5dd8ced-9647-452b-b4d692723006496c>, accessed on October 1, 2023.

Disabilities (2006), the Convention Against Discrimination in Education (1960), the Convention on the Protection and Promotion of the Diversity of Cultural Expressions (2005)".[120] And any other relevant international instruments, recommendations, and declarations. The *"United Nations Declaration on the Right to Development (1986); the Declaration on the Responsibilities of Current Generations Towards Future Generations (1997); the Universal Declaration on Bioethics and Human Rights (2005); and the United Nations Declaration on the Rights of Indigenous Peoples (2007) are also worth mentioning the United Nations General Assembly Resolution on the Review of the World Summit on the Information Society (A/RES/70/125) (2015); the United Nations General Assembly Resolution on Transforming Our World: the 2030 Agenda for Sustainable Development (A/RES/70/1) (2015); the Recommendation Concerning the Preservation of, and Access to, Documentary Heritage, Including in Digital Form (2015); the Declaration of Ethical Principles in Relation to Climate Change (2017); the Recommendation on Science and Scientifics (2017); the Internet Universality Indicators (endorsed by UNESCO's International Programme for the Development of Communication in 2018), including the ROAM principles (endorsed by UNESCO's General Conference in 2015); the Human Rights Council's resolution on "'Privacy in the Digital Age' (A/HRC/RES/42/15) (2019); and the Human Rights Council's resolution on 'New and Emerging Digital Technologies and Human Rights' (2019)."*

Noticing the profound and dynamic effects of artificial intelligence (AI) on ecosystems, societies, the environment, and human lives, including the human mind, in part because of the new ways that its use affects learning, human, social, and natural sciences, culture, communication, and information technology.[121] Although AI technologies have the potential to be extremely beneficial to humanity and that all nations can benefit from them, they also raise some fundamental ethical concerns, including the biases they can encode and aggravate, potentially leading to discrimination, inequality, digital divides, exclusion, and a threat to cultural, social, and biological diversity, as well as social and economic divides; the need for transparency and understanding of algorithmic workings; and the data they were created with. Recognising that AI technologies have the potential to exacerbate existing divides and inequalities in the world, both within and between countries, and that justice, trust, and fairness must be upheld to ensure that no country or person is left behind, either by having fair access to AI technologies and reaping their benefits or by being protected from their negative consequences, while taking into account the unique circumstances of different countries and recognising that some people do not wish to participate in all technology improvements.[122]

Addressing vulnerabilities and ethical issues shouldn't inhibit innovation and progress; rather, it should create new opportunities and promote ethically conducted research and innovation that bases AI technologies on human rights and fundamental

---

[120] Ibid. (US. Government, 2012).

[121] See< https://unesdoc.unesco.org/ark:/48223/pf0000381137?3=null&queryId=c5dd8ced-9647-452b-b4d692723006496c>, accessed on October 3, 2023.

[122] Ibid.

freedoms, values, and moral and ethical thinking. Acknowledging that, in light of the rapid pace of technological change, ethical values and principles can provide guidance for the development and application of rights-based policy measures and legal norms.

To support this process at the national, regional, and global levels, Member States, private sector companies, and civil society organisations are urged to form a network of independent ***AI Ethics Officers with UNESCO's assistance.***[123]

It is believed that globally acknowledged ethical standards for AI technologies, based on complete respect for international law, particularly human rights legislation, can help shape AI-related norms around the world. Essential standards for ethical AI have been identified by the UNI Global Union.

- Transparency in AI systems is a requirement, as are 'ethical black boxes', in AI systems.
- AI must serve people and the environment.
- Use a human-in-command strategy.
- Ensure a genderless, unbiased AI.
- Share the advantages of AI systems.
- Ensure a fair transition and support for fundamental rights and liberties.
- Create a system of global government.

Different degrees of decision autonomy[124] can be found in AI applications and the computer systems that implement them. The German Federal Government's Data Ethics Commission, 2018,[125] for example, divides autonomy into three categories: *algorithmically based, algorithmically driven, and algorithmically determined systems.*

Can you give examples of autonomy in case of AVs?

AI applications that are *algorithmically based* function as pure help systems with no autonomous decision-making ability. However, human decisions are based on (partial) results and (partial) information calculated by them.

Algorithm-driven

AI applications influence human judgements by calculating results. As a result, humans' actual decision-making capabilities and, as a result, their self-determination options are limited.

AI applications that are *algorithmically decided* make decisions independently and so have a high degree of autonomy. Because of the high level of automation, no

[123] See <https://www.caidp.org/reports/aidv-2022/>, accessed on October 3, 2023.

[124] Supra note 88.

[125] Datenethikkommission der Bundesregierung, Gutachten der Datenethikkommission. Berlin: BMI, 2019. [Online]. Available at: https://www.bmi.bund.de/SharedDocs/downloads/DE/publikationen/themen/itdigitalpolitik/gutachten-datenethikkommission.pdf?__blob=publicationFile&v=6, accessed on October1, 2023. [141] See <https://www.pewresearch.org/internet/2018/12/10/concerns-about-human-agency-evolution-andsurvival/>, accessed on October 3, 2023.

human decision is made in individual cases, and automated choices are not reviewed by humans.

People's blind reliance on digital technologies is growing as automated systems get more complicated and elites gain control of them. Because of AI, the majority of people will not be faster and more efficient in 2030.[141] It will not get more autonomous; instead, it will become more automated as it follows the metaphorical GPS line through daily interactions. Individuals do not have control over their breakfast, morning workouts, or commute routes. An algorithm will make these decisions for individuals in a way that maximises efficiency (narrowly defined) and, most likely, the service provider's profits. Individuals may jam more activities and interactions into their days by 2030, but they do not believe this will improve their lives. The greatest danger is that all members of society will be under more pressure to live according to what 'the system' will tell them is 'best for them' to do and not do, i.e., that individuals will lose the autonomy to decide how they want to live their lives and to choose various ways of doing things. With an increase in 'recommendations', 'rankings', and competitiveness based on societal pressure and control, individuals may risk losing fundamental liberties (including, but not limited to, the right to a private life) that have been battled for over decades and centuries.

Suggestions for the Corporate Sectors

It is proposed that member states should encourage public entities, private sector companies, and civil society organisations to include various stakeholders in AI governance, and consider adding the role of an independent AI Ethics Officer or another mechanism to oversee ethical impact assessment, auditing, and continuous monitoring efforts, as well as ensure ethical guidance of AI systems.

Chapter 6
Conclusion

Abstract This chapter will attempt to develop some action-oriented approaches that, if implemented, could increase the civil and criminal regulatory system's responsiveness to liability issues of legal and ethical concerns, like when deciding the proper liability standard for artificial intelligence software, we need to consider both the intended function of the program and how the software is being sold. If the function of the software is potentially dangerous (such as engineering design or item delivery), strict liability should be applied. On the other hand, if the intended function is not risky (for example, providing gardening advice), then the liability standard is determined by how the software is marketed. Lastly, it concludes that where the software is mass-marketed, then strict liability will apply, and if the software is a custom program, then negligence would apply in that case. So, it is in our best interest to continue developing software and increase the benefits of technology.

6.1 Conclusion—Findings

The growing reliance on AI, which serves many beneficial purposes, is not a threat to the legal system. This chapter explains some of the challenges in proving AI-related criminal liability. It suggests that the legal system can respond in various ways, including traditional tort law methods of negligence, vicarious liability, strict liability, and product liability. The chapter also proposes considering AI devices as 'semi-autonomous beings' and even granting them legal personhood. However, none of these options is obvious, and each would require the legal system and its practitioners to understand what AI is, how to regulate it through rules, code, or both, and how to adapt to the increasing complexity of the technological environment.[1]

---

[1] Giuffrida, I., Lederer, F., & Vermeys, N. (2017). A legal perspective on the trials and tribulations of AI: how artificial intelligence, the internet of things, smart contracts, and other technologies will affect the law. *Case W. Res. L. Rev.*, *68*, 747.

S. Fahim, *Ethico-Legal Aspect of AI-driven Driverless Cars*, Frontiers of Artificial Intelligence, Ethics and Multidisciplinary Applications,
https://doi.org/10.1007/978-981-97-6883-7_6

Position in India

In India,[2] there is no specific legislation to manage or regulate self-driving vehicles. The 'Motor Vehicles Act, 1988 and the Consumer Protection Act, 2019' are the two major laws that regulate or govern motor vehicles in India.[3] Even the 'Motor Vehicle (Amendment) Act, 2019' has no clear impact on self-driving vehicles or autonomous vehicles. In India, there have been fewer discussions on the liability of AI.[4] Remarkably, 'NITI Aayog in 2018' released a policy paper on 'National Strategy for Artificial Intelligence', which talks about how AI could be introduced in areas like medical services, horticulture, and automobiles. However, this policy paper neglects to examine the issue of obligation/liability of AI.[5] Presently, the preeminent inquiry that emerges is whether India ought to follow the other countries' model where the proprietor or owner is at risk regardless of whether the AI commits the error, or whether India ought to follow the German model, which forces responsibility on the manufacturer of the vehicle when there is a mistake concerning the AI.[6] The ***'Consumer Protection Act, 2019***, under ***Section 2(34)'*** characterises product liability as "the liability of a product manufacturer or product seller, of any product or services, to make up for any mischief caused to a consumer by such blemished product manufactured or sold or by a lack in service relating thereto." If AI is considered as a product, the manufacturer/producer is responsible for the damage caused by the AI.[7] When it comes to product liability claims involving software failures, complications can arise because computer code is generally considered a 'service' rather than a 'product', and cases seeking compensation for allegedly defective software are more often filed as breach of warranty cases rather than product liability.[8] As products are created, stored, and transported, AI can be considered to be a product if it is mass-produced, off-the-shelf, physical, and valuable for sale.[9] AI is a service if it is not manufactured, stored, or transported due to its intangible nature. Customers come to services, whereas products come to customers. In the same way that self-driving car components are classified as products, car sharing rides are classified as services. For the most part, it is treated as a breach of guarantee/warranty instead of product liability.[10]

---

[2] Tejas Sateesha Hinder and Ritik Kumar Rath, *'Self-Driving Cars And India: A Call For Inclusivity Under The Indian Legal Position'*, NIMIMS University, June 22, 2021.*See also* <https://lawreview.nmims.edu/2021/06/22/self-driving-cars-and-india-a-call-for-inclusivity-under-the-indian-legal-position/>, accesses on October 9, 2023.

[3] Ibid.

[4] Ibid.

[5] Ibid.

[6] *Id.*

[7] Ibid.

[8] Ibid.

[9] *Supra note 2.*

[10] Motorola Mobility, Inc. v. Myriad France SAS, Case No. 11 C 7373; Hallinan v. Fraternal Order of Police of Chi. Lodge No. 7, 570 F.3d 811, 820 (7th Cir.2009).

Another[11] important point is whether the criterion of 'no-fault responsibility', which indicates that a respondent expects to bear responsibility even if he makes no mistake or has no 'problem'.[12] A requirement for appropriate enactment of legislation on AI with a legitimate outline of responsibility is vital as the incidents of AI mishaps are increasing. India tops the world in road crash deaths given the data of more than 400 fatalities per day (WHO, 2018).[13] Road crashes in the last decade alone have injured over 5 million and killed 1.3 million in India.[14] Every year, 4.5 lakh road crashes occur in which essentially 1.5 lakh individuals bite the dust.[15] A new report from the World Bank expresses that India has 1% of the world's total vehicles yet contributes 11% to worldwide passing in road mishaps.[16]

With such[17] astonishing statistics, it will be a fiasco if India permits self-driving vehicles to run on the streets without the appropriate enactment of legislation. Other enormous deterrents will incorporate wrestling with the subject of existing significant provisions of the 'Motor Vehicle Act and the Consumer Protection Act'.[18] Getting the self-driving vehicle into the regulatory framework would require amending these two regulations. Amendment to an explicit section is not enough. It requires an amendment to the degree[19] of broadening provisions that administer issues, not including drivers' faults in essence, to the owners of self-driving vehicles.

Furthermore, a provision should be included that would require a company whose self-driving cars were not intended for Indian roads to impose a severe penalty. On the off chance that the circumstance deteriorates, their licence ought to drop. Then, either the government should make revisions or amendments[20] to 'Motor Vehicles Act, 2019' to incorporate self-driving vehicles, or the public authority should make specific legislation on self-driving vehicles similar to the U.S and Germany where there is a clear connection between laws regarding charging and laws regarding liability in the event of an accident.[21] Additionally, the law ought to force the risk or liability on the manufacturer for any shortcomings of AI, as a similar will give a two-overlay advantage.[22] The vehicle manufacturers are in a vastly improved situation to pay compensation; *nom de plume* for their abundant resources.[23] Furthermore, when

---

[11] Ibid.

[12] Ibid.

[13] See https://documents1.worldbank.org/curated/en/761181612392067411/pdf/Traffic-Crash-Injuries-and-Disabilities-The-Burden-on-Indian-Society.pdf, accessed on October 10, 2023.

[14] *Supra* note 2.

[15] Ibid.

[16] World Bank report on "Traffic Crash Injuries and Disabilities: The Burden on India Society", accessed on October 10, 2023.

[17] *Supra* note 2.

[18] Ibid.

[19] Ibid.

[20] Ibid.

[21] *Id.*

[22] Ibid.

[23] bid.

the manufacturer gives compensation, a more influential and motivating force for them is to make their products blunder-free.[24]

Position in Germany

Germany is one of the world's top nations to concoct enactment to control and direct self-driving vehicles. The 'German Road Traffic (Amendment) Act, 2017' is one of the leading legislation in the world that governs self-driving vehicles. "***Section 1*** *of the Act permits the driver to transfer the control of the vehicle to an automated driving framework if that satisfies the global necessity, as under the Vienna Convention on Road Traffic, 1968.*" In March 2016, automated vehicles have been approved and acknowledged under the Convention, applying to self-driving vehicles. "***Section 63A*** *of the Act determines or specifies that a black box, which is a gadget associated with a GPS framework that tracks vehicle pace, course, and distance voyaged, driving speed, and season of the day, ought to be introduced in the vehicle to keep a record of who was controlling the vehicle at the hour of the accident.*"

Furthermore, with the assistance of this black box, the responsibility will be effortlessly determined. If the mishap is caused because of a failure of the self-driving framework, then, at that point, the fault would move to the manufacturer of the vehicle. Additionally, as per "***Section 12*** *of the German Road Traffic (Amendment) Act, 2017 on account of death or injury because of the self-driving framework, the most significant sum the victim can recuperate is €10 million.*" The German legislation, by making the manufacturers liable for the mishap brought about by their self-driving framework, forces the manufacturer to build a more fault-proof framework, which is helpful for everybody from the vehicle owner to the pedestrian walking on the road.

As a result, German national law has been revised or modified to keep up with the emergence of autonomous vehicle advances in business and technology, allowing it to remain competitive as one of the world's top car industry business areas.

Position in the US—California

The regulations for driverless testing were adopted by the 'Office of Administrative Law (OAL)' on February 26, 2018. The 'California Department of Motor Vehicles (DMV)' oversees the Autonomous Vehicles Program and gives permits to manufacturers who test and deploy autonomous vehicles on public roads. Depending on whether the manufacturer wants to (a) test an autonomous vehicle with a test driver present; (b) test a fully driverless vehicle; (c) post-test deployment of autonomous vehicles with a driver present; or (d) post-testing deployment of fully driverless vehicles, the proposed permitting regime envisions a slightly different process. The regulations also aim to clarify who is responsible for a vehicle's safe operation and adherence to traffic laws: the driver or the manufacturer. The *driver is accountable* in SAE Level 0-3 cases where he or she is obliged to assume control of an autonomous

[24] Ibid.

vehicle or operate it outside of its intended realm. *The manufacturer is accountable* for product failure in SAE Level 4-5 cases when the autonomous system is in command (such as in a completely driverless car).

The draft bill 2016 regulations would try to govern whether a vehicle can be advertised as 'autonomous' or 'self-driving' through the DMV's jurisdiction to enforce fairness requirements under the California Vehicle Code. Only vehicles at ***Levels 3, 4, and 5*** of the SAE International spectrum of automated driving systems—vehicles that can handle some or all driving activities without active monitoring or control by the driver—are defined as 'autonomous vehicles' in the draft bill. Vehicles that do not satisfy this description, such as those with limited driver assistance or advanced safety measures, could not be advertised with the terminology 'autopilot', 'self-driving', 'automated', or similar terminology, according to the draft regulations.

A Critical Analysis between US(California)and Germany:

1. Unlike Germany, the United States does not rely on international treaties or norms/standards, neither on federal or state-level legislation for regulating the law and order concerning autonomous vehicles on traffic rules.
2. Looking at the US and Germany's frameworks of liability, the US is arranged comparatively better for auto collisions, including AVs, because of the application of product liability more often to such cases. Despite that, Germany has unique and more suitable traffic rules and regulatory framework. This is because the 'German traffic law' is controlled on a federal level, and Germany's law is more adaptable or flexible concerning the vehicle proprietor and vehicle keeper roles. The responsibility is consistently a strict liability, which is not the situation in many states of the US, where the responsibility is, for the most part, connected to the negligence of the driver. This practise is not appropriate for autonomous vehicles since the driver will be supplanted by the actual vehicle and become a user. Subsequently, a liability framework dependent on drivers' conduct can no longer be applied concerning driverless vehicles.
3. One significant contrast between the three nations, namely Germany, California, and India is the design of the legislature roles. While in the US, enormous issues happen among the distinctive state-level necessities and principles on self-driving vehicles. Germany has published amended 'Road Traffic Act in 2017' in regards to automated mobility frameworks. Germany does not permit driverless vehicles. As a result, in Germany, highly self-driving cars are being tested on public roads, despite the fact that a driver is always required as an additional operator in such a new vehicle.
4. The investigation of liability during the shift from autonomous framework to operator in Level 3 and Level 4 of the 'International Society of Automotive Engineers by the US Department of Transportation' vehicles will raise similar issues of proving fault or negligence in court as it did previously, so this does not work with liability under the 'Road Traffic Act, 2017'. In any case, the Level 4 altered autonomous vehicles are formally perceived and approved in Germany.
5. Germany is more restrained as to its administrative or legislative process because it is participatory in the international rush hour/traffic gridlock agreement, called

the 'Vienna Convention on road traffic'. Because this treaty does not include self-driving vehicles, Germany's traffic laws do not include them. Convincingly, Germany's traffic law is more complex and appropriate for vehicles up to Level 4, contrasting it with US law. As far as Level 5 vehicles are concerned, the US is more ready or better prepared because, first, they permit them on their public roadways, the federal level gives them a novel assemblage of security norms or safety standards, and many states of US are advancing AVs in delivering proper regulations for them. The US product liability is developed all around; likewise, car collisions and the US are significantly more flexible than Germany can be in setting up new guidelines or regulations on arising technologies encompassing AVs.

6. Germany does not allow driverless autonomous vehicle technology on public roads, not even for a testing purpose, but most states in the US do. Consequently, the US, at the same time, established a framework for a likely market for self-driving vehicles. Lesson or best practise to learn from Germany or California is to bring all the different national legal approaches on mobility and transportation in line, called as 'United Nations Economic Commission for Europe (UNECE)'. Signing of all of these conventions has a significant economic influence on the Indian regulatory or legislative environment on AI. Becoming a signatory to this agreement will make it easier for government entities and agencies to amend and change present rules and regulations to align them with international standards, thereby helping to improve India's road safety situation. India would be able to add to the convention and assume intellectual leadership on the critical matter of 'road safety' if it becomes a signatory.

The Tortious, Criminal, and Ethical Liability in Germany, California, and India

To fix the liability, the following two situations can be considered:

Scenario 1: When a machine is highly and fully autonomous(Level 4-5), acting as both an operator and a tool, the manufacturer bears responsibility. It is proposed that the 100% liability will be on the manufacturer for any product failure. The onus-probandi will be on the manufacturer and/or AI to get to the Artificial General Intelligence and Artificial Super Intelligence stage. Later, the manufacturer may file a second lawsuit against the software programmer/developer or designer for non-compliance with the manufacturer's policies and rules.

Nevertheless, if it is semi-autonomous(Level 2–3), then the burden of proof lies on the party claiming himself/herself innocent and thereby claiming others to be at fault. So, therefore, till it gets proved beyond the preponderance of probability, Fixation of the liability will be in question.

Scenario 2: Where the machine is not fully autonomous (Level 0–3), and there is some manual where the individual takes control of the machine, then the liability will be on the driver—specifically, when it comes to following the principles of '*under the due course of employment*' as defined under the *law of torts*, where both the parties can be sued by the plaintiff upon his/her wishes—whether it is employer or employee. Companies that use and manufacture AI must provide a written disclaimer describing the policies dictating how users should use AI, what it can do, who is qualified to use it, and what operators and other users should expect from it. It will later help both the parties, i.e., the human operators and beneficiaries, get an accurate idea of what to expect from the AI while also protecting the companies that make the AI from future litigation.

Criminal Liability:

Fixing Criminal Liability—At the Levels of Autonomy

Standard J3016 "Taxonomy and Definitions for Terms Related to On-Road Motor Vehicle Automated Driving Systems," published by the Society of Automotive Engineers (SAE International) in January 2014, is now commonly used to categorise AVs. It was amended in 2016 and again in 2018.[25] The terminology used here is from the standard's most recent iteration. The number of federal and state authorities who use this terminology shows that it is the most widely acknowledged standard.

J3016 offers a six-level[26] driving automation taxonomy by the US Department of Transportation,[27] the general public of car manufacturers, which has since become the business standard when alluding to independent vehicles. When it comes to understand AI specifically in terms of AVs, then the best way to understand it is through the help of an example in terms of easy, moderate, and intricate levels and understanding the need of legislation at every level whether and what is the law to regulate or govern each level of AV?

From Level 0–2 it does not require any specific legislation dealing with it because already Germany, California, and India have pre-existing legislation to deal with the Level 0–2 situation and make the driver legally held liable under the criminal legal liability system for his/her negligence act or omission.

[25] "SAE INT'L, TAXONOMY AND DEFINITIONS FOR TERMS RELATED TO DRIVING AUTOMATION SYSTEMS FOR ON-ROAD MOTOR VEHICLES 1 (2018)".

[26] "Society of Automotive Engineers (SAE) is a global association committed to being the ultimate knowledge source for the engineering profession".

[27] *See* https://www.sae.org/news/2022/04/more-demand-for-sae-level-2-adas-tech, accessed on October 8, 2023.

Such as Germany has '**Sections (§§) 69,**[28] **222, 229,315 c, 316**[29] of German Penal Code', which provides for negligence driving, *and* ***Section 15*** *which says "unless the law expressly provides for criminal liability for negligent conduct, only intentional conduct attracts criminal liability."*[30]

California has '**Section 192 (c) (1)** of California Penal Code' which provides for "*driving a vehicle in the commission of an unlawful act, not amounting to felony, and with gross negligence; or driving a vehicle in the commission of a lawful act which might produce death, in an unlawful manner, and with gross negligence."*

India has **Section 106** of **Bharatiya Nyaya Sanhita, 2023** which provides for *"whoever causing death by negligence."*

In this context, 'whoever' refers to a natural or legal person which is true to SAE Level 0–3 but not to a highly and fully autonomous system, because autonomous systems are independent in their actions and reasoning, whereas in SAE Level 0–3, humans control and monitor the AI agent/tool/machine on their own, and human intervention is present to control the AI agent/tool/machine. As a result, the author observed that there is a gap in the legislation that does not specifically cover the highly and fully autonomous system. The author proposes that a proper law be put in place to address the current issue, namely SAE Levels 4 and 5.

At Levels 3 and 4

Where an operator controls the car manually only when an autonomous mode requests to do so.

Since it needs a user for backup(fallback) while levels 4 and 5 do not, level 3 varies qualitatively from them.[31]

---

[28] **"Section 69**: ***Disqualification order***.

If a person has been convicted of an unlawful act he committed in connection with the driving of a motor-vehicle or in violation of the duties of the driver of a motor-vehicle, or has not been convicted merely because he was proven to have acted in a state of insanity or his having so acted could not be excluded, the court shall make a driving disqualification order if the act shows that he is unfit to drive a motor-vehicle. A further examination pursuant to Section 62 shall not be required.

(2) If the unlawful act under subsection (1) above is one of the following misdemeanors.

i. endangering road traffic (Section 315c).

ii. driving while under the influence of alcohol or drugs (Section 316).

iii. leaving the scene of an accident without cause (Section 142) although the offender knows or should have known that a person was killed, seriously injured or significant damage to the property of another was caused in the accident; or.

iv. committing offences in a senselessly drunken state (Section 323a), if the offence committed is one of the offences in Nos 1 to 3 the person shall typically be deemed unfit to drive motor-vehicles.

(3) The driving licence shall cease when the judgment becomes final. A driving licence issued by a German public authority shall be subject to a deprivation order in the judgment.".

[29] *See* <https://www.legislationline.org/download/id/6115/file/Germany_CC_am2013_en.pdf> , accessed on October 10, 2023.

[30] Ibid.

[31] Kyle Hyatt & Chris Paukert, Self-driving cars: A level-by-level explainer of autonomous vehicles, CNET (Mar. 29, 2018), https://www.cnet.com/roadshow/news/self-driving-carguide-autonomous-explanation/.

The degree of independence that an AV has will frequently be a deciding factor in determining culpability.[32] A level 3 AV is capable of operating autonomously in specific environments and situations known as the Operational Design Domain ('ODD'),[33] but a human driver still has the final say over the car's operation and is purportedly ready to take over at any time if the ODD arises[34] conditions are exceeded. The issue in a crash involving a Level 3 vehicle is whether the operator or the vehicle is at fault (or both).

Author is of the view that if it is at SAE level 3, the machine is operating as a tool (product and/or service) rather than an independent entity, and the manufacturer will be held liable right directly. In other types of AI, the same rule will apply in holding manufacturers legally accountable depending upon the degree of independence it has.

In a level 4 or level 5 vehicle, the vehicle operates entirely autonomously under certain (level 4) or all (level 5) conditions (or ODDs), hence the question of whether the vehicle should be held accountable rather than the operator arises in the event of a collision.

Because active safety systems[35] (such as automatic braking) are intended to be activated in an emergency and are not included in the digital development technology, they are not included in these six levels (DDT).[36]

Is that right? If it holds the operator fully or partially liable for using the risk-based product.[37] Similarly, another way to hold the operator liable is when an autonomous mode requests to do so and the operator still not taking control (negligence) of the vehicle. Furthermore, is it possible to take control of the car in all circumstances? Who will be held liable in such worsened situations where the operator will have a manual intervention?

The operator is at fault for the accident in partially autonomous cars.[38]

In California, the 'operator' is defined as "the person who is seated in the driver's seat, or, if there is no person in the driver's seat, causes the autonomous technology to engage."[39]

---

[32] Marchant, G., & Bazzi, R. (2020). Autonomous vehicles and liability: what will juries do?. *BUJ Sci. & Tech. L.*, *26*, 67.

[33] Ibid.

[34] SAE INT'L, TAXONOMY AND DEFINITIONS FOR TERMS RELATED TO DRIVING AUTOMATION SYSTEMS FOR ON-ROAD MOTOR VEHICLES 1 (2018).

[35] *Supra* note 32.

[36] Ibid.

[37] Ibid.

[38] *See* <https://www.shouselaw.com/ca/personal-injury/car-accident/self-driving-car-lawsuit/> , accessed on October 10, 2023.

[39] *"California Vehicle Code 38750(4)—**Autonomous Driver—Operator Definition**".*

Autonomous vehicles[40] must feature a safety alert system, according to **'California Vehicle Code § 38,750'**, that will notify the driver if the autonomous technology fails. The operator must also be able to take full control of the situation, which includes the usage of *Brake, accelerator, and steering wheel are all controls on the car.*

In Germany the new provision '***§1b StVG** of the German Road Traffic Act, 2017* addresses the driver's responsibilities. It goes like this:

"§ 1b. Rights and obligations of the vehicle driver when using highly or fully automated driving functions

(1) *While driving the vehicle, the driver may turn away from the traffic situation and the vehicle control when the vehicle is activated by means of highly or fully automated driving functions in accordance with § 1a; in doing so, he must remain so perceptive that he can fulfil his obligation under paragraph 2 at any time.*
(2) *The driver shall be obliged to take over control of the vehicle again without delay,*

   1. *if the highly or fully automated system prompts him to do so, or*
   2. *if he recognizes or must recognize due to obvious circumstances that the prerequisites for the intended use of the highly or fully automated driving functions no longer exist."*

The majority of self-driving cars on the road have a human in the driver's seat. In most cases, autonomous vehicles are pilot projects that require a human test driver or operator to take instant control of the vehicle in the event of an emergency.

If the test driver fails to take control in an emergency, they may be held responsible for the accident. Similarly, if the operator takes control of the vehicle and causes a crash, the test driver may be held accountable. When the self-driving mode is turned off or the test driver overrides the autonomous mode, the car drives like any other vehicle.[41]

Autopilot is a feature available in some vehicles, particularly Tesla models. Although drivers may treat the autopilot system as a self-driving mode, they must still be able to take control of the vehicle in the event of an emergency.[42]

In the US, rules regarding AVs vary in each state. As stated in the California and Nevada law explicitly that the operator would be held liable (strict liability) for any

---

[40] VEHICLE CODE—VEH, DIVISION 16.6. Autonomous Vehicles [38750–38755] *(Division 16.6 added by Stats. 2012, Ch. 570, Sec. 2.).*

38,750: (2) (A) "Autonomous vehicle" means any vehicle equipped with autonomous technology that has been integrated into that vehicle that meets the definition of Level 3, Level 4, or Level 5 of SAE International's "Taxonomy and Definitions for Terms Related to Driving Automation Systems for On-Road Motor Vehicles, standard J3016 (APR2021)," as may be revised.

[41] *Supra* note 38.

[42] Ibid.

incidents or accidents caused by him because he took the risk of using the AV, so he would be only prosecuted for his acts/omission.[43]

Level 4 vehicles can work in self-driving mode. Be that as it may, until enactment and legislative framework advance, they can just do so inside a restricted region (typically a metropolitan climate where maximum velocities or speed arrive at a normal of 30mph). This is known as geofencing. Most Level 4 vehicles such as Tesla presently are designed for ridesharing.[44]

Alphabet's Waymo, as of late, revealed a Level 4 self-driving taxi service in Arizona, where they had been trying driverless cars–without a security driver in the seat–for over a year and more than 10 million miles.[45]

At Level 5 vehicles do not need human attention–the 'dynamic driving task' is eliminated. Level 5 vehicles will not have directing wheels or speed braking down pedals. It will be liberated from geofencing, ready to go anyplace, and do anything that an accomplished human driver can do. Ultimately independent vehicles are going through testing in a few pockets of the world. However, none are accessible to the overall population.[46]

California has begun accepting applications for completely autonomous vehicles. Permits for driverless testing will allow autonomous vehicles to be tested without the use of human test drivers (or steering wheels, gas and brake pedals, or mirrors).[47]

Furthermore, even in Germany, the current regime's remedy for road traffic accidents in which the driver's responsibility is presumed stays unchanged[48] According to the high standard that is normally imposed here, a driver (who is not always the owner of the vehicle) is likely to be merely pardoned if an unforeseeable malfunction of the automated system caused the accident, for example, did not warn in a timely manner. Although **§1b (1) StVG** allows *"the driver to turn away from the traffic situation and vehicle control when the vehicle is activated by highly or fully automated driving functions,"* it is unlikely that the courts will find such a driver guilty of fault if paying attention to the traffic situation would have prevented the accident.

At Level 5, it requires sui generis legislation to regulate this level, because the pre-existing legislation is not at par with Level 5. Therefore, the proposal is that a proper law be put in place to address the current issue, i.e., regulation of SAE Levels 4 and 5.

Ethical Issues:

[43] Ibid.

[44] Ibid.

[45] Ibid.

[46] *See* <https://www.synopsys.com/automotive/autonomous-driving-levels.html> , accessed on October 10, 2023.

[47] *Supra* note 38.

[48] *See* §§ 7, 18 StVG. Under general tort law (§ 823 BGB) the victim must prove the fault of the driver; s., e.g., G. Wagner, in: *Münchener Kommentar zum Bürgerlichen Gesetzbuch* (7th ed. 2017) § 823 n. 85.

The right to privacy, which is essential to safeguarding human dignity, autonomy, and agency, must be respected, upheld, and encouraged throughout the life cycle of AI systems. Data for AI systems must be collected, utilised, shared, stored, and deleted in accordance with applicable national, regional, and international laws as well as international conventions.

Findings:

The following are the findings of the research questions:

1. In the last five years, artificial intelligence has made immense development which has ignited the debate whether or not AI should be recognised as a Legal Person? AI is a technology or system which can take the form of a robot, an AV, a drone, etc. Hence, whether the form and shape of AI matter in the conferment of legal status?

A '2017 European Parliament'[49] report explored the concept of awarding unique legal standing, or 'electronic personality', to smart robots, notably those that (or should that be who?) can learn, adapt, and act independently. This *'legal personhood'* would be comparable to that which has already been bestowed on corporations around the world, and it would hold AI, not people, responsible for their independent actions, including any potential harm they cause. In the long run, giving robots a unique legal status, such that at least the most sophisticated autonomous AI systems such as robots could be established as electronic persons liable for any damage they cause, and possibly applying electronic personality to cases where robots make autonomous decisions or otherwise interact with third parties independently. Making AI liable is also expected to relieve manufacturers of duties that are legally theirs—posing a danger to AI while allowing manufacturers to avoid legal obligation.

Nevertheless, the supporters of AI autonomy have argued that corporations, idols, and incompetent persons also have some rights in law even though they do not possess true consciousness. As a general rule, corporations have 'deeper pockets' than their stakeholders and can be sued as a single entity. Humans create corporations with their interests in mind. Although legal personhood is not limited to humans, it serves primarily to control how people behave. Legal personality is a technical label for a set of rights and obligations, rather than a single concept. Because of the power put upon them, even an AI would have its own set of rights and obligations after being granted an electronic identity in an effort to bring it on par with humanity.

For the time being, it is important to distinguish between when it is necessary to grant AIs legal personality and when they actually deserve it.

The question of whether or not Artificial Intelligence deserves 'personhood' is intertwined with discussions over accountability, autonomy, and responsibility: who is responsible for the AI's actions and consequences: the AI or the person(s) who designs it? A few creators think of it as a "***recreation of things not thing itself***."

---

[49] TURNER, J. (2019). *ROBOT RULES-Regulating Artificial Intelligence*, London-UK: Palgrave Macmillan, ISBN-978-3-319-96,234-4, pp. 82–102.

This proposal would put many AI systems on the same legal footing as companies, rather than making it easier for AI to be treated as a person in the traditional sense. It's important to emphasise that the legal personality of businesses can shield humans from the repercussions of breaking the law. On the other hand, the 'UNI Global Union' has argued that the creator or designer, not the AI system, is legally responsible and has pushed for a ban on blaming AI.

Fixing liability in the event of any injury or loss caused by AI to humans requires determining the status of AI since autonomous AI will make decisions in the same way that humans do, and it is appropriate to recognise AI as a legal person.

The recognition of an entity establishing its own rights and duties under legal personhood is crucial since AI is more than a machine now and can be improved to the level of Artificial General Intelligence and Artificial Super Intelligence in the future.

2. The security concerns, risks, and challenges concerning the use of AI systems, particularly in the context of an AV such as the following:

Potentials	Risks
Improved transportation efficiency	Driver and car safety malfunctions
Fewer accidents	Algorithmic concerns and malfunctions
Decreased traffic congestion	Vehicle communication and wireless privacy concerns
Increased Highway capacity	Vehicles can be switched off on the road (in rare cases)
Lower Fuel Consumption	Less security when using Internet
Parking ease of mind	Hackers can be changing routes (in rare cases)
Improved mobility for elderly, children, and disabled	In case of failure of Sensors vehicle can create a chance of accidents
Large market and consumer demographic	In rainfall cars cannot recognise traffic signals
Relieving Vehicles	
Determine current location	

Reliance can be placed on AI system because the technology controls the vehicle, and autonomous cars avoid human errors. It eliminates the possibility of distraction, unlike people who are easily distracted. It also employs complex algorithms to determine the proper stopping distance between two vehicles. As a result, the risk of accidents is greatly reduced. But at the same time, the security concern is related to hacking, Autonomous automobiles,[50] which track and analyse the owner's details in real time, could be the next big target for hackers. This could lead to the acquisition of personal information.

[50] *"**Section 66** of The Information Technology Act, 2000- Computer hacking or unauthorized use of computer systems and networks. If found guilty, users could face up to three years in prison and/ or a fine of up to Rs 5 lakh".*

It's possible that when a vehicle is in autonomous mode, the autonomous control disengages[51] due to an error or situations that the system can't handle.[52] Companies testing autonomous technology in California[53] are required to disclose any disengagements of the test vehicles' autonomous systems. The DMV[54] had received 456 Autonomous Vehicle Collision Reports as of April 28, 2022.[55]

The security concerns about the use of AI technology are as follows:

1. A significant area of product liability[56] to which AVs may be subject is failure to warn responsibility.[57] A plaintiff hurt in an AV accident could separately claim that the manufacturer's failure to provide adequate warning about the AV's limitations and risks of crashing contributed to the crash and injuries,[58] regardless of whether the legal factfinder determines the manufacturer's failure to provide adequate warning about the AV's limitations and risks of crashing.[59]
2. In order to succeed in a claim for failure to warn, the plaintiff would[60] need to demonstrate that the warning provided was insufficient and that an accident might have been prevented with a clearer or more obvious warning.[61]
3. Manufacturers of Level 2 or Level 3 semi-autonomous vehicles must issue warnings and demand that the driver be involved and alert.[62] In fact, active warning systems are currently in place to alert the driver to take control, to actively monitor the driver's response, and to carry out a fail-safe manoeuvre[63] to draw the car off the road and to stop it if the human driver is unable to maintain control of the vehicle.[64] If the active warning system performs as intended, it is difficult to see how an AV maker[65] could be held liable for failing to warn the driver to take control[66] in safe circumstances. According to the Restatement, "Users of the Product may not be sufficiently reached, may be inattentive, or may be inadequately motivated to follow the directions or heed the warnings, [which] may result in instructions and warnings being ineffective."[67] A manufacturer

[51] *Supra* note 32.
[52] Ibid.
[53] *Id.*
[54] Ibid.
[55] Ibid.
[56] *Id.*
[57] Ibid.
[58] Ibid.
[59] *Supra* note 32.
[60] Ibid.
[61] *Id.*
[62] Ibid.
[63] Ibid.
[64] Mark A. Geistfeld, *A Roadmap for Autonomous Vehicles: State Tort Liability, Automobile Insurance, and Federal Safety Regulation*, 105 CAL. L. REV. 1611, 1616–17 (2017).
[65] Ibid.
[66] Ibid.
[67] *"RESTATEMENT (THIRD) OF TORTS: PRODS. LIAB. § 2 cmt. l (AM. LAW INST. 1998)".*

of autonomous vehicles is unlikely to be able to foresee the majority of specific accident scenarios. These kinds of accidents are more likely to occur under unanticipated circumstances that the AV operating system had never encountered throughout its training cycle.[68] If a vehicle manufacturer adequately monitors and promptly corrects for such accident situations, there seems to be no basis for failure to warn responsibility.[69]

4. AV accident risks may be more foreseeable in a few specific general driving scenarios, including as bad weather, strange road layouts, or construction zones on major highways. However, there seems to be limited potential for claims and culpability if the AV manufacturer provides advice regarding such unusual scenarios.[70]
5. Even while failure to warn claims is unlikely to be successful in the majority of AV accident lawsuits, manufacturer warnings may feasibly provide AV manufacturers with some liability protection in design flaw liability claims. Some product liability specialists contend that good manufacturers may be exempt from responsibility for design flaws (particularly under the consumer expectation test).[71] A notice is sent regarding any limitations or elimination of manufacturer duty. A warning would not shield the AV manufacturer from liability for other parties, such as occupants of another vehicle struck by the AV, bystanders struck by the AV, or even passengers riding in the AV, as they would only apply to the operator (who would receive the warning when purchasing the vehicle).[72] None of those parties would have missed the warning.
6. Manufacturers of AVs may not be able to predict all possible failure modes and accident scenarios that an AV may experience, and hence they cannot always issue warnings about them.[73] The AV manufacturer could only issue a general warning about the possibility of an unexpected failure as a result.[74] As a result, a plaintiff's expert will claim that, with the benefit of hindsight, the manufacturer should have provided a warning regarding the failure mode for the specific accident at hand.[75] Given the difficulties of predicting every accident scenario, product accountability has struggled to establish the required amount of product warnings that need to be precise.[76] Furthermore, it is well-established under the

---

[68] *See id.*

[69] *Supra note 64.*

[70] Ibid.

[71] *Supra* note 64; See also ("An adequate warning about the safe use and inherent risks of a safely designed autonomous vehicle will absolve the manufacturer from liability for crashes caused by the fully functioning operating system.").

[72] *"RESTATEMENT (THIRD) OF TORTS: PRODS. LIAB. § 2 cmt. i (AM. LAW INST. 1998)".*

[73] *Supra* note 64.

[74] Ibid.

[75] Ibid.

[76] *Supra* note 32; *"RESTATEMENT (THIRD) OF TORTS: PRODS. LIAB. § 2 cmt. i (AM. LAW INST. 1998)"* ("It is impossible to identify anything approaching a perfect level of detail that should be communicated in product disclosures... No easy guideline exists for courts to adopt in assessing the adequacy of product warnings and instructions.").

Restatement that a warning will not suffice to preclude responsibility if a design adjustment may have eliminated or minimised the danger warned about, which is another problem with relying on generic warnings for manufacturers.[77] As stated earlier, a competent plaintiff's expert can often identify a design adjustment to the AV, even if it were simply a few lines of code in the operating system that may have averted the accident.[78]

7. Lastly, the idea that AVs will be safer than human-driven vehicles contradicts a clear warning about the risks they entail. Both the commercial success of AVs and the court's willingness to consider AVs are impacted by the public's perception of safety.[79] These consumer and juror safety messages would be contradicted and undermined by harsh warnings that AVs are intrinsically dangerous.[80] Advocates of using warnings to shield AV manufacturers from accountability for torts use the example of cigarettes,[81] where package labels stating that nicotine is highly hazardous and carcinogenic helped to protect the manufacturers from blame.[82]

"Once the typical customer has been appropriately advised that smoking causes cancer, his or her basic safety expectations would not be violated if that product usage caused cancer," according to tobacco warnings.[83]

However, unlike cigarettes, AVs[84] won't ultimately jeopardise public safety; therefore, the 'warning strategy' utilised by cigarette businesses to evade responsibility would probably 'backfire for AV' companies under the umbrella of punitive penalties.[85]

3. The following questions emerge in case of determining the liability of AI in the context of an autonomous vehicle when a tort occurs:

Who should bear liability manufacturer/ producer, designer, owner, or user?[86]

What changes it could see in terms of '*the principles of negligent design' or 'standard of care'?* As AI keeps evolving, soon it would start making its decisions on its own, so depending on this analogy, it would consider it as an *agent of the developer* in the future, and if, yes, then would that developer becomes liable vicariously, in terms of whatever acts done by AI perhaps resultant into negligence.[87]

---

[77] *Supra* note 32; *See* "RESTATEMENT (THIRD) OF TORTS: PRODS. LIAB. § 2 cmt. 1 (AM. LAW INST. 1998)".*See* Marchant & Lindor, supra note 106, at 1334.

[78] *Id.*

[79] *Id.*

[80] *Supra* note 32.

[81] Ibid.

[82] *Supra* note 64.

[83] *Id.*

[84] *Supra note 64.*

[85] Ibid.

[86] Ibid.

[87] *Id.*

Liability of AI under the Law of Negligence in India

The present research has tried to analyse whether the Indian law is adequate to determine the tortious liability in the case of Autonomous Vehicles especially in the case of Contributory Negligence.

Due to the lack of a driver in an autonomous vehicle, it will be difficult for the plaintiff to prove their claim under contributory negligence in India, or SAE Level 4–5, as this would shift some of the blame for the unfortunate event from the defendant to the plaintiff.

Being a futuristic technology, where it would have its own autonomy in its acts and decision-making capability after decades, where the legal status of AI would be decided, to hold AVs liable for their own actions and to impose contributory negligence liability under tort law.

How does the law define contributing negligence in the context of SAE Level 0–3? The following further explanations are listed as follows:

In **Level 0**, the full-time performance by the human driver of all aspects of the dynamic driving task, even when enhanced by warning or intervention systems. Who, once again, is in charge of steering and acceleration/deceleration? Who will be held accountable for negligence? Another aspect of driving a car is the monitoring of the driving environment, which is done by a human driver. Who is the performing, answer is *the human driver* if a fallback execution of the dynamic driving task is available. Is there any capability (driving mode) in the system? The answer is negative. As a result of the arguments presented by the author, it is believed that only human drivers/operators are liable under the law of negligence because the car is under their complete control.

In **Level 1** (Driver Assistance), the execution of steering or acceleration/deceleration by a driver assistance system is based on data about the driving environment, with the hope that the human operator will handle the other parts of the dynamic driving task. Who will be held accountable for negligence, now that the answer is a human driver and system. Is there any capability (driving mode) in the system? The answer is some driving modes. As a result of the arguments presented by the author, it is concluded that only human drivers/operators are liable under the law of negligence because the car is under their complete control.

In **Level 2** (Partial Automation), the application of steering and acceleration/deceleration by one or more driver assistance systems in accordance with information about the driving environment, with the hope that the human driver would handle the advanced settings of the dynamic driving task. Here the system is in charge of steering and acceleration/deceleration. Who will be held accountable for negligence, in cases where the system is in charge of steering and control?

Another aspect of driving a car is the monitoring of the driving environment, which is likewise done by a human driver. If a fallback execution of the dynamic driving task is available, who is the performing *human driver*. Is there any capability (driving mode) in the system? Who is performing? The system is the answer. It is concluded that only human drivers/operators are liable under the law of negligence because the car is under their complete control.

SAE Level 3–5: Automated driving system ('system') monitors the driving environment.

In **Level 3** (Conditional Automation), in a certain driving mode, the automated driving system will handle every aspect of the dynamic driving task with the hope that the human driver will react appropriately when asked to intervene. Who, once again, is in charge of steering and acceleration/deceleration? Who will be held accountable for negligence now that the answer is a *system*. Another aspect of driving a car is the monitoring of the driving environment, which is done by a *system*. If a fallback execution of the dynamic driving task is available, who is the performing, answer is *the human driver*. Is there any capability (driving mode) in the system? Who is performing? The system is the answer. As a result of the arguments presented by the author, the author contends that the human driver/operator and the manufacturer are both guilty under the law of negligence.

In **Level 4** (High Automation), in a certain driving mode, the automated driving system will handle every aspect of the dynamic driving task with the hope that the human driver will react appropriately when asked to intervene. In this situation, the AI system is in charge of steering and acceleration/deceleration. Who will be held liable for negligence in this situation? Another aspect of driving a car is the monitoring of the driving environment, which is likewise done by a *system*. If a fallback execution of the dynamic driving task is available, who is performing? The system is the answer. Is there any capability (driving mode) in the system? Who is performing? The system is the answer. The author contends that the manufacturer is liable as a result of the arguments presented, but that a sui generis law is required to deal with cases of negligence in India, or that a place should be given under existing legislation to deal with Level 4 autonomous cars, as the existing provisions only deal with human drivers, not machines or autonomous cars.

In **Level 5** (Full Automation), the performance of all dynamic driving task components by a fully automated driving system in all traffic and environmental circumstances that a human driver is capable of handling. Who, once again, is in charge of steering and acceleration/deceleration? Who will be held liable for negligence? Now that the answer is a *system*. The monitoring of the driving environment is another aspect of operating a vehicle and is also carried out by a system. Who is the performing, system if a fallback execution of the dynamic driving task is possible. Does the system have any functionality (driving mode)? All types of driving are the solution. The author contends that the manufacturer is liable as a result of the arguments presented, but that a sui generis law is required to deal with cases of negligence in India, or that a place should be given under existing legislation to deal with Level 5 autonomous cars, as the existing provisions only deal with human drivers, not machines or autonomous cars.

Liability of AI under the Law of Strict and Product Liability in India

Under Sections 2(33), 2(34), 2(10), 2(12), 2(36), 2(37), 2(38), and 2(35) of the Consumer Protection Act, 2019, damage must be caused by the use of a product's defect, the law on strict and product liability would apply in the case of SAE Level

0–5. It establishes a legal framework for product liability. Only a product should be considered if a part is defective. Sections 2(33), 2(34), 2(10), 2(12), 2(36), 2(37), 2(38), and 2(35) of the Consumer Protection Act, 2019 also apply if the car is SAE Level 0–2, with a human driver/operator in charge of the vehicle and monitoring the environment. Even though the car is SAE Level 3–5, if the autonomous driving system monitors the driving environment, this part is sufficient to hold the manufacturer liable under the law of product liability.

Liability of AI under the Law of Vicarious Liability in India

In India, vicarious liability for autonomous vehicles, i.e., SAE Level 4–5, would move from the employer-employee relationship to the owner-manufacturer one.

Vicarious liability will be imposed in situations where an autonomous vehicle is at SAE Level 0 through 3. For SAE Levels 4 and 5, *sui generis law* is required to deal with the case of vicarious liability in India.

Why is it that it is applicable only for the level 0–3? Because, according to SAE Level 4–5, a relationship will be established between the owner of the car and self-driving cars once they become autonomous in nature. Under the category of vicarious liability, self-driving cars will act as an employee who is acting in the regular course of employment.

Indeed, even without making another or extended legislative framework, the current legal framework is, on a fundamental level, fit for covering AI-based advances. The specific test is to cover the space of AI accurately if the current liability framework remains set up for the appraisal of prospective risk.

Liability of AI under the Law of Negligence in Germany

The present research has tried to analyse whether these provisions under the German law are adequate to determine the tortious liability in the case of Autonomous vehicles? The applicability of these provisions to AVs.

A comprehensive analysis of these provisions reveals that existing provisions such as §§ 823 BGB, 823 BGB I, 823 BGB II,823 BGB III, 276 I BGB, 276 I 2 BGB, 839 BGB, 839 I 1 BGB, and 839 I 2 BGB only apply to human drivers or car owners who are held liable for negligence and subject to punitive damages under tort law. ***Whoever causes a person's death by negligence faces a penalty of up to five years in prison or a fine.***

Whoever*, who is considered as a natural and legal person in this context, in the category of SAE Level 0–3 is adequately regulated and governed by the existing provisions. However, in the case of highly and fully autonomous systems, i.e., SAE Levels 4 and 5, the existing provisions and framework to impose liability of any kind are not adequate; in SAE Level 0–3, there is a presence of human intervention to control the AI; whereas in SAE Level 4–5, no human intervention is present.*

CONCLUSION —There is a gap in the legislation that does not specifically cover the highly and fully autonomous system.

PROPOSAL—That a proper law be put in place to regulate SAE Levels 4 and 5.

Now, because it must be viewed from the perspective of SAE Level 0–2, where the car is perfectly under the control of the human driver, the human driver monitors the driving environment in these scenarios. Now author will look at whether the same law applies in cases of negligence ranging from SAE Level 0 to 5 when compared to existing provisions in the law of negligence, such as §§ 823 BGB, 823 BGB I, 823 BGB II, 276 I BGB, 276 I 2 BGB, 839 BGB, 839 I 1 BGB, and 839 I 2 BGB, with SAE Level 0 to 5.

According to the author, it will be used on a frequent basis whenever the situation necessitates it because it is entirely in the hands of the human driver/owner/user of a car, who can monitor the driving environment.

Liability of AI under the Law of Strict and Product Liability in Germany

The law on strict and product liability would also be applicable in the case of 'SAE Level 0–5' because as per '§§ 2, 3 of the German Product Liability Law, 1989', the damage must be produced by the use of a product's defect which provides for law on liability for defective products. A defective part should only be considered a product. If the car is SAE Level 0–2, with a human driver/operator in charge of the vehicle and monitoring the environment, then '§§ 2, 3 of the German Product Liability Law' also applies. Even though the car is SAE Level 3–5, if the autonomous driving system monitors the driving environment, this part is sufficient to hold the manufacturer liable under the law of product liability.

Liability of AI under the Law of Vicarious Liability in Germany

The author has tried to analyse what this provision '§ 831 BGB of the German Civil Code,1900' means in terms of AVs. What role can this section have in determining vicarious liability if an AV is involved in an accident? A comprehensive analysis of these provisions reveals that existing provisions such as § 831 BGB of the German Civil Code,1900 only apply to human driver or/and car owner who are held liable for vicarious liability and subject to punitive damages under tort law. Now, because it must be viewed from the perspective of SAE Level 0–2, where the car is perfectly under the control of the human driver, the human driver monitors the driving environment in these scenarios. Now author will look at whether the same law applies in cases of vicarious liability ranging from SAE Level 0 to 5. So, according to the author, it will be applied on a regular basis whenever the scenario requires it because it is totally in the hands of the human driver/owner/user who is driving a car because the operator can monitor the driving environment. When compared to existing provisions in the law of vicarious liability, such as § 831 BGB of the German Civil Code,1900 with SAE Level 0 to 5.

Liability of AI under the Law of Negligence in California

The criterion used under "Californian law is pure comparative negligence." This means that the plaintiff is entitled to compensation for all losses brought on by the defendants. Even if the plaintiff is substantially at blame, the amount of the award may nevertheless be reduced by the plaintiff's own negligence.

After analysing the provisions under the 'California Civil Code,1988—Section 1714 and California Code of Civil Procedure,1872—Sections 335.1, 338(b) and (c), 340.5 and 0.6' it seems that similar to the German legal framework. The applicability of these provisions to AVs whether or not AI liability can be determined under the existing provisions, particularly when an AV is involved in an accident? If yes, why and how?

A comprehensive analysis of these provisions reveals that existing provisions such as 'California Civil Code Section 1714' only apply to human drivers or car owners who are held liable for negligence and subject to punitive damages under tort law. Now, because it must be viewed from the perspective of SAE Level 0–2, where the car is perfectly under the control of the human driver, the human driver monitors the driving environment in these scenarios. Now author will look at whether the same law applies in cases of negligence ranging from SAE Level 0 to 5. So, according to the author, it will be applied on a regular basis whenever the scenario requires it because it is totally in the hands of the human driver/owner/user who is driving a car because the operator can monitor the driving environment. When compared to existing provisions in the law of negligence, such as 'California Civil Code Section 1714, California Code of Civil Procedure,1872—Sections 335.1, 338(b) and (c), 340.5 and 0.6 with SAE Level 0 to 5', the outcome is even in **Level 0** (No Automation), the full-time performance by the human driver of all aspects of the dynamic driving task, even when enhanced by warning or intervention systems. Who, once again, is in charge of steering and acceleration/deceleration? Who will be responsible for gross negligence? The solution is now a human driver. The monitoring of the driving environment, which is also done by a human driver, is another part of operating a vehicle. Who is the performing human driver if a backup execution of the dynamic driving task is available. Does the system have any functionality (driving mode)? The answer is negative.

As a result of the arguments presented by the author, the author argues that only *human driver/operator* are liable under the law of negligence under 'California Civil Code Section 1714, California Code of Civil Procedure,1872—Sections 335.1, 338(b) and (c), 340.5 and 0.6'.

Liability of AI under the Law of Strict and Product Liability in California

California Product Liability is defined under 'Section 1714.45 of the California Civil Code,1872', the rule on strict and product liability would also apply in the instance of 'SAE Level 0–5'. According to 'Sections 38,755 and 38,750' of the Autonomous Vehicles, division 16.6 of the California Vehicle Code,1993, which creates a legal foundation for product liability, the damage must be caused by the use of a product's fault. Only a defective part should be considered a product. If the car is 'SAE Level 0–2', and there is a human driver/operator in charge of the vehicle and monitoring the surroundings, 'Product Liability § § 2, 3, and 5 of the Restatement (THIRD) of Torts' also apply. Even if the car is 'SAE Level 3–5', if the autonomous driving system monitors the driving environment, this portion is sufficient to make them liable under strict and product liability laws.

Liability of AI under the Law of Vicarious Liability in California

The author has tried to analyse what this provision 'Sections(§§) 423 and 424, §§17,707,17,708 and 38,750 of the California Vehicle Code,1993' and 'Sections 17 and 1714.1 of the California Civil Code,1872' mean in terms of AVs. What role can this section have in determining vicarious liability if an AV is involved in an accident? A comprehensive analysis of these provisions reveals that existing provisions such as 'Sections(§§)423 and 424, §§17,707,17,708, and 38,750 of the California Vehicle Code,1993' and 'Sections 17 and 1714.1 of the California Civil Code,1872' only apply to human driver or/and car owner who are held liable for vicarious liability and subject to punitive damages under tort law. Now, because it must be viewed from the perspective of 'SAE Level 0–2', where the car is perfectly under the control of the human driver, the human driver monitors the driving environment in these scenarios. Now author will look at whether the same law applies in cases of vicarious liability ranging from 'SAE Level 0 to 5'. So, according to the author, it will be applied on a regular basis whenever the scenario requires it because it is totally in the hands of the human driver/owner/user who is driving a car because the operator can monitor the driving environment. When compared to existing provisions in the law of vicarious liability, such as 'Sections(§§) 423 and 424, §§17,707, 17,708, and 38,750 of the California Vehicle Code,1993' and 'Section 17 of the California Civil Code,1872', which talks about the master-servant relationship one person is liable for the actions that caused liability for another person, the 'agent', for acts/actions performed or undertaken by the 'principal'. Based on a legal maxim: *Qui facit per alium facit* per se, which is a Latin legal term that means "*He who acts through another does the act himself*" with the SAE Level 0 to 5, the outcome is even.

2. The first step in determining AI's criminal liability is to evaluate if the principles of actus reus and mens rea apply to AI, particularly when dealing with AVs. And if the answer is yes, then can a machine have its own mens rea to commit any crime per se, and if so, at what level of autonomy does it have? Because if it is seen through the case of autonomous cars level 4–5, where it is highly and fully autonomous—reached the level of AGI and ASI, then the machine will definitely be liable for its acts for making decisions on its own.

In cases where there is still manual intervention and the autonomous vehicle is still at SAE level 0–3, the machine operates as a tool (product and/or service) rather than an independent entity, and the manufacturer will be held liable right directly. In other types of AI, the same rule will apply in holding manufacturers legally accountable.

However, this can be convenient because the significance of 'intention' in India's criminal law jurisprudence is essential to build up AI's legitimate character personality. For example, artificial intelligence will have many rights and duties. To address the inquiry on liability, since AI is viewed as lifeless, a strict obligation that holds the manufacturer or producer of the product liable for the harm, subject for the damage, no-fault liability (regardless of the fault), possibly a way to deal with considering AI's singularity.

Determination of Criminal Liability of AI in India

The present research has tried to analyse whether these provisions under the Indian law are adequate to determine the criminal liability in the case of autonomous vehicles? The applicability of these provisions to AVs.

A comprehensive analysis of these provisions reveals that existing provisions such as Rash Driving or Riding on Public Way under ***'Section 281 of Bharatiya Nyaya Sanhita, 2023'***: *causing death by negligence* under ***'Section 106 of Bharatiya Nyaya Sanhita, 2023'***: *act endangering life or personal safety of others* under ***'Section 125 of Bharatiya Nyaya Sanhita, 2023'***, *causing hurt by act endangering life or personal safety of others* under ***'Section 125(a) of Bharatiya Nyaya Sanhita, 2023'***, *causing grievous hurt by act endangering life or personal safety of others* under ***'Section 125(b) of Bharatiya Nyaya Sanhita, 2023'*** *who are held liable for negligence and subject to punishment under criminal law.* In these circumstances, the human driver monitors the driving environment since it must be regarded from the perspective of SAE Level 0–2, where the car is perfectly under the control of the human driver. Whether the same law applies in negligence situations ranging from SAE Level 0 to 2 and SAE Level 3–5? When comparing existing provisions in the criminal law of negligence connected to traditional driving, such as ***'Sections (281, 106, 125, 125(a), 125(b)) BNS, 2023'***, to 'SAE Level 0 to 5', autonomous driving, the outcome is as follows:

Section 281: Negligent manslaughter— Whoever drives a vehicle or rides on a public route in such a reckless and careless manner as to threaten human life or to be likely to cause harm or injury to another person shall be punished with either imprisonment for a term of up to six months or a fine of up to one thousand rupees, or both. In this context, whoever is considered a natural and legal person is true to 'SAE Level 0–3' but not to a highly and fully autonomous system, because autonomous systems are independent in their actions and reasoning, whereas in 'SAE Level 0–3', humans control and monitor the AI agent/tool/machine on their own, and human intervention is present to control the AI agent/tool/machine. As a result, the author observed that there is a gap in the legislation that does not specifically cover the highly and fully autonomous system. The author proposed that a proper law be put in place to address the current issue, namely 'SAE Level 4s and 5'.

Section 106-Causing bodily harm by negligence—Whoever causes the death of another person by committing any rash or negligent conduct that does not amount to culpable homicide is punishable by imprisonment of any sort for a time up to five years, a fine, or both. In this context, whoever is considered a natural and legal person is true to 'SAE Level 0–3' but not to a highly and fully autonomous system, because autonomous systems are independent in their actions and reasoning, whereas in 'SAE Level 0–3', humans control and monitor the AI agent/tool/machine on their own, and human intervention is present to control the AI agent/tool/machine. As a result, the author observed that there is a gap in the legislation that does not specifically cover the highly and fully autonomous system. It is proposed that a proper law be put in place to address the current issue, namely the regulation of 'SAE Levels 4 and 5'.

Section 125-Endangering road traffic—Whoever does an act so rashly or negligently as to harm human life or the personal safety of others shall be punished with imprisonment of either sort for a term up to three months, or a fine up to Rs. 2500/-, or both. In this context, whoever is considered a natural and legal person is true to SAE Level 0–3 but not to a highly and fully autonomous system, because autonomous systems are independent in their actions and reasoning, whereas in 'SAE Level 0–3', humans control and monitor the AI agent/tool/machine on their own, and human intervention is present to control the AI agent/tool/machine. It has been observed that there is a gap in the legislation that does not specifically cover the highly and fully autonomous system. Hence it is proposed that a proper law be put in place to address the current issue, i.e., regulation of 'SAE Levels 4 and 5'.

Section 125(a)-Driving under the influence of drink or drugs only applies to human drivers or car owners—Whoever causes harm to another person by acting rashly or negligently in such a way as to endanger human life or the personal safety of others is punishable by imprisonment of either description for a time up to six months, or a fine up to five thousand rupees, or both. In this context, whoever is considered a natural and legal person is true to SAE Level 0–3 but not to a highly and fully autonomous system, because autonomous systems are independent in their actions and reasoning, whereas in 'SAE Level 0–3', humans control and monitor the AI agent/tool/machine on their own, and human intervention is present to control the AI agent/tool/machine. As a result, the author observed that there is a gap in the legislation that does not specifically cover the highly and fully autonomous system. The author proposed that a proper law be put in place to address the current issue, namely 'SAE Levels 4 and 5'.

Section 125(b)-Driving under the influence of drink or drugs only applies to human drivers or car owners—Whoever causes serious harm to another by acting rashly or negligently in such a way as to endanger human life or the personal safety of others shall be punished with imprisonment of either sort for a time up to three years, or a fine up to ten thousand rupees, or both. In this context, because autonomous systems are independent in their actions and reasoning, anyone who is regarded as a natural and legal person is true to 'SAE Level 0–3', but not to a highly and fully autonomous system. In 'SAE Level 0–3', humans control and monitor the AI agent/tool/machine on their own, and human intervention is present to control the AI agent/tool/machine. The author concluded that this leaves a legal gap as highly and fully autonomous systems are not specifically addressed in the law. The study suggested 'SAE Levels 4 and 5' as a suitable law to be implemented to address the existing issue.

Determination of Criminal Liability of AI in Germany

Whether these provisions cover AVs also. The present research has tried to analyse whether these provisions under the German law are adequate to determine the criminal liability in the case of autonomous vehicles?

A comprehensive analysis of these provisions reveals existing provisions such as Section 222- *Negligent manslaughter*, Section 229-*Causing bodily harm by negligence*, Section 315 c-*Endangering Road Traffic*, and Section 316-*Driving under the influence of drink or drugs only applies to human drivers or car owners* who are held liable for negligence and subject to punishment under criminal law. In these circumstances, the human driver monitors the driving environment since it must be regarded from the perspective of SAE Level 0–2, where the car is perfectly under the control of the human driver. The author will now investigate whether the same law applies in negligence situations ranging from SAE Level 0 to 2 and SAE Level 3–5. When comparing existing provisions in the criminal law of negligence connected to traditional driving, such as 'Sections (222, 229, 315 c, and 316)', to 'SAE Level 0 to 5', autonomous driving, the outcome is as follows:

Section 222: Negligent manslaughter—Whoever causes the death of another person by negligence suffers a penalty of up to five years in jail or a fine. In this context, whoever is considered a natural and legal person is true to 'SAE Level 0–3' but not to a highly and fully autonomous system, because autonomous systems are independent in their actions and reasoning, whereas in 'SAE Level 0–3', humans control and monitor the AI agent/tool/machine on their own, and human intervention is present to control the AI agent/tool/machine. As a result, the author observed that there is a gap in the legislation that does not specifically cover the highly and fully autonomous system. The author proposed that a proper law be put in place to address the current issue, namely 'SAE Levels 4 and 5'.

Section 229-Causing bodily harm by negligence—Whoever causes bodily harm to another by negligence faces a punishment of up to three years in prison or a fine. In this context, whoever is considered a natural and legal person is true to 'SAE Level 0–3' but not to a highly and fully autonomous system, because autonomous systems are independent in their actions and reasoning, whereas in 'SAE Level 0–3', humans control and monitor the AI agent/tool/machine on their own, and human intervention is present to control the AI agent/tool/machine. As a result, the author observed that there is a gap in the legislation that does not specifically cover the highly and fully autonomous system. The author proposed that a proper law be put in place to address the current issue, namely 'SAE Levels 4 and 5'.

Section 315c-Endangering road traffic—Whoever, in road traffic drives a vehicle while intoxicated or unable to drive safely due to the consumption of alcoholic drinks or other intoxicating substances, or due to mental or physical deficiencies, or in gross violation of road traffic regulations, and causes bodily harm to another by negligence faces a penalty of imprisonment for a term not exceeding three years or a fine. In this context, whoever is considered a natural and legal person is true to 'SAE Level 0–3' but not to a highly and fully autonomous system, because autonomous systems are independent in their actions and reasoning, whereas in 'SAE Level 0–3', humans control and monitor the AI agent/tool/machine on their own, and human intervention is present to control the AI agent/tool/machine. As a result, the author observed that there is a gap in the legislation that does not specifically cover the highly and fully autonomous system. The author proposed that a proper law be put in place to address the current issue, namely 'SAE Levels 4 and 5'.

Section 316-Driving under the influence of drink or drugs only applies to human drivers or car owners—Unless the offence is punishable under 'Section 315a or 315c', whoever drives a vehicle in traffic while intoxicated (Sections 315 to 315e) faces a punishment of imprisonment for a period not exceeding one year or a fine. In this context, whoever is considered a natural and legal person is true to 'SAE Level 0–3' but not to a highly and fully autonomous system, because autonomous systems are independent in their actions and reasoning, whereas in 'SAE Level 0–3', humans control and monitor the AI agent/tool/machine on their own, and human intervention is present to control the AI agent/tool/machine. As a result, the author observed that there is a gap in the legislation that does not specifically cover the highly and fully autonomous system. The author proposed that a proper law be put in place to address the current issue, namely 'SAE Levels 4 and 5'.

The full-time execution of all components of the dynamic driving task by the human driver at Level 0, even when assisted by warning or intervention systems. Humans are once more in charge of steering, acceleration, and deceleration. Who will be responsible for negligence, now that a driver is the solution. The monitoring of the driving environment, which is also done by a human driver, is another part of operating a vehicle. Who is the performing, human driver if a backup execution of the dynamic driving task is available. Does the system have any functionality (driving mode)? The response is no. As a result of the author's reasoning, the author believes that SAE Level 0 is true to traditional driving, and thus the same sections will apply to SAE Level 0, namely Sections 222: Negligent manslaughter, Section 229: Causing bodily harm by negligence, Section 315 c: Endangering Road Traffic, and Section 316: Driving under the influence of drink or drugs.

Determination of Criminal Liability of AI in California

A comprehensive analysis of this provision reveals existing provisions such as Vehicular under Section 192 sub-Section 2(c) of the California Penal Code, 1872, who are held liable for rash, reckless, and negligence driving and subject to punishment under criminal law. In this circumstance, the human driver monitors the driving environment since it must be regarded from the perspective of SAE Level 0–2, where the car is perfectly under the control of the human driver. The author will now investigate whether the same law applies in negligence situations ranging from SAE Level 0 to 2 and SAE Level 3–5. When comparing existing provisions in the criminal law of negligence connected to traditional driving, such as Section 192 sub-Section 2(c), to SAE Level 0 to 5, autonomous driving, the outcome is as follows:

Section 192 (c) (1): negligence driving—"driving a vehicle in the commission of an unlawful act, not amounting to felony, and with gross negligence; or driving a vehicle in the commission of a lawful act which might produce death, in an unlawful manner, and with gross negligence." In this context, driving a vehicle is considered; a natural and legal person is true to SAE Level 0–3 but not to a highly and fully autonomous system, because autonomous systems are independent in their actions and reasoning, whereas in SAE Level 0–3, humans control and monitor the AI agent/tool/machine on their own, and human intervention is present to control the AI agent/tool/machine. As a result, the author observed that there is a gap in the legislation that does not specifically cover the highly and fully autonomous system. The author proposed that a proper law be put in place to address the current issue, namely SAE Levels 4 and 5.

3. To name a few international conventions—the "*Universal Declaration of Human Rights (1948),*[88] *the instruments of the international human rights framework, the Discrimination (Employment and Occupation) Convention (1958), the International Convention on the Elimination of All Forms of Racial Discrimination*

[88] *See* <https://unesdoc.unesco.org/ark:/48223/pf0000381137?3=null&queryId=c5dd8ced-9647-452b-b4d6-92723006496c> , accessed on October 12, 2023.

(1965), the International Covenant on Civil and Political Rights (1966), the International Covenant on Economic, Social, and Cultural Rights (1966), the Convention on the Elimination of All Forms of Discrimination Against Women (1979), the Convention on the Rights of the Child (1989), and the Convention on the Rights of Persons with Disabilities (2006), the Convention Against Discrimination in Education (1960), the Convention on the Protection and Promotion of the Diversity of Cultural Expressions (2005)," other relevant international instruments, recommendations, and declarations also mentioned and so forth.[89]

Noticing the profound and dynamic effects of artificial intelligence (AI)[90] on ecosystems, societies, the environment, and human lives, including the human mind, in part because of the new ways that its use affects learning, human, social, and natural sciences, culture, communication, and information technology.[91] Although AI technologies have the potential to be extremely beneficial to humanity and that all nations can benefit from them, they also raise some fundamental ethical concerns, including the biases they can encode and aggravate, potentially leading to discrimination, inequality, digital divides, exclusion, and a threat to cultural, social, and biological diversity, as well as social and economic divides; the need for transparency and understanding of algorithmic workings; and the data they were created with. Recognising that AI technologies[92] have the potential to exacerbate existing divides and inequalities in the world, both within and between countries, and that justice, trust, and fairness must be upheld to ensure that no country or person is left behind, either by having fair access to AI technologies and reaping their benefits or by being protected from their negative consequences, while taking into account the unique circumstances of different countries and recognising that some people do not wish to participate in all technology improvements.[93]

Addressing vulnerabilities and ethical issues shouldn't inhibit innovation and progress; rather, it should create new opportunities[94] and promote ethically conducted

---

[89] Ibid. *The "United Nations Declaration on the Right to Development (1986); the Declaration on the Responsibilities of Current Generations Towards Future Generations (1997); the Universal Declaration on Bioethics and Human Rights (2005); and the United Nations Declaration on the Rights of Indigenous Peoples (2007) are also worth mentioning the United Nations General Assembly Resolution on the Review of the World Summit on the Information Society (A/RES/70/125) (2015); the United Nations General Assembly Resolution on Transforming Our World: the 2030 Agenda for Sustainable Development (A/RES/70/1) (2015); the Recommendation Concerning the Preservation of, and Access to, Documentary Heritage, Including in Digital Form (2015); the Declaration of Ethical Principles in Relation to Climate Change (2017); the Recommendation on Science and Scientific Researchers (2017); the Internet Universality Indicators (endorsed by UNESCO's International Programme for the Development of Communication in 2018), including the ROAM principles (endorsed by UNESCO's General Conference in 2015); the Human Rights Council's resolution on 'Privacy in the Digital Age' (A/HRC/RES/42/15) (2019); and the Human Rights Council's resolution on 'New and Emerging Digital Technologies and Human Rights' (2019)".*

[90] *Supra* note 88.

[91] Ibid.

[92] Ibid.

[93] Ibid.

[94] Ibid.

research and innovation that bases AI technologies on human rights and fundamental freedoms, values, and moral and ethical thinking.[95] Acknowledging that, in light of the rapid pace of technological change, ethical values and principles can provide guidance for the development and application of rights-based policy measures and legal norms.[96]

To support this process at the national, regional, and global levels, Member States,[97] private sector companies, and civil society organisations are urged to form a network of independent ***AI Ethics Officers with UNESCO's assistance.***[98]

It is believed that globally acknowledged ethical standards for AI technologies, based on complete respect for international law, particularly human rights legislation, can help shape AI-related norms around the world. Essential standards for ethical AI have been identified by the UNI Global Union.

1. Transparency in AI systems is a requirement, as are 'ethical black boxes', in AI systems.
2. AI must serve people and the environment.
3. Use a human-in-command strategy.
4. Ensure a genderless, unbiased AI.
5. Share the advantages of AI systems.
6. Ensure a fair transition and support for fundamental rights and liberties.
7. Create a system of global government.
8. Although the existing provisions in the legal and regulatory framework of Germany, California, and India can be applicable to a certain extent in crimes and torts involving AI, however, there are gaps in the law/regulation due to which the AI system including the AVs are not effectively governed or regulated. For instance, there are laws of tort and criminal law, but having separate legislation on AI will help the State to impose liability on the wrongdoer and for that, it needs a sui generis legislation on fault among product manufacturers/sellers, AI designers/suppliers, and AI purchasers/users from the nonattendance legislation administering AI in California, State councils will create numerous AI laws before improving a Uniform Artificial Intelligence Act. It is presumed that the first state assembly will move towards AI advancement exclusively. Along these lines, when AI authorities become more regular, assemblies will create laws to administer AI manufacturers. As a result, it should admit what California has to give about self-driving vehicles each time: There are presently no AI-related laws in place. In any case, as more AI is developed, that assurance will become less accurate. States may conclude that they do not need a mixed bag of laws and guidelines administering AI distinctively in vehicles versus experts versus legal advisors. It is expected that there will be a uniform legal or regulatory regime on AI like the numerous other uniform Acts that oversee deals and

[95] Ibid.

[96] Ibid.

[97] Ibid.

[98] Ibid.

exchanges, trusts, controlled substances, and so forth. This will give exceeding guidelines to AI and licence more explicit laws overseeing specific types of AI as necessary. The Uniform Act can also appear as a government act, adding layers of regulatory requirements to each state's requirements. Another possibility is that a government agency, such as the Consumer Protection Agency, adopts a Uniform AI Act developed by an industry group or an American Bar Association warning board as a model law. The Uniform AI Act and the explicit AI Act leading the way will almost certainly take risk into account. Gray Scott, a futurist, adds, "When will we develop an artificial intelligence bill of rights is the actual question. What exactly will that entail? Also, who will draw that conclusion?" When deciding on a regulatory and legal structure, the government should evaluate if the number of AI in the world is adequate to provide them the Right to Exist. When deciding on a regulatory and legal structure, the government should assess if the degree of AI in human existence is sufficient to grant AI the Indian Constitution's rights to privacy, non-discrimination, and life and dignity. States must practise Laissez-faire when it comes to reforming new developments that touch living souls—human lives. However, they are unable to become observers because the government's help to human existence remains their primary goal. The introduction of autonomous vehicles could reduce greenhouse gas emissions because they could be programmed to follow eco-driving principles during a travel, decreasing fuel consumption by up to 20% and greenhouse gas emissions by a similar amount.[99] Autonomous vehicles could potentially help to minimise traffic congestion by suggesting alternate routes and the quickest routes possible, as well as exchanging traffic information with other vehicles on the highway, resulting in lower fuel use.

AI has applications in the conservation field as well. Deep learning technology, for example, might be to analyse photographs of wild animals acquired by motion-sensor cameras.

This data might then be utilised to offer precise, thorough, and up-to-date information about the location, number, and behaviour of wild animals, which could help to improve local biodiversity and conservation efforts.[100]

4. Different degrees of decision autonomy[101] can be found in AI applications and the computer systems that implement them. The German Federal Government's Data Ethics Commission, 2018,[102] for example, divides autonomy into three categories: *algorithmically based, algorithmically driven, and algorithmically determined systems.*

---

[99] Iglinski et al., 2017).

[100] Norouzzadeh et al., 2018.

[101] W. Wahlster, "Künstliche Intelligenz als Grundlage autonomer Systeme". Informatik-Spektrum, 40, pp. 409–418, 2017.

[102] Datenethikkommission der Bundesregierung, Gutachten der Datenethikkommission. Berlin: BMI, 2019. [Online]. Available at: https://www.bmi.bund.de/SharedDocs/downloads/DE/publikationen/themen/it-digitalpolitik/gutachten-datenethikkommission.pdf?__blob=publicationFile&v=6, accessed on October12, 2023.

Can You Give Examples Of Autonomy In The Case Of Avs?

AI applications that are *algorithmically based* function as pure help systems with no autonomous decision-making ability. However, human decisions are based on (partial) results and (partial) information calculated by them.

Algorithm-driven

AI applications influence human judgements by calculating results. As a result, humans' actual decision-making capabilities and, as a result, their self-determination options are limited.

AI applications that are *algorithmically decided* make decisions independently and so have a high degree of autonomy. Because of the high level of automation, no human decision is made in individual cases, and automated choices are not reviewed by humans.

People's blind reliance on digital technologies is growing as automated systems get more complicated and elites gain control of them. Because of AI, the majority of people will not be faster and more efficient in 2030.[103] It will not get more autonomous; instead, it will become more automated as it follows the metaphorical GPS line through daily interactions. Individuals do not have control over their breakfast, morning workouts, or commute routes. An algorithm will make these decisions for individuals in a way that maximises efficiency (narrowly defined) and, most likely, the service provider's profits. Individuals may jam more activities and interactions into their days by 2030, but they do not believe this will improve their lives. The greatest danger is that all members of society will be under more pressure to live according to what 'the system' will tell them is 'best for them' to do and not do, i.e., that individuals will lose the autonomy to decide how they want to live their lives and to choose various ways of doing things. With an increase in 'recommendations', 'rankings', and competitiveness based on societal pressure and control, individuals may risk losing fundamental liberties (including, but not limited to, the right to a private life) that have been battled for over decades and centuries.

Bibliography

Books

Abbott R (2018) The reasonable computer: disrupting the paradigm of tort liability, 86 Geo Wash L Rev, 1

AJ Kurki V (2017) Legal personhood: animals, artificial intelligence and the unborn (2017 ed.). (T. Pietrzykowsk, ed.) Cambridge, UK: Springe

Artificial Intelligence, The Law Dictionary (n.d.) https://thelawdictionary.org/artificial-intelligence/[https://perma.cc/5bpn-ybte

Calo R (2016) Robots as legal metaphors, 30 HARV. J L TECH, 209

103 *See* <https://www.pewresearch.org/internet/2018/12/10/concerns-about-human-agency-evolution-and-survival/>,accessed on October 12, 2023.

CHRISTOPHER KUNER, * FRED H (2018) Cateexpanding the artificial intelligence-data protection debate international data privacy law, Vol 8, NO 4

George Wright R (2019) The constitutional rights of advanced robots (and of human beings), 71 ARK L Rev 613

Halkimoral R (2019) Responsibility of robots and hybrid agents the monist 102(2):259–275

IRIAGIUFFRIDA, FREDRIC LEDERER& NICOLAS VERMEYS, a legal perspective on the trials and tribulations of AI: how artificial intelligence, the internet of things, smart contracts, and other technologies will affect the law, 68 CASE W RES L REV 747 (2018)

Iriagiuffrida, Lederer F, Vermeys N (2018) A legal perspective on the trials and tribulations of AI: how artificial intelligence, the internet of things, smart contracts, and other technologies will affect the law, 68 CASE W. Res L Rev 747

Kaplan J (2016) Artificial intelligence (2016 ED.). 198 Madison Avenue, New York, NY 10016, United States of America: Oxford University Press

KAREN YEUNGFIVE fears about mass predictive personalization in an age of surveillance capitalism international data privacy law 8(3) (2018)

Khoury AH (2017) Intellectual property rights for HUBOTS: on the legal implications of human-like robots as innovators and creators, 35 CARDOZO ARTS &ENT. LJ 635

Lawrence DR, Palacios-Gonzalez C, Harris J (2016) Artificial intelligence the shylock syndrome, 25 Cambridge Q. Healthcare Ethics 250, 261

Lawrence DR, Palacios-Gonzalez C, Harris J (2016) Artificial intelligence the shylock syndrome, 25 Cambridge Q Healthcare Ethics 250:261

Nick BOSTROM Eliezer YUDKOWSKY the ethics of artificial intelligence Cambridge handbook of artificial intelligence, eds. William Ramsey, and Keith Frankish Cambridge University Press (2011)

Nunez C (2017) Artificial intelligence and legal ethics: whether ai lawyers can make ethical decisions, 20 TUL J Tech Intell Prop 189, 204

Pagallo U (2013) The laws of robots (2013 ED.). Torino, Italy: Springer Dordrecht Heidelberg New York London, ISBN: 978-94-007-6563-4, PG

ROMAN DREMLIUGA, PAVELKUZNETCOV& ALEXEY MAMYCHEV, criteria for recognition of Ai as a legal person, 12 J. POL. & L. 105 (2019)

Sartor G (1998) Judicial applications of artificial intelligence (reprinted from artificial intelligence and law 6(2–4)1998 ed.). (K. Branting, ed.) AA Dordrecht, The Netherlands: 1998 Kluwer Academic Publishers

Turner J (2019) *Robot rules*-regulating artificial intelligence, London,-UK: Palgrave Macmillan, ISBN: 978-3-319-96234-4, PG.

Vladeck DC (2014) Machines without principals: liability rules and artificial intelligence, 89 WASH L REV, 117

Walton D (2013) Argumentation methods for artificial intelligence in law (2013 ed.). Winnipeg, Manitoba R3B 2E9, Canada: Springer Berlin Heidelberg New York

Articles Referred

Dremliuga R, Kuznetcov P, Mamychev A (2019) Criteria for Recognition of AI as a legal person, 12 J Pol L 105

Executive Office of the President (2016) Artificial intelligence, automation and the economy. Washington, DC, USA

European Parliament, European Civil Law Rules In Robotics, (Dec. 8, 2019, 11:30 PM) REGULATION (EU) 2016/679 OF THE EUROPEAN PARLIAMENT AND OF THE COUNCIL of Apr. 27, 2016, on the protection of natural persons about the processing of personal data and the free movement of such data, and repealing Directive 95/46/EC (General Data Protection

Regulation) (Dec. 9, 2019, Karen YeungFive fears about mass predictive personalization in an age of surveillance capitalism International Data Privacy Law 8(3) (2018)
Frank LevyComputers and populism: artificial intelligence, jobs, and politics in the near-term Oxford Rev Econ Policy 34(3):393–417 (2018)
Goksu BB, Oze U (2020) Responsibility for damages caused by artificial intelligence. 23 GSI Articleletter 64
Ilková V, Ilka A (2017) Legal aspects of autonomous vehicles—an overview. Conference: 21st international conference on process control (PC)At: Štrbské Pleso, Slovakia. https://doi.org/10.1109/PC.2017.7976252
Keller P (2018) Autonomous vehicles, artificial intelligence, and the law. J Robot Artif Intell La 1:101–109
Marchant G, Bazzi R (2020) Autonomous vehicles and liability: what will juries do? (2020) 26(1) Boston Univ J Sci Technol Law, 67
Richter K (2019) Product liability, legal transplants, and artificial intelligence, 2019 harmonious: J Legal Soc Stud Se EUR, 292
Rzeczycka H, Kovac M, Autonomous self-driving vehicles—the advent of a new legal era? King's Student Law Rev 10(I)
Rachel Wither, The EU Is Trying to Decide Whether to Grant Robots Personhood." European commission high-level expert group on artificial intelligence, policy, and investment recommendation on trustworthy AI
Scherer MU (2016) Regulating artificial intelligence systems: risks, challenges, competencies, and strategies. Harv J Law Technol 29(2). Spring
Santa Clara Law Review, Volume 33; Ronald B. Desilets, Jr., Note, Software Vendors' Exposure to Products Liability for Computer Viruses, 9 COMPUTER/L.J.509,524 (1989)
The future computed: artificial intelligence and its role in society, Microsoft (2018) Rachel Metz "And the award for most nauseating self-driving car goes to … I rode in a bunch of autonomous cars, so you don't have to"
US Defence Science Board, "*Summer Study on Autonomy*," (US Department of Defence, 2016.
Walpert JD (2017) Carpooling liability: applying tort law principles to the joint emergence of self-driving automobiles and transportation network companies, 85 Fordham L. Rev 1863

Statutes And International Agreements

Un convention on road traffic, 1948
Vienna convention on road traffic, 1968
German road traffic (Amendment) ACT, 2017
German civil code, 1900
German product liability law, 1989
California civil code, 1872
California vehicle code 1993
California code of civil procedure, 1872
Consumer protection ACT, 2019
Motor vehicle ACT, 1988
Motor vehicle (AMENDMENT) ACT, 2019
Consumer protection ACT 1986
LAW of tort
Bharatiya Nyaya Sanhita, 2023
Constitution of India

Reports

National Strategy for Artificial Intelligence #AIFORALL—Discussion Paper (NITI Aayog, June 2018)

2016–2019 Progress report: advancing artificial intelligence by artificial intelligence research & development interagency working group, November 2019

Working Document: Enforcement Mechanisms for Responsible #AIforAll 2020: Towards Responsible AI for All (Part 1)

Mckinsey global institute---notes from the Ai frontier modeling the impact of Ai on the world economy, September 2018.

Corporate partnership board report: governing transport in the algorithmic age by. International transport forum, December 2018 at the OECD in France.

Recommendation report of the council on artificial intelligence—OECD Legal Instruments 2020.

NTDPC, India transport report: moving India to 2032.

Future of Jobs in India: a 2022 perspective (2017)

Websites

http://legalinstruments.oecd.org
https://www.nitrd.gov/pubs/National-AI-RD-Strategy-2019.pdf
https://www.whitehouse.gov/ai/ai-american-innovation/
https://www.nitrd.gov/about/.
www.mckinsey.com/mgi.
www.medium.com
www.CSRankings.org
https://heinonline.org/HOL/License
www.harvardbusinessreviewpress.com
www.nytimes.com/section/technology
https://www.bloomberg.com/technology
https://www.sae.org/standard

The manufacturer's authorised representative in the EU is Springer Nature Customer Service Centre GmbH, Europaplatz 3, 69115 Heidelberg, Germany. If you have any concerns regarding our products, please contact ProductSafety@springernature.com

Printed and bound by CPI Group (UK) Ltd, Croydon, CR0 4YY
01/10/2026
02225987-0012